Red Hearts and Roses?

Red Hearts and Roses?

Welsh Valentine Songs
and Poems

RHIANNON IFANS

UNIVERSITY OF WALES PRESS
2019

www.uwp.co.uk

British Library CIP Data
A catalogue record for this book is available from the British Library
ISBN   978-1-78683-371-6
eISBN   978-1-78683-372-3

The University of Wales Press acknowledges the financial support of
the Welsh Books Council.

Designed and typeset by Chris Bell, cbdesign
Printed by the CPI Antony Rowe, Melksham

Acknowledgements

I AM GRATEFUL for the assistance of the following family members and friends while I was preparing this volume: Huw Ceiriog, Dr Martin Crampin, Dr D. Islwyn Edwards, Professor E. Wyn James, D. Geraint Lewis and Professor William Marx. I am particularly indebted to Dr Rhidian Griffiths for reading the original typescript and for many valuable comments regarding the music; Miss Mair Jenkins of Waunfawr, Aberystwyth, for her kind permission to photograph and publish a series of family Valentine cards; Ric Lloyd of Cleftec for the preparation of the music for publication; and Dafydd Ifans for compiling the General Index. I wish to thank the staff of the National Library of Wales for their professional assistance, and I am grateful to Dr Llion Wigley and his colleagues at the University of Wales Press for their support throughout the publishing process.

Contents

List of illustrations

List of abbreviations

Bangor Manuscript held in Archives and Special Collections, Bangor University, Bangor.

Cerddi Bangor Welsh ballads held in the Bangor University Library, Bangor.

Cardiff The Cardiff Central Library Manuscripts, Cardiff.

CG Canu Gwerin (Folk Song) (Cymdeithas Alawon Gwerin Cymru/ The Welsh Folk-Song Society, 1978–).

Cwrtmawr The Cwrtmawr Manuscripts collection, held at the National Library of Wales, Aberystwyth.

JWFSS Cylchgrawn Cymdeithas Alawon Gwerin Cymru/Journal of the Welsh Folk-song Society (1909–77).

NLW The National Library of Wales Manuscripts collection, held at the National Library of Wales, Aberystwyth.

NLW Baledi a Cherddi Welsh ballads held at the National Library of Wales, Aberystwyth.

Peniarth The Peniarth Manuscripts collection, held at the National Library of Wales, Aberystwyth.

J. Lloyd Williams Papers Dr J. Lloyd Williams Music MSS and Papers, held at the National Library of Wales, Aberystwyth.

Introduction: Who was Saint Valentine?

THE NOVEL *A Misalliance* by Anita Brookner opens with the sentence, 'Blanche Vernon occupied her time most usefully in keeping feelings at bay.'[1] Countless others behave in precisely the same way for the greater part of the year, but there are occasions in life when those defensive walls come tumbling down. Saint Valentine's Day on 14 February may be one such occasion.

Who is this saint who gave his name to the festival of lovers? And slightly more perplexing, why was it a saint that was given this honour?

Martyrologium Romanum, The Roman Martyrology, a catalogue of martyrs and saints listed according to their feast days, commemorates two saints named Valentinus on 14 February, both martyred. The former was a priest in Rome, martyred on the Flaminian Way during the persecution of Emperor Claudius II Gothicus;[2] the latter was bishop of Terni, some sixty miles from the capital city, and whose death is recorded in the *Martyrologium Hieronymianum*, the Martyrology of Saint Jerome. In their present form there is no strong historical foundation for either of these chronicles, and their content should possibly be listed with the legendary rather than the historical. Both records may, however, have an historical basis and it is possible that they offer two slightly different accounts of the martyrdom of one saint.

Whether there were actually one or two Valentines is disputed. O. Marucchi held for two. H. Delehaye felt that Valentine of Terni may have been brought to Rome for execution and that two cults, one at Rome, another at Terni, sprang up to the same martyr.[3]

This study allows for one Saint Valentinus, born on the Via Flaminia, and martyred on 14 February *c*.269.

It is of little consequence whether there lived one saint or two as we text and e-mail our Valentine wishes in the twenty-first century; choosing Valentines on this day bears only an accidental relation

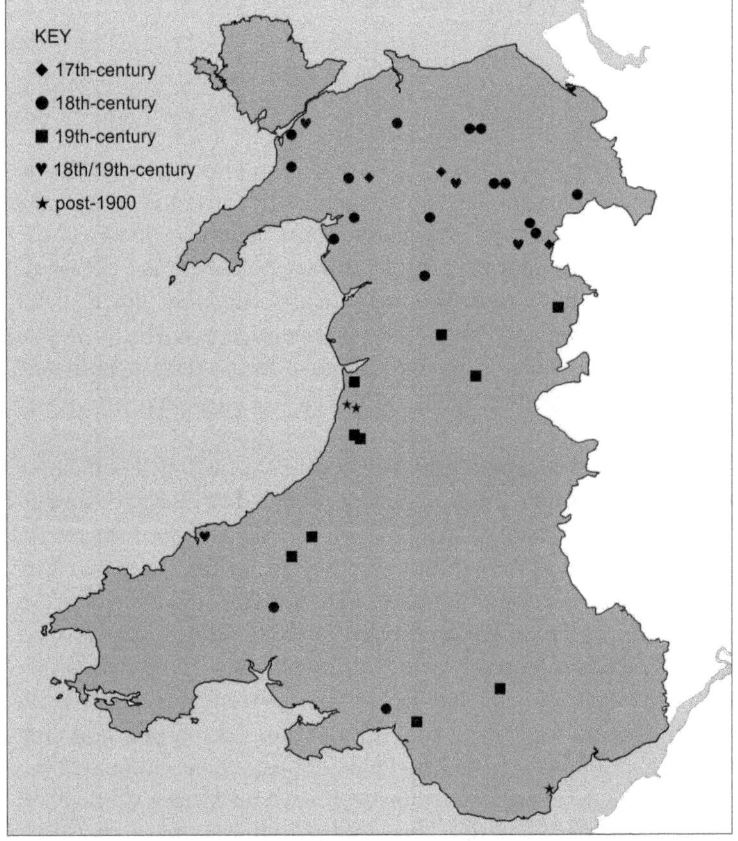

Geographical distribution of Welsh Valentine songs and poems.

to saints. It is far more likely that Saint Valentine was a chaste and sober man who was never once stung by Cupid's arrow. Disappointment awaits those who hope that he enjoyed a brief romantic chapter and that subsequently his name became synonymous with lovers in every age and nation. No such record exists.

On the contrary, Valentinus was famed for professing Christ during the reign of an anti-Christian governor. Valentinus valiantly and unfailingly served those Christians who suffered persecution in Rome under Emperor Claudius II, a service regarded as a crime and for which he was imprisoned. Duly called to answer the accusation, he addressed the court fearlessly, impressing many, to the extent that the emperor's officers attempted to turn Valentinus's loyalty towards the pagan gods of the Romans, but with no success. For refusing to adopt those pagan gods he was clubbed, stoned and executed outside the Flaminian Gate, *c.*269. According to legend, the saint became friendly with the prison warder's blind daughter. Valentinus restored her sight, and on the eve of his execution is reported to have written her a note signed 'from your Valentine'. This engaging story should be regarded as a fictional, though charming, anecdote.

What, then, is the source of this custom of presenting gifts to loved ones in mid-February? Once again the Italians provide an answer. Following the Roman conquest of Britain the ancient spring festival of Lupercalia,[4] celebrated on 15 February, was transported to Britain. When the Romans returned to their own country early in the fifth century this was one of the many traditions they left behind. The Lupercalia was a pastoral festival, held to ward off evil spirits and to promote health and fertility, its rituals carried out by priests called Luperci.

Each Lupercalia began with the sacrifice by the Luperci of goats and a dog, after which two of the Luperci were led to the altar, their foreheads were touched with a bloody knife, and the blood was wiped off with wool dipped in milk; the ritual required that the two young men laugh. The sacrificial feast followed, after which the Luperci cut thongs from the skins of the sacrificial animals and ran in two bands around the Palatine hill, striking with the thongs at any woman who came near them. A blow from the thong was supposed to render a woman fertile. In 494 CE the Christian church under Pope Gelasius I appropriated the form of the rite as the Feast of the Purification.[5]

According to some sources, no particular god was honoured by this custom. Other sources name Lupercus as the venerated god, and Faunus is often cited as the central figure of the tradition in modern conjecture.

Since the Lupercalia was so popular, the Church found it almost impossible to eradicate. Scholars have suggested that a compromise was reached by combining the celebration with the Valentine feast day, thus moderating much of its effect.[6] This has been accepted uncritically and often repeated. The custom of throwing the names of the beautiful women of Rome into a love urn was retained. One by one the young men of Rome would choose a name from the urn by lot. The person named would be his Valentine for the day and, having become 'drawn', would remain his Valentine for the year. In some instances this would develop into a betrothal.

During the Middle Ages it was a popularly held belief that mid-February, according to the historic Julian Calendar,[7] was a melodious time when the sound of birdsong gathered a new momentum. In rhythm with, and inspired by, this enthusiasm humans conformed with the calendar of birds as regards matchmaking. The first reference to Saint Valentine's Day as a special day for lovers is Chaucer's dream-vision poem, 'The Parliament of Fowls', written sometime between 1372 and 1386, in which a conference convened on the feast of Saint Valentine is described, and at which each bird is invited to choose a mate.

Jack B. Oruch's survey of the literature finds no association between Valentine and romance prior to Chaucer. He concludes that Chaucer is likely to be 'the original mythmaker in this instance'.[8]

> For this was on Seynt Valentynes day,
> Whan every foul cometh there to chese his make,
> Of every kynde that men thynke may,
> And that so huge a noyse gan they make
> That erthe, and eyr, and tre, and every lake
> So ful was that unethe was there space
> For me to stonde, so ful was al the place.

> And right as Aleyn, in the Pleynt of Kynde,
> Devyseth Nature of aray and face,
> In swich aray men myghte hire there fynde.
> This noble emperesse, ful of grace,
> Bad every foul to take his owne place,
> As they were woned alwey fro yer to yeere,
> Seynt Valentynes day, to stonden theere.[9]

The birds' enthusiasm for pairing is quite evident, as is their indebtedness to Saint Valentine and to the sun for driving away the winter with its long, dark nights.

> Saynt Valentyn, that art ful hy on-lofte,
> Thus syngen smale foules for thy sake:
> [Now welcome, somer, with thy sonne softe,
> That hast thes wintres wedres overshake.][10]

Literary critics believe that the poem includes a personal allegory, but there is little agreement between the various attempts to explain the identity of the birds taking part in the conference, or their mates. It is wiser not to limit the interpretation, for it is not crucial to personalise the birds in the poem for it to be a success; there is also a definite suggestion, but no direct evidence, that similar movements in the spheres of birds and humans were expected in mid-February in Britain by the fourteenth century.

The second reference to Saint Valentine's Day as a day for lovers appears in a poem by John Lydgate (?1370–1449) entitled 'The Flower of Courtesy' composed for Saint Valentine's Day. In it Lydgate hears the skylark calling lovers to renew their support for the excellence of love on Valentine's Eve. The birds have already chosen a mate, he notes, but it will not be as simple for him:

> For I my herte have set in suche a place
> Wher I am never lykely for to spede.[11]

He then opens his heart and describes his love, 'the floure of courtesye'.

The earliest known surviving Valentine is a medieval French poem written by the 21-year-old Charles, duke of Orléans, to his wife Bonne d'Armagnac while he was imprisoned in the Tower of London following his capture at the Battle of Agincourt. Written in 1415, it is housed in the manuscript collection of the British Library in London. The oldest known Valentine message in the English language is also at the British Library;[12] written in Norfolk the love letter dates to February 1477 and was from Margery Brews to her fiancé John Paston (1444–1504). In it she describes John as her 'right well-beloved valentine', and explains that her mother had tried unsuccessfully to persuade her father to increase her dowry. However, all ended well and they were eventually married.

Not only did poets concern themselves with the patron saint of lovers, but he was also favoured by artists. It seems that the first portrait of Saint Valentine to appear in print is that found in the *Nuremberg Chronicle*, a book of images printed in Nuremberg by Anton Koberger in July 1493, and which purports to chronicle the history of the world from the Creation. The original publication, by Hartmann Schedel, was in Latin and is referred to as *Liber Chronicarum*, but within five months it had been translated into German by Georg Alt, as *Die Schedelsche Weltchronik*. Both the Latin and German editions:

> are lavishly illustrated with 1804 xylographical images created from 641–643 woodblocks by the Nuremberg artists Michael Wolgemut (circa 1434/37–1519) and Wilhelm Pleydenwurff (circa 1450–1494), a map of the world, showing the Gulf of Guinea discovered by the Portuguese in 1470, and a map of Northern and Central Europe by Hieronymus Münzer (circa 1437/1447–1508). The woodcut illustrations of a number of copies, both in Latin and in vernacular, were also supplied with hand colouring by contemporary German artists. The alleged involvement in the creation of the woodblocks of Albrecht Dürer (1471–1528), has now been rejected on the documentary evidence that he only worked as an apprentice in Wolgemut's workshop between 1486 and 1489, well before the beginning of the production of the Chronicle.[13]

One woodcut print depicts the saint with long curly hair, carrying a palm branch symbolizing his martyrdom.[14] The story of his death is retold concisely in the days of Claudius II, and his feast day given as

16 March; no mention is made of his patronage of lovers. The same entry, in effect, is found in December 1493, with the distinction that Saint Valentine's feast day had been moved to 14 February.

The only known image of Saint Valentine on view in Wales is a stained glass window dating from 1994 set in the north wall of the chancel at St Mary's Church in Swansea (see figure 1). This memorial window was given in memory of Helyn Mary Rose, who died on Saint Valentine's Day 1991 aged twenty-two; the window 'depicts her interests and love of the sea' and is a 'two-light window with various motifs. St Valentine is shown holding a crown with birds, a double bass with flowers in front of a sea scene with a sailing boat and lighthouse. Upper cinquefoil with a letter H and birds, with leeks(?) arranged around it.'[15] The window was designed by Colwyn Morris of Glantawe Studios.

The seventeenth century

Several references to Saint Valentine in the context of the season of love appear in English and European literatures from the medieval period onwards, but Welsh poets and prose writers make no mention of the subject until the seventeenth century. *A Dictionary of the Welsh Language* records the first example of the word 'falendein' in a seventeenth-century context. Evolved forms were in common usage by the nineteenth century: the form *balant* in south Ceredigion, a variant form of *malant* (compare *benyw/menyw*); other forms include *'ffolant, ffalant* (Montgomeryshire), *folant lan* and *folant salw* (sentimental and comic valentines) (Llanwenog), *malant, malantau salw* and *molantau ysmala* (Pren-gwyn), *folant* (Llandyssul).'[16] Trefor M. Owen notes that, however tempting it might be 'to conclude from this that the custom was new in the seventeenth century and that in the course of more than a hundred years it had become entrenched in the Welsh countryman's pattern of life and thus in his vocabulary', there is no hard evidence for that surmise.

Edward Morris (?1633–89), a cattle trader from Perthi Llwydion near Cerrigydrudion in the county of Conwy, is the author of two surviving seventeenth-century Valentine poems and possibly a third; two other poems and possibly a third are the work of Huw Morys

(1622–1709); and Siôn/John Ellis the Harpist is the possible author of a poem requesting a Valentine's gift. All seven poems are undated, but it is reasonably safe to conclude that poems 1–7 in this collection were composed during the seventeenth century.

Edward Morris's *cywydd*[17] of eighty-eight lines was written on behalf of David Davies, requesting that Mrs Margaret Wynne should be his Valentine.[18] In this instance the Valentine is a person (rather than a card or a letter), although the word is synonymous with a gift in a second poem by Edward Morris.[19] The poet acts as spokesman for David Davies as he attempts to charm Mrs Margaret Wynne, a neighbour living at Cwm Main, south of Cerrigydrudion.

The poem describes how the ritual of 'tynnu Falentein' (drawing a Valentine) was practised in seventeenth-century Wales.[20] The date on which the custom was held is woven into his *cywydd* by interposition:

> *Y pedwerydd dydd*, diau,
> Wir adde' clod, *ar ddeg* clau
> *O Chwefror* oedd a chyfri,
> Ddwyn mawr ddaioni i mi.[21]

> [*The fourth day*, doubtless, | Sincerely acknowledging praise, *on ten* swiftly | *Of February* it was by count, | That brought me great goodness.]

It was on 14 February that this 'great goodness' came about. In the Cerrigydrudion area names were drawn on the saint's day, not on Saint Valentine's Eve as Lydgate describes, and unlike the custom recorded on 13 February 1661 among the English gentry: 'to Sir W. Batten's; whither I sent for my wife and we chose Valentines against tomorrow'.[22]

Edward Morris describes the Welsh custom thus:

> Honno ei gwir henw y ges,
> Lleuad doniau, lle tynnes
> Valentine, foliant hynod,
> Clo des dawn, clau destun clod,
> Foesgarwch, o fysg eraill,
> I gyd o'r llaw, gado'r lleill.[23]

[She, her very name I received, | Moon of talents, as I drew [the name of my] | Valentine, exceptional praise, | Knot of warm moral virtue, ready subject of praise, | Refinement, from among others, | Entirely by hand, leaving the others behind.]

Lleuad (moon) is used figuratively, signifying a woman of outstanding beauty, and typifies that which cannot be reached, rather than fickleness or inconstancy as in the following quotation (also from 1661): 'Och! Och! dwyn yr ydym ni ormod o'r lleuad, hynny yw Anwadalwch, yn ein dwyfronnau'(Woe! Woe! we carry too much of the moon, that is Fickleness, in our breast).[24]

The poem describes how a paper (line 57), on which appeared the name of the one to be addressed as the young man's Valentine (line 63), was drawn from an urn. The suitor exhibits eager enthusiasm in this novel situation: 'Neidiais … fel hydd | … o wir lawenydd' (I leapt … like a stag | … out of true joy) (lines 65–6). He is so thrilled with his choice of paper that he wishes to gild it with molten gold (lines 60–1). Further:

Gwasgu y wnawn, yn llawn lles,
Henw'r fun hon i'r fynwes,
A'i gusanu, gais hynod.[25]

[I would press, with abounding profit, | This woman's name to the bosom, | And kiss it, excellent request.]

The promise of this woman's company for the foreseeable future is far more desirable than any gift.

The *cywydd* elaborates on another of the responsibilities of a Saint Valentine's Day partner: he is expected to adorn himself with a ribbon as a visual sign that he is bound to another. Since that other was a married woman in this instance the lover would need to respect the rituals of *amour courtois*. The woman's surname, Wynne, suggesting 'white' or 'fair', prompts the man to wear a white ribbon in her honour.

Ruban gwyn ar ben ei gwas,
Lliw a wisga i'n 'wyllysgar,
Lliw hon pob calon a'i câr.[26]

[A white ribbon on her young man's head, | A colour that I will readily wear, | Every heart adores the colour of this woman['s complexion].]

No further mention is made of the obligations that stem from the great privilege of partnering Mrs Wynne save that the poet asks the woman's forgiveness for taking upon himself 'y rhyfyg mawr' (the great presumption) of asking her favour (line 88).

The custom of men drawing partners by lot is often mentioned in Welsh Valentine poems. Certain couples were expected to become betrothed and married, but in this case an already-married woman's name is acquired, a woman married to the vicar of the parish at that.[27] Samuel Pepys reports a similar practice in London. Born in 1633, the same year as the believed date of birth of Edward Morris, Pepys lived into the following century, and died in 1703 (Edward Morris died in Essex in 1689). They were contemporaries, but one lived in rural Cerrigydrudion, the other (the son of a London tailor) in the metropolis. Between 1 January 1660 and 31 May 1669 Pepys kept a diary and fashioned a number of entries in which he noted his experience of the Saint Valentine's Day festival, or more often than not the experiences of his wife. In his entry for 22 February 1661 he writes: 'my wife to Sir W. Batten's, and there sat a while – he having yesterday sent my wife half-a-dozen pair of gloves and a pair of silk stockings and garters, for her Valentine's gift'.[28] Over a week had gone by before Mrs Pepys received her gifts on 22 February, and it is clear from the diary that gifts were not necessarily presented on the saint's day, and that the extravagant gift Mrs Pepys had received was a repayment of that which Samuel Pepys had given to his Valentine, Sir W. Batten's daughter, on the eighteenth of the month. The following year Pepys states that he avoided Sir W. Batten's home over the Saint Valentine's Day period to avoid drawing his daughter as a Valentine for a second time. Relations between the two families had grown tense by February 1662.

According to the Pepys diaries, women and young girls too would draw Valentines. On 16 February 1667, two days after the feast day, Pepys finds that 'Mrs. Pierce's little girl is my Valentine, she having drawn me – which I was not sorry for, it easing me of something more that I must have given to others.'[29] A girl could claim a gift from the hand of whomsoever she drew as a Valentine.

Such papers, revealing the name of a partner, could be the fore-runners of the modern Valentine card as the entry for 14 February 1667 seems to suggest: 'This morning came up to my wife's bedside, I being up dressing myself, little Will Mercer to be her Valentine; and brought her name writ upon blue paper in gold letters, done by himself, very pretty – and we were both well pleased with it.'[30] In a further entry on 16 February of the same year:

> But here I do first observe the fashion of drawing of Motto's
> as well as names; so that Pierce, who drew my wife, did draw
> also a motto, and this girl drew another for me. What mine was
> I have forgot; but my wife's was (*Most virtuous and most fair*);
> which, as it may be used, or an Anagram made upon each
> name, might be very pretty.[31]

The Edward Morris *cywydd* suggests a similar custom in Wales, using gilded paper. The addition of a romantic verse, flowers and other adornments to create a card in the eighteenth-century fashion was fast approaching.

In 1668 Mrs Pepys had attracted more than one Valentine:

> There comes also my Cosen Rogr. Pepys betimes, and comes to
> my wife for her to be his Valentine, whose Valentine I was also,
> by agreement to be so to her every year; and this year I find
> it is likely to cost 4 or 5*l* in a ring for her which she desires.[32]

Samuel Pepys was equally popular. On 27 February 1668 he writes: 'took up my wife to the Exchange and there bought things for Mr. Pierces little daughter, my Valentine; and so to their house, where we find Knipp, who also challengeth me for her valentine'.[33] It is likely that the most popular girls would have their names drawn in more than one circle, and attract gifts from more than one source.

The Edward Morris *cywydd* is an analogy between Margaret Wynne and the workings of nature in a beautiful garden. The first part of the poem describes the garden as 'Ail i Eden oleudeg' (Comparable with Eden fair and beautiful) (line 3). The beautiful Garden of Eden, or Paradise, is described in the Book of Genesis (chapters 2 and 3), and described in the Book of Ezekiel (28:13) as 'Eden, the garden of God'. Although only mid-February, the flowers named in the Valentine *cywydd* are primroses (which carry connotations of a special love), clover (meaning 'be mine' and symbolizing a long and prosperous marriage), daisies (a symbol of loyal love), one damask rose (a symbol of beauty and love) and a cherry blossom (portraying femininity); a plait of Margaret Wynne's fair hair in a 'blaenglwm bleth' (plait knotted at the front) (line 18) is compared to the golden yellow saffron, a spice derived from the crocus flower, sometimes referred to in Dorset as 'the flower of Saint Valentine'.[34]

Edward Morris references the Song of Solomon in the Old Testament, the description of the desired Margaret Wynne corresponding to Solomon's description of the Shulamite woman who is deeply loved and loves deeply, and suggests a story of courtship and consummation:

> A garden inclosed is my sister, my spouse; a spring shut up, a fountain sealed. Thy plants are an orchard of pomegranates, with pleasant fruits; camphire, with spikenard. Spikenard and saffron; calamus and cinnamon, with all trees of frankincense; myrrh and aloes, with all the chief spices: A fountain of gardens, a well of living waters, and streams from Lebanon. Awake, O north wind; and come, thou south; blow upon my garden, that the spices thereof may flow out. Let my beloved come into his garden, and eat his pleasant fruits.[35]

Exotic plants have been exchanged for the more familiar Welsh varieties in the Edward Morris *cywydd*, nevertheless it exudes the same abundant appreciation and praise. It further references verses in the Song of Solomon in lines 11–12:

> Marged Wyn, mawr gadwyni,
> Meini claer i'w mwnwgl hi.

> [Margaret Wynne, long chains | [And] shining gems [hang] about her neck.]

This compares favourably with the countenance of Solomon's spouse: 'Thy cheeks are comely with rows of jewels, thy neck with chains of gold' (Song of Solomon 1:10), and again: 'Thou hast ravished my heart, my sister, my spouse; thou hast ravished my heart with one of thine eyes, with one chain of thy neck' (Song of Solomon 4:9).

A second poem written by Edward Morris serves a different purpose. It is a poem of gratitude for a Valentine gift, written on one of the most popular of the Welsh free metres, *tri thrawiad*, of obscure origin.[36] Its message is clear enough: the poet feels duty-bound to thank his Valentine, in the first instance, for revealing her generous love for him:

Am ddangos mor weddedd eich cariad helaethedd
Trwy fwynedd, ddiomedd dda i mi.[37]

[For manifesting in such a becoming way your abundant love |
By means of your tender, ungrudging goodness towards me.]

She is referred to as 'seren y Teirsir' (star of the three counties), possibly a reference to the historical counties of Anglesey, Caernarfonshire and Merionethshire (now the Isle of Anglesey and Gwynedd) and her kindness is unequalled.[38] She is comparable with Gloria and Rosa, two unknown women the relevance of whose names is unclear, but it may be safely assumed that it is a comparison of praise.[39]

The poet's second task is to thank his benefactress for her gift. He does not specify its exact nature, but assures her that:

Er mwyn eich gwir gofio mi gadwa nhw er gwirio
Y rhodd tra parhao, er clirio ar eich clod.[40]

[In order to remember you truly I will keep them so that
I can attest to | The gift for its duration, so that your praise
is made clear.]

'Nhw' (they) manifests the plurality of the gift, suggesting that it has several parts or features, and could well be a pair of gloves.

The young woman is not named in full – Edward Morris calls her by the pet name El – and the manuscript provides no further clues as to her identity. A prime example of the Welsh poets' stock technique for forming stanzas, the woman's name is repeated using a different adjective to emphasize her waxing stardom.

El eurwych, El ara', El glirwen, ail Gloria,
El rasol, ail Rosa, chwi roesoch, main dw',
Rodd imi.[41]

> [Beautiful and excellent El, patient El, bright and blessed El, comparable with Gloria, | El full of grace, comparable with Rosa, you have given me, slim of build, | A gift.]

A poem included in an anthology of poems by Huw Morys makes use of a similar technique by weaving into the poem the initials of the woman's name 'A geinwen ac E' (splendidly pure A and E).[42] Furthermore her lover states that he will wear those letters in honour of her fine figure, which is brighter and purer and more brilliant than any jewel. This poem was typical of those sung between the middle of the seventeenth century and the close of the eighteenth. Welsh poets avidly set their lyrics to contemporary popular tunes, some of them Welsh in origin, some English, some from France and other European countries, others from even further afield.

> There were two metrical developments in this type of poetry. Firstly, the musical phrase was always very strictly observed and the words made to conform to the framework of the tune. Hence the intricate pattern of the stanzas. Secondly, *cynghanedd* was abundantly introduced, though it belonged traditionally to the strict metres and was, by its very accentuation, alien to the free metres. Full use was also made of rhyme to denote the end of musical phrases and even to mark a break in the phrase. Such verse was always meant to be sung, not read or spoken, and it can fairly be said that such a perfect blend of words and music has rarely been achieved.[43]

Speaking specifically of Huw Morys (using the variant spelling Morus):

> Huw Morus's deft manipulation was, however, lacking in many of his successors, and though the ability to fit words to tune remained, there was a tendency to use a good deal of 'padding', which seriously impaired the standard of the verse.[44]

Another Welsh Saint Valentine's Day poem dating from the seventeenth century formally requests a Valentine gift, in this instance from 'Jonett Willm' as the title notes, or Janet/Sioned Williams, whose name the suppliant had happily drawn for his Valentine, and he solicits her to give in accordance with her pleasure. The poem was written on behalf of Humphrey Lloyd of Hafod Ysbyty, near Beddau Gwŷr Ardudwy (The Graves of the Men of Ardudwy), Ffestiniog in Gwynedd, and was copied into a manuscript from the Trawsfynydd district, Cwrtmawr 128A, a manuscript dated 1738.[45] Since Humphrey Lloyd died on 7 April 1702 and his wife, the 'Sioned … Williams' mentioned in this poem (lines 11, 13), died in 1710 it is reasonably safe to conclude that this is a seventeenth-century poem.[46] The title notes that it is to be sung to the tune 'Consêt Arglwydd Straenee'.[47] This unusual tune is thus described by John Parry 'Bardd Alaw' (1776–1851):

> 'Hoffder Arglwydd Strain,' or *Lord Strain's Delight*, is an air very little known, I believe; I never, however, recollect to have heard it played. It is in the style of the 'Queen's Dream,' but the division of the strains (or parts) is unequal, the first consisting of 18, and the second of only 16, bars or measures. This irregularity often perplexes the singers, who are obliged to rest, or hurry over a few bars, in order to finish with the harper.[48]

'Consêt Arglwydd Straenee', or 'Hoffter Arglwydd Strain' is discussed by Meredydd Evans and Phyllis Kinney who note that the seventeenth-century ballad entitled 'Myfyrdod, neu Ddeusyfiad Cantores, am gael ei gwisgo a rhai o'r prif Geinciau, yn lle Dillad' (Meditation, or request of a female Singer to be dressed in some of the chief Tunes, instead of Clothes) includes a reference to the tune 'Streins Morus'.[49] Evans and Kinney argue that if 'Streins Morus' is another title for 'Hoffter Arglwydd Strain', then it is likely that it is a Morris dance tune.[50] Daniel Huws standardizes the form of the title to 'Stane's Morris', and notes the occurrence of the title in *Playford's Dancing Master*.[51]

The poem is accompanied by an ambivalent note, 'Siôn Ellis y Telyniwr a'i gwnaeth medd rhai, eraill a ddywedant nad e' oedd yr awdwr' (John Ellis the Harpist wrote it according to some, others say that he was not the author). Humphrey Lloyd was a descendant of Siân Prys, daughter of Edmwnd Prys, the author of *Salmau Cân* (1621), metrical psalms in a metre well adapted for setting to music. Humphrey Lloyd was a cultured man, a poet and harpist, well versed in the art of *cynghanedd* according to Ellis Rowland's commemorative poem to him.[52] It is possible that Lloyd wrote this Saint Valentine's Day poem himself if indeed it is true that its author was not Siôn/ John Ellis.

Only one poem in the collection of seventeenth-century Saint Valentine's Day poems can be classed as religious.[53] Composed by an anonymous author, it is recorded in NLW 11990A, a manuscript dating partly from the seventeenth and partly from the eighteenth century. A second copy of the text can be found in NLW 9B, a manuscript in the hand of Dafydd Jones of Trefriw in Conwy, dated between 1736 and 1755. A third copy appears in Cwrtmawr 171D and is a copy of NLW 9B, in the hand of J. H. Davies and dated 1902. The poem is untitled in NLW 11990A, but in NLW 9B the title 'Carol y Valentine' (Valentine Carol) was added by a later hand and this title was copied into Cwrtmawr 171D. Edward Morris, Perthi Llwydion, is the author of the two poems that precede this poem in NLW 9B, and another of his poems follows this Valentine carol. It would be unwise to attribute this poem to him with no attestation of authorship. However, it bears the marks of the seventeenth century and on this premise it is placed with the seventeenth-century poems.

Although the first stanza speaks of the beauty of birdsong during fine weather, overall the poem's message is rather more solemn. It is a dialogue poem between the poet and a blackbird, in which the blackbird hands out advice to his companion. This genre has a long literary lineage. Numerous Welsh medieval poems are exchanges between a wise counsellor, advanced in years, who offers advice, inspiration and consolation to a naive young man. The one of superior wisdom or understanding is starkly juxtaposed with the one who has little knowledge or experience, and such conduct literature enjoyed a secure place in the European medieval literary tradition.[54]

The advice offered by the wise old blackbird is that no amount of distress for a lost love can influence the outcome of the young lover Harri's circumstances. A tormented soul cannot shorten or prolong life.

> 'Estyn dim nid elli ar d'oes,
> Na wna yn fyrrach, leiach loes,
> Gad ti hynny i'r Gŵr a'th roes,
> A ddioddefodd ar y groes
> I safio dy einioes di.'[55]

['You cannot add anything to your lifespan, | Do not make it shorter, or less painful, | Leave that to the One who made you, | Who suffered on the cross | To save your life.']

Reference is made (line 32) to Joshua, the faithful leader of the Israel-ites following the death of Moses and the man who led the conquest of Canaan. At Shechem, shortly before his death, Joshua renewed the covenant made between God and the Israelites and urged Israel to continue to worship Jehovah rather than the gods of the Amorites.[56] The blackbird encourages the poet first of all to repent and then to follow the paths of righteousness. His advice is welcomed:

> Dy gyngor, maith ordor, a'th eirda,
> Fwyalchen d[d]u gefen, a gofia.[57]

> [Your advice, ambitious command, and your good word, |
> Black-backed blackbird, I shall bear in mind.]

The poet has one last request:

> A ddoi di 'r ha i goed y rhiw,
> Nyni ein dau, i ganu i'n Duw
> O byddwn ni byw yn y byd?[58]

> [Will you come in summertime to the wooded slope, |
> We two, to sing to our God | If we are [still] alive in the world?]

It is decided, in response to the blackbird's sage words concerning Harri's loss in love, that time will bring full deliverance.

At the heart of this intriguing 'Carol y Valentine', whether aptly titled or not, lies a didactic impetus that offers instruction on how a young man may win good repute in this world and aspire to live a wiser life. No mention is made of Valentine, of his celebration day, or of the Saint Valentine's Day ritual. However, in its advice regarding matters of the heart and the perils of unrequited love, the poem demonstrates a close affinity with the day-to-day business of the saint who is much venerated on 14 February.

The earliest Saint Valentine's Day poems preserved in the Welsh language are survivors from the seventeenth century. At a time when ritual singing on a love-saint's feast day was taking hold in Wales, Europe was losing interest in it. The custom of writing Saint Valentine's Day poems draws to an end in several European countries during the seventeenth century, but continued in the United Kingdom and later in America following the great surge of emigration there.

The eighteenth century

Eighteenth-century Welsh Valentine poems frequently offer a narrative element. That story is sometimes placed within the context of the seasons, noting the significance of the spring season in man's story. As spring starts to unfold, the invisible forces of nature bring about certain expectations of hope and reawakening. At this appointed time of mid-February, Arthur Jones the sexton notes that the richly attired birds, in accordance with the laws of nature, go courting.[59] In much the same way, the poet hopes to be transformed from being wintry of heart to being swiftly joined together with his love. Thomas Edwards writing on behalf of Peter Jones alludes to February as 'mis du' (the black month), but a month nonetheless which, once the feast of Saint Valentine has dawned, brings to light the fact that spring is on the increase. The flesh of every bird and fish realizes its desire, and human friendships flourish too, by the ordinance of Providence.[60] Moreover, Thomas Edwards concludes that this should not cause surprise: boys (or young men) will be boys, he insists.

An anonymous dialogue poem[61] copied into an undated manuscript in the Penrice and Margam Collection (no. A72) held at the National Library of Wales, Aberystwyth,[62] a Valentine poem which probably dates from the eighteenth century, forms part of the traditional genre of sending a bird as a messenger – a common convention in Welsh love poetry. In this case the message-bearer of love is the nightingale.[63] Described as being matchlessly fluent, and as one that performs long, loud, magnificent boasts to potential mates, the nightingale sings a song of exquisite praise, and is indeed the captain of the forest. No finer messenger could greet the poet's love: the bard could do no better himself. The message the nightingale should convey is that the poet is proudly wearing the young woman's name as a Valentine garland. How was that accomplished? It becomes clear that the poet, on one occasion and in company, randomly drew her name from a cask or box – the usual means of drawing a Valentine, as attested in a number of songs from the seventeenth and eighteenth centuries.[64]

The anonymous poet is unsure of his fate at the hands of this young woman. It was her prerogative to accept or reject any name presented to her, and she would possibly have received a number of offers from various eager potential lovers. But although the poet is taking a step into the unknown by sending this bird as a go-between, he lives in hope that the woman will be true to him; and if she is not, it cannot be helped – after all, she can only act in accordance with her own mind and conscience.

There is room to speculate, however, whether drawing lots was genuinely what it seemed. Was it a situation governed by chance? Or could fortune have been offered a helping hand in the task of choosing partners in rural Wales? The drawing of lots was probably an addition to the already popular custom of regarding the first person of the opposite sex sighted on Saint Valentine's Day as that person's Valentine for the following year. A woman of status might not wish to find herself in the company of a workman for the coming year; Mrs Pepys in fashionable London refused to look at painters who were working in her home for fear a tradesman would become her Valentine. Drawing Valentines successfully and without embarrassment was often a prearranged procedure in order to avoid being disadvantageously paired. Edward Edwards writing (in English) in 1757 was conscious of a mismatch between his own fortunes and those of his chosen partner:

> As you are maid of high degree
> Pray be not angered now with me;
> It was my fortune at this time
> To draw you for my Valentine.[65]

Richard David of Llanymawddwy, however, boasts his luck at the urn of love:

> Eich enw llon a ddaeth i'm llaw,
> Hawddgara' bun, yn un o naw
> Ymysg ifienctid trefnid traw,
> Hardd fenyw hylaw, hwylus;
> Yn tynnu Falentine gytûn,
> Gwawr radol, fun gariadus,
> Y fi fu heno, blode ha,
> Rwy'n leicio, yn fwya lwcus.[66]

[Your happy name came into my hand, | Most pleasant young woman, one of nine | From among [the names of] the young people arrayed there, | Beautiful, skilful [and] friendly woman; | In drawing [the name of] an agreeable Valentine, | Gracious dawn, loving young woman, | It was I who was this evening, choicest [one] of summer, | I am so pleased, the most lucky.]

A man pleased with his Valentine would invite the woman to walk with him on love's paths. But should she feel that the suitor is too feeble for her she is advised not to feel offended; she should simply burn the lottery paper. Edward Edwards urges Mrs M. E. thus on Saint Valentine's Day 1757:

A heart of gold, new love of mine,
I draw you for my Valentine,
Your lot was cast and so I drew
And fortune said it must be you
I drew you from amongst ye rest,
The reason was I loved you best
And if you do these lines refuse
Ye paper burnt and me [excuse].[67]

Two references are made to the custom of greeting the hoped-for partner by letter, one by Ioan Siencyn and the other by E.W. This could be a reference to the paper selected from the urn, or to a follow-up letter of invitation to become the lover's partner. It is unclear whether such a document contained a message of love, or a Valentine's Day poem or note, possibly declaring the name selected and claiming a gift.

Having obtained the woman's agreement to become paired for the duration of the festival, the young man's chief delight is to wear the woman's name. Richard Thomas states clearly:

I wisgo eich enw gwastad
    Rwy'n gofyn cennad, clywch y cwyn,
A hyn o dasg dan ddyddie'r Pasg,
    Y ganaid feinwasg fwyn.[68]

[To wear your agreeable name | I ask permission, heed the plea, | And this task [I will undertake] until the days of Easter, | The radiant, slim-waisted, gentle one.]

It is emphasized that it is not for gain that the lover wishes to bear that name, but for love. Not all eighteenth-century Welsh Valentine poems demand material gifts. Indeed a few declare that such gifts are unnecessary. John Jenkin states that he desires K.R. as his Valentine, not in order to obtain a payment of great worth, but out of sincere love for a greatly esteemed young woman (who later became his wife). An anonymous poem states that there is no desire for a material gift, but that the poet be allowed to greet his love, and to contemplate her beauty.[69] Arthur Jones, the sexton of Llangadwaladr in Denbighshire, fostered a similar ambition. Even if he were a rich man, and could choose on a rich man's whim, Arthur Jones would stay true to his lovely M.R.

> Petawn i berchen mil o bunne mi rown fy meddwl yr
>   un modde,
> Am fod hyd ange yr dynged imi dy gael yn gowled,
> Coelia hyn o faled fer;[70]

> [If I possessed a thousand pounds I would [still] set my mind in the same way, | So that it were destined that I should have you in my embrace unto death, | Give credence to this short ballad.]

The woman's name is worn until Easter. Lent bridges Saint Valentine's Day and Easter, and is a forty-day period of fasting in preparation for the Easter celebrations and in commemoration of Christ's fasting in the wilderness. The penitential character of Lent made it a time of great restraint. Bearing a woman's name could have meant being close to her, yet being physically apart. Several weddings would be celebrated at Easter, following this period of penitence.

Many Valentine's Day poems were written to married women. Edward Edwards addresses Mrs N-M to ask her permission 'I'ch gwisgo yn ffri', to wear her name freely.[71] Single women were occasionally courted through the medium of such poems. Indeed, Ioan Siencyn's poem could be read as a proposal of marriage, no less; entitled '. . . Valantine i'w gariad, a'i wraig yn ôl hynny' (. . . a Valentine to his sweetheart, and his wife after that) it is not clear whether he is choosing K.R. simply as his Valentine partner, or as his life partner:

> K. R., rwyf fi'n dy ddewis di
> Fod i myfi'n gydmares,
> Fy nuwies gynnes, gu.[72]

[K. R., I choose you | To be my partner, | My warm, dear goddess.]

Wishing to wear the woman's name in public as a mark of love, Jonathan Hughes writing on behalf of and in the persona of Evan Evans reports that he will place the revered name of his true love, Jane Lewis, '[y]ng nghopa fy nghapan' (on the crown of my cap):

> Eich enw da chwi fydd mowredd i mi
> Dros ddeufis neu dri, y lili oleulan,
> Yng nghopa fy nghapan, nid bychan fy mri![73]

[Your good name will be my greatness | Over two or three months, the pure bright lily, | On the crown of my cap, I shall not be of little esteem!]

Nor would Evan Evans deem it inappropriate were he to receive a kiss or two from Jane's shining lips. It is the custom of the land, he assures her, to be on the lookout for pleasure and merry-making from Valentine's festival until Easter and this 'clefyd' (line 43), ailment, has overcome him too. So much so, that all the good intentions regarding the solemnity of Lent have been put aside.

A highly impassioned poet might ask for a lock of his lover's hair. It was popular among European men to wear a lovelock, usually plaited and made to rest over the left shoulder (the heart side), to show devotion to a loved one. Women in history have regularly presented a lock of hair for a loved one to appreciate and cherish in their absence.[74] Dafydd Jones of Trefriw has a single request:

> Cael un o'ch gwallt chwi i'w roi ar 'y mhen i …
> Ac yna bydd hardd i'ch weled eich bardd
> A'i gorun fel gardd.[75]

[To have one lock of your hair to place on my head … | And then it will be comely for you to see your poet | With the crown of his head like a garden.]

Wearing a lock of a woman's hair is a symbol of loyalty and undying faithfulness, but also commands power over that individual. Should the poet not be bold enough to request a lock of hair he could adorn himself with flowers:

Eich enw, gwawr wen, fel blodau pêr bren,
G'leuni heb drueni yw fy mhwysi yn fy mhen.[76]

[Your name, white dawn, is like the blossom of a fragrant tree, |
My posies on my head are uninterrupted light.]

The Edward Morris seventeenth-century *cywydd* states that Welsh suitors selected a ribbon as adornment.[77] Such decorations were the outward signs of becoming 'tan nod', being under obligation to a woman, or becoming her servant; this is consistently found in Welsh Valentine songs, a situation proclaimed with pride and great amusement. In the medieval Welsh laws 'gŵr nod'[78] was a person eligible to act as a sworn witness to the innocence or good character of an accused person: a man of distinction, an illustrious person. Valentine songs claim the same freedom to proclaim a woman's praise. However, the poet would expect payment for his loyalty. In the seventeenth century Huw Morys was quick to remind his Valentine of her duties:

Blode gwlad Troea, yn ddigysgod mi a'ch gwisga,
Dewises y lana', hawddgara' wrth ei grudd;
Chwi wyddoch y gyfreth am hyn o wasaneth,
Mae imi daladigeth yn digwydd.[79]

[The most superior in the land of Troy, I will wear you[r name
openly and] without shadow, | I have chosen the most beautiful, most amiable by [the blush of] her cheek; | You are acquainted with the custom as regards this duty, | A remuneration is to be made to me.]

The exact nature of the payment is not stated, but the woman has a moral obligation to repay the honour of having her named indicated so clearly. If 'cyfraith' here carries the meaning 'law' rather than 'custom', then it holds a more serious significance. Similarly in the eighteenth century, Cadwaladr Morus insists that his Valentine has a legal obligation to gift him – possibly a tongue-in-cheek statement and perhaps not meant to be taken seriously.

> rwy'n gwisgo'ch enw,
> Cri air croyw, loyw lein:
> Ceisiwch, gwenfron, lunieiddlon lili,
> Lwyr gyflawni ffansi, rhag ffein;
> Parliament mwyngu sydd yn barnu,
> Cyfraith mabiaeth meibion Cymru,
> Y dylech dalu eich Falendein![80]

[I wear your name, | A word of sweet entreaty, [in a] pol-ished line [of poetry]: | Attempt, white-breasted young woman, graceful and joyous lily, | To wholly fulfil a fancy, for fear that [you are penalized with] a fine; | [The] tender and amiable parliament has decreed, | Law of frivolity of the young men of Wales, | That you should pay your Valentine [gift]!]

During the seventeenth century and in most instances during the eighteenth century 'Valentine' or 'Valant' referred to a person, but can also refer to a Valentine's gift. Ioan Siencyn, writing at the behest of Thomas Lewis of Pant Hwdog, Cynwyl Elfed, Carmarthenshire in 1743, demonstrates that legal steps would be threatened on anyone, man or woman, for withholding repayment of gifts. The poem 'Cwyn-fan merch a dalodd Valantein' (The plaint of a woman who paid a Valentine) tells the story of a woman who received a 'Valant | Oedd galant ei gweled' (a Valentine [gift] | That was a splendid sight [to behold]) from Rhys Dafydd, and she honoured him with a groat's worth of garters in return.[81] Unfortunately:

> Pan cas e'r gardyson
> O gwmpas ei goesau
> Fe drows arna' ei gefen,
> Gu feinwen, gwae finnau:
> Merch arall a'i hudodd
> Ac yntau yn anwadal,
> Am dorri ei addewid
> Fe ddaw arno ddial …
> Myfi yn ei drwsio
> A hi['n] mynd â'i bleser.[82]

[As soon as he placed the garters | About his legs | He turned his back on me, | Loving, fair-complexioned slim one, woe is me: | Another girl charmed him | And he was fickle, | For breaking his promise | Revenge will come upon him … | I clothing him | And she receiving his sensual gratification.]

She vows to bring the culprit to justice and the trial would be held in Hereford at the Court of Great Sessions where all criminal offences were heard, to be dealt with by a judge and jury. There is a clear note of exaggeration in this poem: it seems highly unlikely that felonies and serious misdemeanours committed in the village of Cynwyl Elfed (in Carmarthenshire) or in its vicinity would be prosecuted in Hereford, over one hundred miles away, when the Court of Great Sessions also met twice a year at Carmarthen, within six miles of the alleged criminal's home. However, cases of greater consequence were frequently tried on the English circuits, for example at Hereford, 'for the advantage of trying a cause at Hereford is not merely the having of a better judge, but, among other things, the having a better jury' than Carmarthen, in the Court's estimation, could typically produce.[83] Wherever the case was heard, the plaintiff would have the satisfaction of seeing Rhys Dafydd brought down: it would have been much wiser, she reflects, for Rhys Dafydd to have taken her as his gentle, most perfect partner.

Several eighteenth-century Saint Valentine's Day poems requesting a favour or gift have survived: John Jones (*fl.* second half of the eighteenth century[84]) of Llanddeiniolen's undated poem of gratitude is the only extant example of a poem expressing appreciation for such a gift. On the popular *tri thrawiad* metre he thanks Siân Humphrey for her unspecified offering, which he vows he will wear openly, possibly a pair of gloves.

Mi gefais rodd hynod, yn Falandine barod,
Yn ôl y pur amod, gwych eurglod fo i chwi,
A diolch yn dirion o w'llys fy nghalon,
Mun ffyddlon nod union, amdani.[85]

[I have received an excellent gift, a prepared Valentine, | In accordance with the sincere promise, magnificent golden praise be to you, | And I thank you tenderly from the bottom of my heart, | Faithful young woman of honest renown, for it.]

Essentially, eighteenth-century Valentine's Day songs and poems communicate the everyday human qualities of love and friendship. With a view to gaining credit for furthering their emotional impact by imaginative use of poetical genius, eighteenth-century poets often introduced a few extravagant gestures into their line structure to attract the attention of their chosen partners. One such strategy was to intertwine the letters of the Valentine partner's name within their poem's lines. The following example features the name of Mari Morys:

Fel hyn **MA**e henw'r lodes
Fwyneiddia e**RI**oed a weles,
Mi a'i sgrifennes, gynnes gannwyll,
MOR gymw**YS**, hwylus, haela.[86]

[This is the **MA**iden's name, | Fai**R**est that **I** ever saw, | I wrote it down, affectionate candle, | **MO**st proper, f**R**iend**lY**, most generou**S**.]

Dafydd Jones of Trefriw wrote in a similar manner, working the letters of the young Valentine's Christian name, Jane, and the letters of her surname, Foulk, into his poem. He delights in the pleasure of being able to wear the nine beautiful letters that spell out the name of his sweetheart.

J ac A, heulwen ha', hoyw wen serchog,
Yw f'angyles enwog, E ac N, walches wen,
A ga' dros ben hawddgarwch byd;
F ac O, drefnus dro, drwyadl ei 'madroddion,
Lana erioed a welson, U, L, K, *vowels* da,
Galonnog o'r lawena i gyd.[87]

[J and A, summer sunshine, cheerful [and] affectionate young woman, | Is my renowned angel, E and N, blessed noble woman, | That I will take, over and above the world's loveliness; | F and O [in their] correct order, eloquent her expression, | The fairest that we ever saw, U, L, K, good vowels, | The most sincere of all the most delightful [women].]

The letters need not necessarily appear in order if the needs of the rhyming scheme are to be easily accommodated. John Thomas, Penffordd-wen (1757–1835) sets down, in no particular order, the nine letters that form the name of his heart's delight. He then challenges his audience to solve the mystery of this riddle: who is it that he loves?

> Rhof R ac O, i ledio i lawr,
> N, E, dwy A, rai gwycha'u gwawr,
> Dwy S, a J, sy'n ola'n eilio[88]

[First I will set down R and O, | N, E [and] two As, of most excellent hue, | Two Ss, and J, that interweave finally.]

The poet requests R + O + N + E + A + A + S + S + J (= Sara Jones) to be charitable and to present him with a gift before Easter Day so that God and man can witness the young woman's generosity.

Women utilized the same technique. The following quotation is from an eighteenth-century Saint Valentine's Day poem written by an anonymous woman to her lover, Lewis Jones, requesting a Valentine. If she were given the choice of any man on this island, she would choose Lewis Jones and she weaves the initials of his name into the opening lines of her poem:

> Hyd atoch, hafedd gannwyll Gwynedd,
>   Gore ei fonedd o Gaer i Fôn,
> L E diledieth, W I diwenieth,
>   Ac S eilweth mewn sylwedd sôn,
> I O diamhur, N E dan awyr,
>   Ac S dda ei gysur mewn synnwyr sydd
> Yn flode meibion[89]

[Unto you, summery light of Gwynedd, | Of the best lineage from Chester to Anglesey, | Eloquent L E, sincere W I, | And S to speak of [you] again [as one] with substance, | Pure J O, N E beneath sky, | And S of good comfort who is in every sense | The most superior of young men.]

Occasionally the suitor's home environment is noted in the poem. Evan Evans of Cwm Eger, Bryneglwys, in south Denbighshire, introduces himself and his home thus:

Un Evans wyf, clywch, o garmon oer guwch,
Nid oes un wlad uwch, ces goruwch cwr Lloeger
Fy magu yng Nghwm Eger dan lawer o luwch.[90]

[I am Evans, listen, a lover with a cold frown, | There is no
higher country, I was, above England's border, | Brought up in
Cwm Eger under many snowdrifts.]

At times both the suitor's address and that of his Valentine are men-
tioned. Thomas Edwards 'Twm o'r Nant' writes on behalf of Peter
Jones of Prion in the parish of Llanrhaeadr-yng-Nghinmeirch, Den-
bighshire, introducing both Peter Jones and his Valentine Beti Rob-
erts, Buarth Mawr, Prion:

A m'fi, *Peter Jones*
O Brion, sy â'm bron
Yn hoffeiddlon goffáu
Hen arfer, hoen wirfodd,
A glymodd yn glau.
Chwychwi, *Beti Rob[er]ts*,
Yn bert sydd i'm bodd
Yn Valandein dyner,
Wir haelber ei rhodd.
Drwy eich gwirfodd a'ch gwawr
Rwy' yn erfyn cynhorthwy
Borth mwy'r *Buarth Mawr*.[91]

[And I, *Peter Jones* | *Of Prion*, do in my heart | Lovingly and
joyfully call to mind | An old custom of voluntary passion |
Which has swiftly tied together [in marriage]. | You, *Beti Rob-
erts*, | Please me prettily | As a tender Valentine, | Truly
generous and pure of gift. | Through your readiness and
your radiance | I beg the assistance, | The greater aid, of
Buarth Mawr.]

Compare this formula with lines from a seventeenth-century
poem that names the loved one in a less flamboyant manner. The
poet here indulges in tmesis, possibly in imitation of the style of the
cywyddwyr (poets of the *cywydd*), which entails the division of the

two elements of a personal name such as Sioned Williams by inter-
vening words:

> *Sioned* wyd y seined wych,
> Lliw distrych ar y don,
> *Williams* eilwaith helaeth wyd,
> Lloer annwyl, deg ei bron.[92]

> [*Sioned*, you are the noble signet, | [One with a complexion]
> the colour of white-crested waves at sea, | *Williams* you are
> repeatedly generous, | Cherished moon, fair of breast.]

Classical references

Country poets and rhymesters were an integral part of the Welsh cul-
tural landscape, but the more skilled the poet the greater the embel-
lishments. This was true of the poets of the early free-metre poetry[93]
and of the *cywyddwyr*, the strict-metre poets of the late medieval and
early modern periods. Many adorned their poems with references to
the heroes and heroines of Greece and Rome, and similar references
are found in Welsh Valentine poems.

Venus and Helen of Troy are the two most popular figures men-
tioned. No details are offered; it is assumed that the audience is well
acquainted with their beauty and attractiveness to men from time
immemorial. Venus, the Roman goddess of beauty and sensual love, is
mentioned by Huw Morys, Jonathan Hughes, Rees Lloyd, John Rees,
Ellis Rowland and in three anonymous poems.[94] She shares her posi-
tion at the heights of the popularity charts with Helen of Troy, the
Greek model of beauty and feminine charm. Helen is named twice
by Ellis Rowland,[95] by an anonymous poet[96] and is referred to as Elen
by two other anonymous poets.[97] She is cited indirectly by Jonathan
Hughes, who mentions the one who is from Troy, the fortified city of
Homer's *Iliad*, besieged by the Greeks when Helen, the wife of the
king of Sparta, was abducted.[98] Another anonymous poet (possibly
Huw Morys) describes his love as '[b]lode gwlad Troea' ([t]he most
superior in the land of Troy), the fairest and most beautiful young
woman ever seen.[99]

Ellis Rowland (*c*.1650–*c*.1730) cites various models of beauty
and excellence in his poem requesting a Valentine's gift from Lowry

William.[100] The poem appears on a ballad sheet printed in Shrewsbury by John Rhydderch for the seller, Owen Williams. John Rhydderch was a printer in Shrewsbury during the years 1715–33, and the printing of this Valentine song can be dated to that period, but not necessarily its date of composition.

Ellis Rowland cites Helen of Troy twice, Aurora the goddess of dawn in Roman mythology once (line 10) and Venus three times (lines 11, 21, 34); he states that Lowry William has surpassed even the standard of excellence achieved by the legendary Phoenix, the fire bird that is resurrected from the ashes of his predecessor (line 13). Greek poet Homer (line 15) and Roman poet Virgil (line 17) could both be firmly relied on to compose epic poems in honour of Lowry William, it is claimed. Orpheus (line 18), an archetype of the inspired singer in ancient Greek religion and myth, would love to make music to Lowry William, as would the nine Muses (line 19) who in Greek mythology were believed to be the inspiration of literature, science and the arts.

The Judgement of Paris is alluded to in this poem (lines 21–30), and the beauty contest between three of Olympus' most alluring goddesses for the prize of the golden apple. Aphrodite (identified with the planet Venus), Mars and Juno are the three contestants mentioned: Paris of Troy was asked to decide which of them was the most beautiful and he chose Aphrodite (Venus), influenced by her promise to give him Helen for his wife. Ellis Rowland declares that had Lowry William entered the contest for the golden apple then she would undoubtedly have been the victor.

Cupid, the Roman god of love often portrayed as the son of the love goddess Venus, and the equivalent of the Greek Eros, is referenced twice in Welsh Saint Valentine's Day poems, once by Huw Morys who holds Cupid responsible for not having turned back the tide of love, causing the poet to suffer great affliction because of his violent passion for a beautiful woman; the second reference is by Arthur Jones of Llangadwaladr who suffers in a similar vein.[101]

Biblical role models

Greek and Roman heroines are not the sole point of comparison: Welsh women are compared favourably with biblical women. In a poem written by Rees Lloyd on behalf of Richard Foulk of Bwlch-y-ddâr near Llanrhaeadr-ym-Mochnant, it is claimed that his love, 'E dwbwl W' (E double W),[102] Elisabeth Williams, the daughter of Green Hall on the outskirts of Llanfyllin, was comparable with Sarah, Abram's wife in the Old Testament.[103] Abram remarks of his wife 'thou art a fair woman to look upon'; the Egyptians were equally impressed and 'when Abram was come into Egypt, the Egyptians beheld the woman that she was very fair'.[104] Not only was Sarah beautiful, she was also a shadow of the covenant of grace.[105] Elisabeth Williams is also a veritable rose of Sharon,[106] praise indeed, implying extreme beauty and an intoxicating fragrance.[107]

In an anonymous poem (poem 22) the object of the poet's love, the generous and excellent Elsbeth, is described not only alongside Helen, but also in the company of two highly respected biblical women, Rachal (Rachel) and Martha, and with Susannah from the Apocrypha. Tuana is an unknown woman; Rachel (in the Old Testament) was the daughter of Laban, the favoured wife of Jacob and the mother of his favourite children, Joseph and Benjamin: 'Rachel was beautiful and well favoured.'[108]

Martha (in the New Testament) is not remembered so much for her beauty as for being a much cherished, conscientious woman who cared for her home and family: her sister Mary and brother Lazarus. Jesus Christ was a close family friend and they shared several important episodes in his life. The family's home was in Bethany, close to Jerusalem, and Jesus often stayed there while visiting the Jewish festivals in Jerusalem. On one occasion he had cause to chasten Martha for being overly concerned with her domestic duties, and for being distracted by too much serving at tables and neglecting to feed her soul.[109]

The brief story of Susannah is told in the Greek but not the Hebrew manuscripts of the Book of Daniel in the Old Testament; the Book of Susannah is considered by many to be apocryphal. She is described as being beautiful and righteous, trained in the law of Moses (verses 2–3). In sixty-four verses, the story of how she was falsely accused of adultery unfolds, and how she received deliverance by the hand of Daniel. Susannah became a symbol of a soul saved by grace. This anonymous, highly skilled poet was possibly familiar with the *cywydd* written by Dafydd ap Dafydd Llwyd in which he lists the names of virtuous biblical wives, for example Rebecca, Judith, Hannah, Anna, Mary, Sarah and Susannah:

> Gwraig Abram ddinam oedd dda
> Henwydd siwr hon oedd Sara
> A Rebecca oedd dda ddoeth
> A i gweddi ar Dduw gwiwddoeth
> Siwsana dan sias iawn wr
> Bu feinir gywir iw gwr
> A Judeth wiw lyweth lan
> A ddugwyd yn ddiogan
> Anna mi Cofid nid Cel
> Di siomwaith oedd fam Sam'wel
> Anna eilfodd anwyl-ferch
> Oedd a gair a Mair ei merch
> Ni ddown o ben ei henwi
> Y da wragedd rhinwedd rhi.[110]

[Faultless Abram's wife was virtuous; | She, Sarah, was of unquestionable pedigree, | And Rebecca was good [and] wise | And she prayed to God [who is] worthy and wise; | Susannah, courted by a righteous man, | Became a true gentlewoman to her husband; | And Judith, beautiful and devout lock [of hair], | Was irreproachably led; | Hannah, it is remembered, it is not a secret, | Without disappointment, was the mother of Samuel; | Anna in the same manner was a woman beloved [of God] | [She] prophesied a message to her daughter Mary. | I will never be able to complete [the task] of naming | The good wives of regal virtue.]

The *cywydd* is written in answer to 'Cywydd Duchan i Wragedd' (A *cywydd* of satire on women), in which Roger Cyffin (*fl. c.*1587–1609) criticizes the deceitful nature of women and condemns their flighty spirit.[111] He lists heroes destroyed by women throughout the ages.[112]

There is a single reference to Eve in seventeenth-century Welsh Saint Valentine's Day poetry. Eve is a figure in the Book of Genesis and was the first woman, created from the rib of a man.[113] Huw Morys praises her for her beauty.[114]

Women, too, praise their suitors in biblical terms. The woman who fell for Lewis Jones describes him as being comparable with Solomon in the Old Testament. Solomon, King David's son of Bathsheba, was best known for the splendour of his ways and for the excellence of his plans, particularly in the context of the work of building the temple in Jerusalem. Solomon was also renowned as a wise and prudent man, peaceable of nature, with one outstanding gift: his insight as a lawmaker. In this poem his loyal faith in God is praised, even though the Old Testament accuses him of the sins of idolatry and of turning away from the God of Israel.[115]

Occasionally a poet sings his own praises. Dafydd Jones assures a certain woman that, should she give him one strand of her hair in order to raise his esteem, he would be so happy that he could be compared to Absalom.[116] This is rather a dubious comparison. While it is true that Absalom was his father King David's favourite son, and that he was the most handsome man in Israel having a full head of heavy curly hair, there was also rebelliousness in him, for which he was punished by death: hanging between two oak trees suspended by his attractive hair Absalom was killed by Joab, who took three spears and thrust them into Absalom's heart.

Genealogy

Genealogy and family history have always played a prominent part in the Welsh psyche. It is surprising that only two poems mention the founding families of the women revered in these Valentine songs, even though extolling the virtues of the ancestral family was a feature of Welsh medieval praise poetry: it voiced an admiration of the patron, his family and his lineage. In a Valentine poem written on behalf of Peter Jones, Thomas Edwards 'Twm o'r Nant' (1739–1810) boasts that Beti Roberts, Buarth Mawr, Prion in Denbighshire, was in the noble lineage of Cynfarch ap Meirion,[117] possibly a scribal error for Cynfarch ap Meirchion,[118] father of Urien Rheged.[119] There is, however, a church in the vicinity of the poet's home and that of the two lovers that was dedicated to a Saint Cynfarch:

> but became afterwards, in Norman times, dedicated to the Blessed Virgin Mary. We mean the church of Llanfair Dyffryn Clwyd, where there was at one time a figure of 'Sanctus Kynvarch' in one of the windows. We have here, as in many other cases, an instance of an obscure Welsh saint having to give way to the favourite saint of Latin Christianity.[120]

This is by far the most likely explanation for the reference.

Similarly in his two Valentine stanzas Thomas Lewis describes a certain Mary as being 'lleuad Llywarch' (the moon of Llywarch), possibly a reference to Llywarch Hen, a prince and poet in the Old Northern Celtic kingdom of Rheged, an area of south-western Scotland today; certainly a paean of praise to Mary.[121]

With the close of the eighteenth century the vocal tradition of singing tender stanzas of intimacy to a loved one was fast disappearing. Love stanzas were moving towards the literary, written world of commerce. In England *The Young Man's Valentine Writer* was first published in 1797 offering suitors pre-prepared verses with which to entice partners, whereas Welsh hopefuls still had to write their own verses or depend on the local 'bardd gwlad' (country poet).[122] But a new century was about to dawn on five continents, one that would present its own Saint Valentine's Day delights and challenges.

The nineteenth century

Affectionate love poetry with its references to pure love and generous gifts was still in vogue during the nineteenth century. Love stanzas written by men are more numerous than those written by women, and the custom of inviting a man to write a poem on behalf of a woman was still a common occurrence. David Evans writing under the pen name 'Dewi Dysul' composed (for an anonymous woman) two *englynion*, quatrains composed in the Welsh strict metres, to be sent to Morgan Evans, shopkeeper. Judging from these two *englynion* Dewi Dysul was a poet of unremarkable accomplishment, yet the message is clear: the woman had set her heart on Morgan Evans and Cupid's arrows had pierced every corner of her being so that she was plagued daily by the pains of love.[123]

Not all advances were well received. A poem rejecting advances made by a male suitor was penned by John Jenkins 'Cerngoch' (Redcheek), a Cardiganshire farmer, on behalf of an unnamed young woman.[124] The poem captures the outpourings of the woman's heart as she admits to having tender feelings for the suitor: he is the man whom she loves. But he is also untrustworthy, a man with a twist in his tail, one who will throw her aside, deeming her unworthy of his love once he reaches the dizzy heights of personal ambition.

Gifts were still part of the Saint Valentine's Day celebrations even though they were not always appreciated. In 1876 a certain John sent his sweetheart Mary a pair of gloves, but she took offence because the gloves were too big and sent John a nightcap in return. Others were more kindly received. In the same report it is noted that Liza Jones bought a beautiful Valentine card and enclosed within it a piece of ribbon worth two shillings; on the following morning she was requited with the same amount of ribbon and a pretty card.[125] A Saint Valentine's Day card from the historical county of Glamorgan was accompanied by a stanza (in English) and a ring; this was possibly meant as a specific proposal of marriage, or perhaps as a simple courtship tradition in the same vein as the giving of gloves.

> This little Ring I offer you
> > Conveys to you my Heart
> 'Tis wounded – but I know my dear
> > You soon can heal the smart.[126]

Some lovers gave their sweetheart a lock of hair, perhaps secretly in a fit-for-purpose brooch or locket. Receiving hair as a keepsake from a loved one was common in various cultures, but the practice evolved on a large scale in the United Kingdom during the Victorian era when hair was an important signifier of love. Victorian women exchanged locks of hair between close friends, so much so that hair jewellery manufactured in silver and gold became very common. Tiny snippets of hair could be accommodated in pendants, but a braid would need to be arranged in a bracelet or brooch, or even displayed prominently under glass. By the last quarter of the nineteenth century the most popular piece of hair jewellery in Wales was a silver brooch, inexpensive and practical, sometimes engraved with the lover's name or with the words 'Cofiwch fi' (Remember me); 'Mizpah', Hebrew for 'Lord watch over me',[127] was another favourite inscription, and marked an agreement between two people with God as their witness. Such jewellery was loved by the Victorians, and by men and women even up to the First World War.[128]

Poets of a more benevolent nature, however, desired no material gift, they simply wanted to be kindly remembered:

Gwnewch gofio amdana i'n dyner,
  Feinwen syber, Fenws wen,
Ymhob rhyw le nes mynd i'r ne,
  Ac felly minne, Amen.[129]

[Remember me kindly, | Wise, slender young woman, bright
Venus, | In every place until you reach heaven, | And so will
I do [you], Amen.]

The drawing of lots was in decline by the nineteenth century and
was considered to be a practice observed predominantly by women.
In 1919 one pensive Welshman, as he reminisces on the customs of
the nineteenth century and mourns the loss of the forgotten Saint
Valentine's Day practices, records that it was *gwyryfon* (unmarried
women) who used to congregate to choose their Valentine during
the nineteenth century. Each woman wrote the name of her favoured
suitor on a piece of paper, each paper was placed in a hat or shoe (a
downgrade from the original Roman urn), and which, having been
given a good shake, was passed around for each in turn to choose a
piece of paper. This was done three times and should a woman have
chosen the same name three times then it was inevitable that the per-
son named would lead her to the altar in due course.[130]

The nineteenth century brought with it great changes. The very
meaning of the word 'Valentine' was changing. By about the first
quarter of the nineteenth century a 'Valentine' could well be a poem
rather than a person or gift. Robert Davies (1769–1835) of Nantglyn in
Denbighshire sends John Simon, on behalf of an anonymous young
woman, 'berffaith, lanwaith *line* | O Falendein' (A perfect, well-
wrought line | Of a Valentine).[131] It was during this century too that
'Valentine' also came to mean the letter or card in which the poem
was sent, initially a home-made card, later factory-manufactured in
England. A poem by John Rees of Llanrhaeadr-ym-Mochnant, entitled
'Pennill i'w roi mewn Ffalendine i'w ganu ar fesur a elwir "Follow my
Fancy"' (A stanza to be placed in a Valentine to be sung on the meas-
ure known as 'Follow my Fancy'), certainly suggests this.[132]

In Wales the earliest examples of Valentine cards date from the
beginning of the nineteenth century. The move from the handcrafted,
labour-intensive card (see figure 2) to the factory-manufactured greet-
ing card was gradual, and the collection of Welsh Valentine cards

held at St Fagans National Museum of History (Cardiff) suggests that there was an intermediate form of hand-decorated card in use until the mid-nineteenth century;[133] however, '[t]he period 1840–60 when the embossed and perforated lace valentine was in vogue has justly been called the golden age of valentines'.[134] Cards were sent to one special, secretly admired person, but also to a wider circle of family and friends in general.

> Little Miss, not yet in her teens, with an apron full of love missives, her elder sister pondering over that elaborate work of art, that the postman had to carry under his arms so mighty its proportions, mentally 'tossing up' whether Charles or Algernon sent it. Grandma, too, is not forgotten, but sits in her chair smiling over some floral compliment ... sent by child or grandchild. Even the kitchen is in a state of tumult during the day, and the cook will not be comforted, for she has received an ugly one, she knows, from that perky housemaid opposite.[135]

The old custom, *clymu cwlwm cariad*, or tying a lover's knot,[136] once popular in Wales as part of the divination customs of Winter's Eve, became part of the Saint Valentine's Day custom during the nineteenth century. In Glamorgan, Marie Trevelyan notes that the knots were distributed 'like favours' on this festive day: 'These were sent anonymously, and great was the amusement, and sometimes the consternation of the youths and maidens when these favours appeared on the bodice or coat of anybody present at the revels.' Trevelyan notes that in 'the old Mabsant times dancing was the greatest feature of the [Valentine] festivities'.[137] The lover's knot was later incorporated into the factory-manufactured Valentine card designs.

Drawing lots was no longer crucial to the Saint Valentine's Day custom in Wales. Several accounts note that young men took part in the day's activities without drawing lots, favouring the Valentine card. Looking back at the nineteenth century, Jini Jôns in 1914 writes that there was something quite becoming about the lovely Valentine cards sent to and by young men and women. She also remarks that the day proved advantageous to any young man who loved a fair maid and was perplexed as to how to make that known to her without an introduction. Jini Jôns is convinced that an indeterminate number of couples had been united by means of the pretty, sweet-scented Valentine card and its romantic verse.[138] Mary Russell Mitford in her sketches of rural life in the Berkshire hamlet of Three Mile Cross near Reading (published 1824–32) also concludes that 'many a village beau hath broken the ice of courtship' by means of a Valentine card. Furthermore:

> There is something like sincerity ... even in a Valentine; – as witness the number of wooings begun on the Fourteenth of February, and finished in that usual end of courtships and comedies – a wedding – before Whitsuntide. Our little lame clerk, who keeps a sort of catalogue *raisonnée* of marriages, as a companion to the parish-register, computes those that issue from the bursting Valentine-bag of our postman, at not less than three and a half per annum – that is to say, seven between two years.[139]

No similar statistics exist for Wales.

As new elements appeared in nineteenth-century Valentine poetry, walking the paths of love was becoming far more hazardous than previously. A fondness for mischief-making was transforming the character of the old Valentine custom with its love poetry and kind gifts, as a wide selection of less affectionate Valentine cards appeared in Welsh homes on 14 February. Some messages could be classed as gently teasing, others were of a harsher nature. With the arrival of the postal service, resentful, spiteful verses could be sent anonymously to the one who had disappointed a prospective lover during the year. For a man or woman who held a grudge it was an ideal way of punishing the perceived wrongdoer, of projecting hostility and aggression, of expending some of the bitterness. The postman's visit was eagerly awaited in each town and village, at times with much trepidation. Valentine verses could be extravagantly scornful and could wound the hardiest soul. Since it was the receiving party that paid the postage, doubly embittered feelings rankled in those who had received surly messages and had had to pay for the privilege. The postal service received complaints from several irate fathers who had been forced to pay for the unkind communications sent to their allegedly unattractive daughters. As these painful messages became more and more commonplace Sir Francis Freeling, the secretary of the Post Office, was compelled to report on the matter on 16 February 1824:

> I am induced to bring the subject of the postages charged on *Valentines*, sent by Post, before your Lordship [the Postmaster-General], more especially as I have this day 8 or 10 applications from the Country, claiming a return of such postage.

> I must premise that from time immemorial the Post Office has *not* refunded postage on any thing of that description, but that in the year 1817 I made it a distinct question to the Law Officer of the Department, his opinion which, I now enclose, is clear and to the point, and has hitherto justified the old and immemorial practice of not returning the postage.

> We have however invariably relieved the applicants when there was any thing gross or personally offensive in the communication, and I have even proceeded further by ordering the postage to be reduced to a single letter when the Valentine has been sent in an Envelope.[140]

Placing the letter in an envelope meant that delivery costs doubled as the number of papers carried, as well as the distance travelled, were taken into account when assessing the total cost. However, following Rowland Hill's efforts at reforming the postal system, in 1840 the Uniform Penny Post was established and a letter weighing half an ounce could be sent anywhere within the United Kingdom. During the 1870s the introduction of the halfpenny postage for postcards and unsealed envelopes acted as an added stimulus to Valentine activity. David Vincent estimates that the number of cards sent in London alone peaked at 1,500,000 in the 1870s.[141] And so the hurt remained. It was reported in the *Evening Express*, a daily English-language newspaper supportive of conservative politics that circulated in Cardiff, that: 'At Highgate, London, on Monday, two prepossessing looking girls applied for summonses against the senders of uncomplimentary valentines. The Bench refused the application amid laughter.'[142]

Because of the offensive nature of the verses that were sent anonymously it is hardly surprising that very few were kept. Cheaply printed and crudely coloured by hand, they rejected partners outright. Sent to men, they mocked their trades, professions and appearance; sent to women they were scornful of their appearance, habits and character. Women in particular are accused of breaching conjugal fidelity and happiness, and of scandalmongering. With the advent of printed Valentine cards, not only could one send a noxious stanza, but also a disagreeable image to accompany it, representative of the recipient. Purposefully denouncing and shaming a specific individual for particular weaknesses such as alcoholism, being a 'puppy dog' with no backbone or a 'cur' that is aggressive and unkempt, comic Valentines were impressively cruel. The suggestiveness of anonymous caricaturists and the slander of uncomplimentary anonymous verses have survived in many countries. In Scotland:

> Such caustic productions are sometimes referred to as 'vinegar' valentines or 'penny dreadfuls' … Various trades and professions are satirised, each character being cruelly derided as unworthy of receiving love; many are depicted as drunkards with swollen noses. Satirical valentines were apparently popular with the lower classes and therefore may be described as being examples of 'street literature'. As such, their study can give us an insight into Victorian popular culture.[143]

Various museums in England hold collections of satirical poems that caused great consternation in many households. In Wales the pretty, flamboyant, fussy and sentimental poems were safely kept and highly prized by their recipients: it is possible that the strongly religious nature of the country following the Methodist Revival meant that the more repugnant elements were omitted from Welsh Valentine poems. It is also possible that they are harder to come by 'because, as a rule, they were used more by the lower classes, and by a section of society unable to keep souvenirs of this type over the years'.[144] But a few examples of comic Valentine poems have survived and a small number of a more 'grotesque and venomous' nature have also been kept: 'the comic valentine served as a vehicle for anonymous social criticism as the series of lithographed sheets attacking human foibles and trade shortcomings in the [St Fagans] Museum's collection suggests'.[145]

Among those stanzas of a personal nature is the following English stanza held at St Fagans National Museum of History, Cardiff (see figure 3): the card depicts a woman carrying a stylish umbrella and inelegantly showing off her underwear under a hooped skirt:

> Ears like Donkey, Eyes like cat
> To be genteel, you are too fat
> While there's another in the land
> I'll never claim your mutton hand.[146]

Even though 'the dishonest practice of using dress to imply a social station not possessed' is a recurrent feature of the comic cards,[147] and applies equally to men and women, the following anonymous poem entitled 'Y Folant salw' (The ugly Valentine) from the parish of Llanwenog in Ceredigion, taunts Tomos on account of his unkempt appearance and wishing that he would imitate the neat and fashionable Ianto Cati in dress and deportment:

> Mae'r Folant yma'n dangos
> Shwt fachan wyti, Tomos;
> Pwy all roi cusan fyth ar swch
> Sy'n fwrfwch fel yr andros?
>
> Mi rown lapswchad iti
> Pe gwisget shilcen deidi,
> A britsh ben-lin, a gwasgod flot
> A cot fel Ianto Cati.[148]

[Stanza 1: This Valentine shows | The sort of lad you are, Tomos; | Who can ever plant a kiss on a snout | That is devilishly hairy?

Stanza 2: I would give you a long wet kiss | If you would wear a tidy silk hat, | And knee breeches, and a plaid waistcoat | And a coat like Ianto Cati.]

Romantic relationships could be endorsed by exchanging cute photographs, possibly to be exhibited in a piece of jewellery such as a locket or brooch. Not all photographs, however, were held in high regard. The following poem, entitled 'Y Falenten Hyll' (The Ugly Valentine), is addressed to a certain Catrin: in good faith she had ventured to send her lover a photograph of herself, only to have him laugh at it derisively. Any previous enthusiasm for her had vanished and to stem her eager interest in him he writes:

Rwy'n diolch am eich darlun,
	Y mae e'n ddarlun da;
Rwyf wedi torri'm hesgyrn
	Efo Ha! Ha! Ha!
Pwy wnaeth eich darlun, Catrin,
	Darlun mor dda?
Mae'n werth y byd o chwerthin,
	O Ha! Ha! Ha!

Yr wyf yn fachgen gwirion,
	Heblaw yn fachgen da,
Oherwydd torri'm calon
	Efo Ha! Ha! Ha!
Ni thorraf byth fy nghalon
	O eisiau 'ch llaw fach wen,
Ond gallaf dorri'm calon
	Wrth chwerthin am eich pen.[149]

[Stanza 1: I thank you for your picture, | It is a good picture; |
I have broken my bones | With Ha! Ha! Ha! | Who drew your
picture, Catrin, | Such a good picture? | It is worth the [whole]
world in laughter, | Oh Ha! Ha! Ha!

Stanza 2: I am a simple boy, | As well as being a good boy, |
Because my heart has been broken | With Ha! Ha! Ha! | I shall
never break my heart | For the want of your small white hand, |
But I can break my heart | By laughing at you.]

Macaronic verses from a ballad bearing the English title
'Valentine's Day' and containing English words amidst the mainly
Welsh lines, describe Dick the Postman's journey through a Welsh
town, probably Cardigan in the county of Ceredigion in west Wales,
delivering cards and parcels on 14 February 1879:

Daeth darlun hynod i'r tŷ draw
I'r luniaidd Hannah Murphy,
Sef clamp o garw, goeliaf fi,
A'i drwyn fel cynffon milgi;

Am hyn mae Hannah, druan un,
Yn wallgo rodio allan,
A bygwth mae *Poor Dick* y Post
Am gludo'r darlun aflan.[150]

[A remarkable picture arrived at the house over there | [Addressed]
to the comely Hannah Murphy, | Namely a great big deer, so
I believe, | With a nose like a greyhound's tail; | And because
of this, Hannah, poor girl, | Has stormed off in a fury, | And is
threatening Poor Dick the Post | For delivering the vile picture.]

Moreover, a local farmer's daughter received an image of a baby in
the post:

Ca'dd merch lân rhyw *farmer* 'r anrhydedd, medd Mam,
O dderbyn trwy'r post *pretty baby*;
A 'nawr y mae honno *in practice to come*
A splendid and beautiful Mammy.[151]

[A farmer's pretty daughter had the honour, so Mam says, | Of
receiving in the post [an image of] a pretty baby; | And now she
in practice is to become | A splendid and beautiful Mammy.]

Not all women were astute enough to realize the insult of receiving
a card that contained a satirical portrait. Rhys Dafydd reports the
story of an anonymous woman who received such a Valentine card:
so delighted was she that, almost deranged with pleasure, she could
hardly put it down. She walked from house to house, sharing her
good luck with her neighbours, who agreed that it was a good like-
ness of her, a beautiful woman – with two faces. 'Tro rhyfedd oedd
iddi ei dangos i'r sawl a'i gyrodd. Hwyl garw sydd gan y gwragedd
efo y llun ardderchog' (A pretty pass that she showed it to the one
who sent it. The women had great fun with the splendid portrait). To
add to the merriment, the inscription on the Valentine card was, as
the recipient describes, in 'grammar' and she had to cross the road for
help to read it as she was no scholar herself.[152]

Humorous Valentine poems were sometimes circulated in
nineteenth-century broadsides. One such poem by the musician
William Thomas Rees 'Alaw Ddu' had great marketing potential.[153]

Sung with a refrain, the poem is to be sung by and supports the cause of the unmarried woman, delights in the spinster status and casts cold water on the ideal of married life as a standard of excellence. The poem ridicules the life of the married man:

> Edrycha o'i gwmpas gan sythu mor *larch*
> Â phe bai o wedi ei drochi mewn *starch*;
> A gwnewch iddo giniaw, ni thâl hi ddim byd,
> Mae gormod neu fychan o rywbeth o hyd.

> Cytgan:
> Mi fyddaf hen ferch, mi fyddaf hen ferch,
> Mor hyfryd yw bywyd a rhyddid hen ferch.[154]

[He looks about him and stands up straight as a larch | As if he had been immersed in starch; | And cook him a dinner, it won't do at all, | There is always too much or too little of something or other.

Refrain: I'll be an old maid, I'll be an old maid, | How lovely is the life and the freedom of an old maid.]

The poem is entitled 'Valentine 'r hen ferch' (The old maid's Valentine), or as a more detailed title claims, 'Can newydd a gyfansoddwyd pan ar fordaith i America: Valentine 'rhen ferch' (A new song composed during a voyage to America: the old maid's Valentine); it is subtitled: 'Siân Llwyd, Bwth Unig, at yr hen lanc, Siôn Wmffre, Llwyn Dedwydd: y Bwthyn yng nghanol y Wlad' (Jane Lloyd, Lonely Cottage, to the bachelor, John Humphrey, Grove of Contentment: the Cottage in the depths of the Countryside). Could this declaration act as a catalyst that might cause Siôn Wmffre to try to win over this woman? Siân Llwyd of Bwth *Unig* (*Lonely* Cottage) may have a two-fold outlook on love, taking one stance in her poem, but at the same time suggesting the opposite view: that she has her eye on the old bachelor of Llwyn *Dedwydd* (Grove of *Contentment*).

Betsan Jones describes the nineteenth-century Valentine cards as being very similar to people: some ugly and some pretty. She states that the ugly ones were terrifyingly ugly, 'yn ddigon a chodi ofn ar ddyn pren ac weithia mi roedd na lygodan neu lyffant wedi marw a phetha cas felly tu fewn iddyn nhw' (enough to frighten a wooden man and sometimes there was a dead mouse or frog and suchlike awful things inside them).[155] A young woman would often retire to her room and lock the door before opening a Valentine parcel that arrived in the post 'I farnu a oedd yn un dlws' (To judge whether it was a pretty [valentine]).[156] Twr y Dderi reported that on Saint Valentine's Day 1876 Nelly Jones received a box measuring six inches by three inches, and three inches in depth. All her friends and family gathered around to congratulate her and to see what her sweetheart had sent. Nelly happily opened the gift; sadly it was a dead owl. When the stanzas were read she paled, blushed and laughed in anguish.

> Nelly annwyl, mawr fu'm ffwdan
> I gael darlun o dy hunan,
> Y tebycaf gefais allan
> I dy lun yw llun dylluan.

> Cymer hon, a dod hi'n gynnes,
> Ddarlun cywir, yn dy fynwes
> Nes y caffot un fwy tebyg
> I foddloni dy ddychymyg.[157]

[Stanza 1: Dear Nelly, I have gone to great trouble | To find a picture of you, | The item I found that is most | Like a picture of you is the picture of an owl.

Stanza 2: Take this, and place it warmly, | True picture, in your bosom | Until you find one that is more likely | To satisfy your imagination.]

Nelly promptly threw a shawl over her shoulders and stalked out. Her mother was in a foul temper and shouted angrily that she would rather lose the best cow from the cowshed than not know who had sent the offensive package. Nelly's family believed the Valentine parcel had been sent by the son of the neighbouring farmer, but local rumour suggested that it was Nelly's jealous cousin who was responsible, in the hope of gaining the farmer's son for herself. The inevitable reply arrived at the farmhouse in two days' time. It contained a dead bat, the owl's tongue pulled from its roots and the following stanzas:

Mae dy rodd yn ddiogel ddigon
A chredaf ddyfod hon o'th galon,
Ond pam anghofiaist gadw'i thafod
I grio'r nos ar ôl rhianod?

Ystlum du y nos a wrendy
Gri'r ddylluan rhwng y llwyni;
Cymer rhain a gweld a ddaw
'R noson nesaf y cei groesaw.

Myn rhai adael eu perthnasau
Ar y plwy i dreulio'u dyddiau;
Yn lled debyg mynnaist tithau
Daflu'th nain i'm cwpwrdd innau.[158]

[Stanza 1: Your gift is safe enough | And I believe that it came from your heart, | But why did you forget to keep its tongue | To cry after the young women at night?

Stanza 2: The black bat of the night listens to | The cry of the owl in the woods; | Take these and see if it comes | The next night when you are welcomed.

Stanza 3: Some insist upon leaving their relatives | To spend their remaining days on the parish (i.e. in receipt of poor relief); | In quite a similar vein, you insisted on | Throwing your grandmother into my cupboard.]

Jini Jôns sums it up when she says that sending a 'falantein hull' or ugly Valentine was a system whereby one neighbour could express his true feelings towards another neighbour in a written testimonial that was often a malicious character assassination.

Doedd dim llun na geirie yn rhu shocin i'w rhoi ar y rhein. Hefo y rhein y bydden ni yn mesur ac yn pwuso ac yn dadgymalu ac yn x-reo ein gilidd, ne yn cynal 'trengholiad' ar ein giludd cin i'r ymwahaniad gymrud lle.[159]

[There was no picture or words too shocking to put on these. It was with these that we would evaluate and dismember and x-ray one another, or hold an inquest on one another before the separation.]

On the morning of 14 February, as Jini Jôns records, the faces of some men and women who ventured out into the street were a veritable sermon on sour bread. Knowing full well that the person who had sent the ugly Valentine was on the watch for them, they could hardly keep the indignation from their faces. And although the world had settled down and become a wiser place since then, according to Jini Jôns, she surmises that sending such a Valentine would do no harm at all to the occasional 'startshi benuchel' (arrogant starchy) that disfigured the valley, or to the fast girls running all the way to destruction or the slanderous gossips who were corrupting the air about them, not to mention anyone or anything of greater importance.

One rarely encounters contemporary reports written in dialect, but nineteenth-century vernacular was superb as regards content, exceptional in style and not confined to women journalists from north Wales. One anonymous male contributor offered the following report to his weekly newspaper *Tarian y Gweithiwr* (The Worker's Shield) in Aberdare in the Cynon Valley in south Wales:

Trw bo fi wedi dechra gweid pethach bothti garu a phido prioti, fe weta air bach yto am y ffashwn sy'n arfadd bod yn y mish hwn, yn enwetig ar y 14eg o hono, o ala Falanteins. Ma pob short a honynt idd u cal, a ma nhw iddi gweld nawr wth y milodd yn ffenestri'r shopa. Fe fydd y merched a'r bechgyn yn ala shew o arian ar y trash hyn cyn diwedd y mish, a ma llawar o bethach insyltin yn cal u doti yndi nhw amball waith, os bydd cwpwl wedi bod yn jocan caru sha'u gilydd a wedi cwmpo mas. Fe fydd y ferch yn ala llun salw o rwpath ar lun dyn, a thrwyn coch mawr seis dwrn Sylifan, a coesa cam a dicon o le i wagan briwari fynd rhyngti nhw, er mwyn profoco'r hen sponar; a fe fydd ynta *by return* yn ala pictwr o hen fenyw a'i gwallt hi'n shang-di-fang, fel sa fa heb gal u gripo am dair wthnos, a bocsad o snyff yn i llaw, a brwsh parth wth i ochr hi, er mwyn poeni ticyn ar ysbryd yr hen wedjan. Weti'n, i wella ticyn ar erchylldra'r photagraphs fe fydd pishis o ganu yndi nhw, yn trin caritors u gilydd, a

ma'r steil ma nhw wedi cal u gneid yn ddisgres i dalent fardd-
onol Belsabyb. Llethir y Postmen druen gen dynelli o stwff
felna am ddyrnota nes bydd u hysgwydda nhw yn blistro.
Ma'n bryd i ienctyd yr os ola hon dowli'r hen ffashwn hon
naill ochor am byth, a ma'n dda gen i nag os dim cymaint o'i
dilyn hi nawr ag odd slawar dydd. Din nhw dda i ddim ond
i ala teimlada cas rhwng merched a bechgyn a'u dysgu nhw i
drin i gilydd yn lle caru'r naill a'r llall. Ma Falenteins o short
arall hefyd wedi cal u gneid yn bert rhyfeddol, ac yn cal i ala
fel cenhadon serch i'r ferch a'r bachan. Dw i ddim yn selog
yn erbyn rhai felna os bydd rhw ferch fach deidy yn dewish
ala un i fi mwn box neis a dicyn o sent yn weddol tu fewn i'r
Postman gal gwinto ta nid Falentein gas fydd hi, yn towli slyr
ar y ngharitor carwriaethol i. Ag os aliff hi i adres tu fewn, os
bydd hi yn y mhleso i, a'r fenyw lle w i yn lodjo, falla alaf ina
un nol iddi hitha, wath ma atnod yn gweid:

> 'Cân di benill mwyn i'th nain,
> Fe gân dy nain i titha.'[160]

[Since I have started to comment on courting and not getting
married, I will comment a little further regarding the fashion
that is practised during this month, particularly on the 14th, of
sending Valentines. There are all sorts on offer, and they are
to be seen now in their thousands in shop windows. Young
women and men will spend good money on this trash before
the end of the month, and many insulting things are put inside
them sometimes if a couple have been courting one another
in jest and have fallen out. The woman will send an ugly
photograph of something resembling a man, with a big red
nose the size of Sullivan's fist, and bandy legs with plenty of
room for the brewery waggon to move beween them, in order
to provoke the old boyfriend; and he will send by return a
photograph of an old woman, her hair higgledy-piggledy,
as if it had not been combed for three weeks, with a box of
snuff in her hand, and a broom beside her, in order to torment
the old girl's spirits. Then, to improve on the vileness of the
photographs, fragments of poetry are included, slandering one
another's character, and the style in which they are written is

a disgrace to the poetic talent of Beelzebub. The Postmen are overwhelmed by tons of such stuff for days, until their shoulders blister. It is high time that the youth of this enlightened age threw aside this fashion forever, and I am glad that it is not followed as closely now as it once was in the past. They are good for nothing but to create bad feeling between young women and men, and to teach them to slander one another instead of the one loving the other. There are Valentines too of a different sort that have been created to look amazingly pretty, and they are sent as love messengers to the woman and to the man. I am not zealously opposed to such things if a tidy little woman chooses to send me one in a nice box with a little decent scent inside so that the Postman can sniff that it is not a vinegar Valentine, one that is a slur on my amatory character. And if she sends her address inside, if she pleases me, and the woman where I lodge, perhaps I will send one back, for there is a Bible verse that says:

'Sing a sweet verse to your grandmother,
Your grandmother will sing to you.']

Birds are a feature of nineteenth-century Welsh Valentine's Day songs, for example 'Y Folantein' (The Valentine) by Daniel Evans 'Daniel Ddu o Geredigion' (1792–1846), a song popular in the Mynydd Bach district (Trefenter and Blaenpennal in central Ceredigion) during the mid-nineteenth century. It speaks of the birds choosing a mate and of the poet's desire to follow their example. He names the beautiful Gwen as his only true love and in the two closing stanzas ardently encourages her to turn to him:

O tro yn awr, tra'n iraidd,
I rwymyn cariad puraidd;
Cawn fyw mewn tes yn gynnes, Gwen,
A'n byd yn hufen hafaidd.

Mae'r gwanwyn ar egino,
Daw blodau'r haf i'w rhifo,
Anturia, Gwen, mae natur gain
Yn cymell sain cydsynio.[161]

[Stanza 1: O turn now, while young and fresh, | To the knot of pure love; | We shall live affectionately in the summer heat, Gwen, | And our world will be like summer cream.

Stanza 2: The spring is about to swell into bud, | The summer flowers will [soon] come to be counted, | Venture, Gwen, [since] beautiful nature | Compels a note of agreement.]

Occasionally birds feature as love messengers and are referred to as Valentines. Two such stanzas have survived from the parish of Llandysul, generic verses that could well be used year upon year for courtship purposes. Stanzas of this nature were ready to hand and available for use, fulfilling their purpose effectively if perhaps lacking in inspiration.

Folant fach, O! cerdd yn fuan,
Paid ag aros dim yn unman;
Disgyn lawr ar bost y gwely
Lle mae nghariad fach i'n cysgu.[162]

[Dear Valentine, O! travel swiftly, | Do not tarry at all in any place; | Alight on the bedpost | Where my dear love sleeps.]

A variant of the stanza was used by John Owen in his (sadly unsuccessful) courtship of Eleanor Pritchard. Miss Mair Jenkins of Waunfawr, Aberystwyth, is the proud owner of six ornately printed Valentine cards dating from the second half of the nineteenth century. They came into her possession through her great-grandfather, Hugh Hughes, who had married the aunt of Eleanor Pritchard, the original recipient of the Valentines. The sender, John Owen, added his own handwritten verse and message, determined to woo Eleanor Pritchard, the woman he cherished above all others. This series of Valentine cards offers a fascinating glimpse of a true-life love story.

Of the six cards, three have been signed by John Owen; one card is unsigned but contains a handwritten message; two are blank (one bearing the printed message 'Guess who sends this' (see figure 4)) and it can only be surmised that he sent a gift with these cards but no greeting, or that the greeting was possibly written on a separate piece of paper, now lost. The second blank card is padded and perfumed and has a dark green scent-bottle nestled into its cushion (see figure 5), an expensive Valentine.[163] The handwriting and orthography suggest little formal education, as does the way in which the line-endings of the love stanzas are independent of the rhyme, suggesting that they were written down from memory. Two envelopes bear the recipient's name and address: Miss Elinor Pritchard/Miss E. Pritchiard of Wern-deg near Tal-y-bont, nine miles north of Aberystwyth, in Ceredigion (see figures 6 and 7). The postal dates are 1872 and 1874; John Owen was aged thirty-five and thirty-seven at this time.

Eleanor Pritchard (1845–1923) was the daughter of Vaughan and Ann Pritchard, Panthaul, Cwm Eleri. According to the 1851 Census of England and Wales, Vaughan and Ann had three children living at home, John (17), Jane (9) and Eleanor (6). The family later moved to Werndeg, Tal-y-bont, and it was there in her new home that Eleanor Pritchard received her Valentine cards. She later moved to Carreg-cadwgan Farm, elderly and blind. Her gravestone in Tal-y-bont records that she died, unmarried, in 1923 at the age of seventy-eight.

John Owen (1837–89) was the son of John and Susannah Owen, Nant-y-nod in Cwm Ceulan, not far from Tal-y-bont. In the 1851 Census, John and Susannah are recorded to have seven children living at home, Anne (20), Elizabeth (17), John (14), Edward (12), Margaret (10), William (7) and Hugh (4). The 1881 Census records that John Owen lived at home in that year, aged forty-four and unmarried. He died aged fifty-two and was buried in the neighbouring village of Llandre.

It is impossible to determine in which order Eleanor Pritchard received the greetings on the four inscribed cards. The card bearing the printed motto 'I'll be constant & true' (see figure 8) opens to reveal a centre panel, framed by a wide cut-out lace border of gold, showing an image of a taunting cat sitting on a stool and a playful, slightly fawning dog looking up at her; the printed message reads 'Let us be happy together' (see figure 9). John Owen added his own handwritten message:

> dyma ffolant yr wif fi yn anfon gyda serch ag wllis galon gan obeithio y cyraiddith i llaw fy ngariad yn llwiddianis – hin yn fir oddi wrth eich gariad [see figure 10]

> [Here is a valentine which I send with love and with all my heart hoping that it will arrive favourably into my love's hand – this in brief from your love].

An image of two hand-clasping lovers enclosed in a delicate white fringe and placed behind an arrangement of roses, evergreen foliage, jewels and silvered cut-out lace, expresses John Owen's desire for Eleanor (see figure 11). Bearing the printed motto 'Constancy', the card expresses the maxim adopted by John Owen as his rule of conduct; he also offers the following handwritten message:

> fy anwil gariad yr wif yn anfon hin o bisin bach attoch i dist gofio
> fy bod I ar gal eto hed y ffolant rhed yn fian paid ag aros dim
> yn in man disgin lawr wrth post y gweli lle mae ngariad fach I
> yn cysgi mae llawer cnwc a llawer pant a llawer cant obethai a
> llawer twmpath bach o frwin rhwngddwi a nghariad ar hin brid.
> hin yn fir oddi wrth eich anwil gariad [see figures 12 and 13]

> [My dear love I send you this short note to testify that I am yet
> available fly valentine travel swiftly do not tarry at all in any
> place alight on the bedpost where my dear love sleeps there
> are many hillocks and many valleys and many hundreds of
> things and many little clumps of rushes between me and my
> sweetheart at this time. this in brief from your dear love].

Red roses and forget-me-nots in a frame of silvered lace adorn the card that bears the following words [see figure 14]:

> hed y folant hed yn fian paid ag aros dim yn in man disgin lawr
> wrth post y gweli lle mai ngarid fach yn gysgi hin fir oddi wrth
> eich anwil gariad [see figures 15 and 16]

> [fly valentine travel swiftly do not tarry at all in any place alight
> on the bedpost where my dear love sleeps this in brief from
> your dear love].

And finally:

> Fy anwyl gariad dirion yr wyf yn cael y cyfle hwn o ddanfon
> hyn o garedigrywydd i chwi yr oeddwn wedi meddwl eich
> gadael chwi heb yr un ond mi feddylias eich gadel chwi heb yr
> un i lodes mor grasawgar a chwi er fy wedi cael wedi cael fy
> anfoddloni yn fawr ynoch chwi [see figure 18]

[My dear gentle love I take this opportunity to send you this
kindness I had thought of leaving you without one but I thought
of leaving you without one to a young woman as welcoming
as you although I have I have been greatly displeased in you].

Whatever troubles and misfortunes came their way, Eleanor Pritchard
went to her grave unmarried and nothing has yet been discovered to
suggest that John Owen did otherwise.

The presence of the word 'Valentine' in a poem's title does
not necessarily mean that the poem bears any relation to the Saint
Valentine's Day rituals. 'Valentine', written by the tailor-poet Robert
Williams 'Trebor Mai' (1830–77) and published in *Gwaith Barddonol
Trebor Mai* in 1883, addresses a newborn baby, making clear the
author's long friendship with the baby's grandfather.[164] Although not
specifically noted, the child may well have been born on the saint's
day. The chubby little baby boy, William, replete with rosy cheeks
and a smile brighter than the sun that shone over his home in New
Inn, Llanrwst, is cherished by the author, and he wishes him long,
blessed days and a gold sovereign in his pocket.

The volume *Gwaith Barddonol Trebor Mai* also includes a series
of poems by various authors, entitled 'Yr ysmaldod Dirwestol' (The
foolishness of Temperance), and is a poetic debate concerning the
wisdom or otherwise of teetotalism, in particular the establishing of
temples throughout Wales to counteract the effects of a perceived
increase in drunkenness. Established in Central New York in 1851,
The Independent Order of Good Templars quickly spread and by
1872 there were six lodges in Swansea.

The Good Templars, ignoring the beneficiary feature place no
motive before a person for joining them but to be reclaimed
if fallen, or to be saved, or to save others from falling; and we
try to get possession of the heart, and then, through the heart,
rather than the purse, carry on our operations for good.

Principles.–Total abstinence, enforced by a life-long pledge,
and the absolute prohibition of the manufacture, importation,
and sale of intoxicating drinks.

Policy.–Broad, allowing lodges to act according to locality,
times, and circumstances.

Basis.–Non-beneficiary, the object being to do good rather than to receive benefit. The funds of each lodge are at its own disposal.[165]

The debate sees John Williams of Llangernyw (1827–1909),[166] a miller by profession, arguing on the side of total abstinence from intoxicating drinks, and David Roberts 'Dewi Havhesp' (imprisoned for offences committed under the influence of drink) arguing against. Two poems which form part of the debate feature the word 'Valentine' in the title: 'Valentine i Dewi Havhesp' (A Valentine to Dewi Havhesp) by John Williams; 'Valentine Dewi Havhesp' is Dewi's reply.[167] Neither poem bears any relation to the rituals of Saint Valentine's Day.

Nor does the poem entitled (in translation) 'Valentine, presented to my dear friend Mr John Pritchard Parry, Melbourne, Australia (formerly of Bryntirion, Nanmor, February 14th, 1885' bear any relation to the St Valentine's Day ritual. In this poem the author greets a friend currently living in Melbourne, having emigrated there for non-specified reasons. The first Welsh settlers in Australia were convicts, later followed by ambitious single men wanting to profit from the gold rushes from the 1850s onwards: it is possible that Mr Parry may have been one of those entrepreneurial young men.[168] The poem attempts to entice John Pritchard Parry home from Australia by extolling the virtues of his homeland, and by reminding him of the past glorious and happy days of his young life in rural Wales. The poet admits that he is in contravention of the Saint Valentine's Day courtship rules:

> Torraf reol fanol ffasiwn
> 'Cyfraith caru' mab a merch,
> Ond disgwyliaf y caf bardwn
> Am wneud hyn at 'wrthrych serch';
> Wel, fy annwyl hen gydymaith,
> Sut mae'n dyfod – wyt ti'n iach?
> Wyt ti dywed ar 'dir gobaith'
> Ar ôl gadael Cymru fach?[169]

[I am breaking the detailed rule of habit | [Regarding] 'courtship customs' between a young man and woman, | But I expect to be pardoned | For this [since] it concerns a 'love object'; | Well, my dear old friend, | How is it going – are you well? | Are you, tell me, in the 'land of hope' | Having left dear Wales?]

By the end of the nineteenth century and the beginning of the twentieth, the tradition of sending Valentine cards containing romantic or comic verses and messages was in decline. An entry in the weekly paper *Y Cymro* (The Welshman) expresses surprise that a custom that enjoyed such popularity in the 1860s had dwindled to almost nothing by the end of the century. Of the Valentine cards he states, 'Ni welais gynifer ag un ar werth yn ystod yr wythnos. Y mae Cardiau'r Nadolig wedi disodli'r Falentein, a heddwch i'w llwch.'[170] (I did not see so much as one on sale during the week. Christmas Cards have ousted the Valentine, may it rest in peace.)

Christmas cards had indeed taken over from the Valentine card. The *Evening Express* declared in 1900 that the custom of sending Valentines on 14 February was almost obsolete. 'Such is the point of decadence now reached that the Cardiff Post-office officials were scarcely aware that it was a day specially marked on the calendar at all. There was no extra pressure of work, and not a single extra man had to be employed on the staff.'[171] Andronicus, writing in 1892 when Saint Valentine's Day fell on a Sunday, maintains that postmen in every town and village in Wales could attend church or chapel as their work for the day was finished in good time.[172]

Post-1900

The twentieth century

John Jones 'Myrddin Fardd' (1836–1921), an antiquarian scholar from Llangïan in the historical county of Caernarfonshire (now Gwynedd), maintained that in his native county the sending of St Valentine's Day cards was vigorously popular at the beginning of the twentieth century. He states confidently that 'cannoedd o filoedd' (hundreds of thousands) of cards changed hands:

> rhai yn hardd a deniadol yr olwg arnynt, yn gyfryngau serch; a'r lleill yn hagr a dirmygus, fel cyfryngau cenfigen a dygasedd; yn profi fod dygwyl Valentine yn boblogaidd iawn gydag ieuengctyd ein gwlad.[173]

> [some beautiful and visually attractive, channels of love; and others repulsive and scornful, as channels of jealousy and

animosity; proving that Valentine's Day is very popular with the youth of our land.]

This is highly questionable and is possibly the result of the writer's excessive pride and satisfaction in his home county. But the sending of ornate Valentine cards did survive in some areas of Wales into the twentieth century, albeit in more modest numbers. In the Pren-gwyn district, near Llandysul in Ceredigion, young men would pay two shillings or half a crown, a substantial proportion of their weekly wage, for a Valentine card. 'These were trimmed with a border of silk thread and ribbons, and flowers of all colours, and were packed in boxes. The girls used to keep these carefully and place them on the dresser after marrying and establishing a home of their own.'[174] Nor did the sending of Valentine stanzas become obsolete in Wales during the twentieth century, but the tradition was lacklustre enough for many decades.

Stories of Saint Valentine Day's excitement, jealousies and misadventures were still told during the opening years of the twentieth century, but it was far more common to report that the world was at best transient and its people inconstant in love. In 1910, Betsan Jones was of the opinion that people knew far more about melancholia than about the Valentine (malancolia/malantein) tradition, and she had not heard of one person who had sent or received a card, the previous Monday being Saint Valentine's Day. She remembers a different culture in Wales, however, 'mae na blant go fawr rwan na chlywson nhw rioed son am ffashiwn beth. Oes y Crismas cardia a'r pictiwr postcards ydi hi, ac mae'r hen falantein wedi ei gyru o'r ffashiwn yn lan' (there are now quite big children that have never heard mention of such a thing. It is the age of Christmas cards and picture postcards, and the old Valentine has been driven completely out of fashion).[175] The Postmaster General commented in 1906 that as far as the Post Office was concerned, Saint Valentine's Day was finished.[176]

Nevertheless, references were still made to the saint's festival, for example by Lewis Valentine, a student studying Semitic languages at the University College of North Wales, Bangor, but whose student days were interrupted by the First World War. During the war he kept a diary that he later published under the title 'Dyddiadur Milwr' (A Soldier's Diary) in *Seren Gomer* (The Star of Gomer) during the years 1969–72, a newspaper that he himself was editor of from 1951 to 1974. In January 1916 Lewis Valentine enlisted in the Royal Army Medical Corps and in his diary entry for 14 February of that year he notes, 'Un hwyrddydd, Dygwyl Falentin, 1916, cyraeddasom Landrindod o Sheffield' (One evening, the Feast day of Saint Valentine, 1916, we arrived in Llandrindod from Sheffield).[177] In 1917 he writes, 'Ar ŵyl Falentin teithio dan ein beichiau o Varennes trwy Hédauville ac Aveluy' (On Valentine's feast day travelling heavily laden from Varennes through Hédauville and Aveluy).[178] Later that year, in October 1917, he inhaled poisonous gas as he was treating wounded soldiers at the battle of Passchendaele; blind, deaf and dumb, he was hospitalized in England and later in Belfast, but recovered and returned to his studies at the end of the war, and in January 1921 was ordained a Baptist minister. Acknowledgement of the feast day of the patron saint of love may have had as much to do with his surname as with his desire to celebrate the saint's festival.[179]

During the 1960s there was a marked revival in the custom of sending Valentine cards, mostly consisting of English verses. In spite of a valiant effort by Welsh nationalists and other supporters of the language to resurrect (or possibly invent) St Dwynwen's Day as the Welsh equivalent of Saint Valentine's Day,[180] the celebrations of Dwynwen, the saint of Welsh lovers whose festival day is honoured on 25 January, failed to sweep aside the observance of Saint Valentine's Day.

During the closing few years of the twentieth century, two Welsh Valentine poems were written in response to a competition set up by the owners of the Waunfawr Post Office in Aberystwyth, Ceredigion. That Valentine poems had become the subject of a competition in itself speaks volumes concerning their status. The initial purpose of the competition was to attract new customers and for the amusement of the established clientele, and such poems were undoubtedly fashioned as a source of merriment rather than as poems of genuine love and affection.

The competition was established in 1996. The Waunfawr shop and Post Office were at the time located in an area brimming with students who lived in self-catering hostels owned by Aberystwyth University. A great number of Welsh-speaking local people also supported this business venture, Dafydd Ifans from the village of Penrhyn-coch (some five miles out of town) among them. He would visit the shop regularly during his lunch break and would speak with the owner and with Mrs Jane Ebenezer at the Post Office counter. As he entered the shop one lunchtime a piece of paper was forced into his hand with the greeting, 'You write poetry – write a Valentine poem by tomorrow.' And so it was that Dafydd Ifans wrote a poem to the friendly lady who stood behind the Post Office counter.

A few days previously a radio talk by Mrs Ebenezer's husband, Lyn, had been broadcast, revealing that Lyn Ebenezer's favourite cinema idol was Jane Fonda – which explains the reference in the first two lines of the poem. Dwynwen, the fifth-century Welsh patron saint of lovers whose feast day is celebrated on 25 January, is cited in lines 5–6; line 9 describes the poet as being a 'Cardi', the name given to natives of Cardiganshire and which alludes to their allegedly tight-fisted and miserly nature; Kevin Davies, cited in line 12, owned a florist's shop in Aberystwyth and was a pillar of Aberystwyth society; and Ted, the soft and furry teddy bear with a bow and red heart around its neck which was offered as the main prize, is referred to in line 23. This was the winning entry for 1996.

Cerdd Ffolant i'r Beirniad

Yr wyt ti, Jên, yn ferch fach glên,
Yr wyf reit Fonda 'honat
A wir, rhen Siân, i ti mae nghân,
4   Ie wir, ti yw fy Ffolant.
Fe geisiais gofio'n santes *ni*
Yn Ionawr, ond anghofies
A nawr ar ŵyl yr estron Val
8   Fe geisiaf anfon neges.

Rwyf fi'n hen Gardi, weli di,
Meddyliais anfon cerdyn,
Fe wnes i 'styried bocs o *chocs*
12   A blode o siop Kevin,
Ond gan fod papur Gaynor fach
Mor lân a gwyn a handi
Fe steddes lawr a llunio cerdd
16   A dyma fi'n barddoni!

Wel cofia nawr, pan weli fi
Yn prynu stampiau'n ddyddiol,

Tu ôl i'r gwydr dyro wên,
20   'Rhen Jên, i ddyn bach fforddiol;
      Ac os mai fi enillith Ted
      Yn atgof bydd i aros,
      Cans rhatach cadw tedi bêr
24   Na gwraig a'i gêr, a phlantos.[181]

[A Valentine Poem to the Adjudicator

Stanza 1: You, Jane, are a fine young woman, | I am quite Fonda you | And indeed, dear Siân [= Jane], my song is for you, | Yes indeed, you are my Valentine. | I tried to remember *our* saint | In January, but I forgot | And now on the foreign Val's feast | I will try to send [you] a message.

Stanza 2: You see, I am an old Cardi, | I had considered sending a card, | I thought of a box of chocs | And flowers from Kevin's shop, | But as dear Gaynor's paper | Is so clean and white and handy | I sat down and wrote a poem | And here I am writing poetry!

Stanza 3: Now remember, when you see me | Buying stamps every day, | Behind the glass partition, give a smile, | Dear Jane, to a miserly little man; | And should it be I who wins Ted | He will be a permanent reminder [of our love], | For it is cheaper to keep a teddy bear | Than a wife and her gear and little children.]

A well-known and much-respected poet took the laurels in 1997, Vernon Jones of Bow Street, a village three miles north-east of Aberystwyth. His chosen metre was the *pennill telyn* (literally: verse for harp), a traditional quatrain popularly used to convey wit and wisdom. Used most widely during the eighteenth century, this old poetic metre was given new life by Vernon Jones, who injected a new vocabulary into this dinosaur of Welsh traditional poetry. Never before had curry and spice been used in the context of Welsh love poetry.

O na bai fy mhen yn feipen
Fel y gallet dan fy nhalcen
Lunio llyged, trwyn a gwefus
Sydd wrth fodd dy gusan melys.

> O na bait yn llyn o gyrri
> Llawn o sbeis a ffrwythau lyfli,
> Llosgi nghorff a llosgi nhafod
> A byth yn blino byta gormod.[182]

[Stanza 1: O that my head were a turnip | So that you could, under my forehead, | Craft eyes, nose and lip | That are pleasing to your sweet kiss.

Stanza 2: O that you were a lake of curry | Full of spice and lovely fruit, | Burning my body and burning my tongue | And never tiring of eating too much.]

The two stanzas were added to and entered for a National Eisteddfod of Wales (2017) competition for six stanzas entitled 'Cariadon' (Lovers). A few years previously the same two opening stanzas had served as the beginning of a longer series of stanzas entered for a similar competition at the Eisteddfod.[183]

The twenty-first century

It is no surprise that the tradition of posting Welsh Valentine cards via snail mail is now virtually obsolete. In an age when the courting conventions of old are not always considered relevant, speed dating, text messaging and dating apps are the popular mode of the day – with the occasional Valentine card sent only now and again. Welsh cards veer towards being Valentine cards that can double as Dwynwen cards, and carry generic messages such as 'Caru Ti' (Love You); 'Caru Ti/Lyfio Chdi'; 'Caru Ti am Byth, Byth, Bythoedd' (Love You for Ever, Ever, and Anon). In England the following messages have appeared on twenty-first century cards: 'You are not bad'; 'There is nobody else I'd rather lie in bed and look at my phone next to'; 'I'm gonna call you dandelion'; 'I'm obsessed with you in a non-creepy way', with the occasional stanza sometimes sported:

> Roses are red
> Violets are blue
> Your farts smell like eggs
> But I still love you.

In Wales, two *englynion* by John Emyr, a published author of both prose and poetry, were composed specifically for (what little remains of) the Valentine celebrations of this century. One of his *englynion*, 'Aberystwyth *I Gwen* (ar Ddydd Gŵyl Sain Folant)' (Aberystwyth *To Gwen* (on Saint Valentine's Day)), was composed in 2013 at a writing class in *cynghanedd* led by Robat Powell.[184] John Emyr looks back on his student days in Aberystwyth where he and his wife Gwen met in the early 1970s. Not technically part of a courtship structure, this *englyn* provides a link to the cultural and social celebration of the saint's day. The other *englyn*, entitled 'Ar Gerdyn Gŵyl Sain Folant' (On a Saint Valentine's Day Card), was written in 2005: it not only expresses the appropriate sentiment for the saint's day, but also links to the commercial significance of the festival in contemporary Wales.[185]

According to research carried out by Royal Mail in 2017, 67 per cent of respondents intended to send a Valentine card. The main recipients of those cards were husband/wife/partner (92 per cent) and children (4 per cent). Ignoring the fact that many send themselves a card, it can be estimated that 4 per cent use a Valentine card as a step in the courtship process; of that 4 per cent not all write love poetry, so that fewer than 4 per cent write an accompanying stanza to convey their love.

Does twenty-first century Wales need courtship? To set aside time during which two people determine whether they are a good match? Many are sceptical. In twenty-first century Wales it appears that writing love stanzas to send to a loved one on Saint Valentine's Day is something for oldies and archivists, or else a class exercise in writing *cynghanedd*. The modern 'lyfio chdi' (love you) seen on generic cards that double as Dwynwen and Valentine's Day cards, and that certain purists find an unspeakable slur on Welsh grammar, is far more convenient than a stressful half-hour spent in rhyming and alliteration.

Conclusions

The earliest surviving Welsh Saint Valentine's Day poems are seven songs and poems dating from the seventeenth century: they request Valentine gifts or give thanks for such generosity. The known authors are Edward Morris, a cattle trader; Huw Morys, traditionally thought to have been apprenticed to a tanner but who later returned home to assist his father on the farm; and possibly Siôn or John Ellis the harpist. Two of the Huw Morys poems are to be sung to the popular 'Sunselia' (poems 3 and 4); a further two poems could be sung to 'Leave Land' although that is not specifically noted (poems 2 and 5); and the tune 'Consêt Arglwydd Straenee'/'Lord Strain's Delight' is noted for the singing of the harper's song, although it is difficult to see how any version of this tune offered by John Parry in *Antient British Music* is suitable – 'Stanes Morus' might be more appropriate. A further two poems remain, a *cywydd* (poem 1) that may or may not have been intended to be sung, and an anonymous Valentine carol (poem 7) in the form of a dialogue poem in which the wise blackbird hands out advice to the young poet, but for which no tune is suggested. Edward Morris is the author of the two poems that precede this poem in NLW 9B, and another of his poems follows this anonymous Valentine carol. As far as is known, the extant seventeenth-century songs were composed in Cerrigydrudion (in Conwy County), the Llansilin area (in Powys) and Ffestiniog (in Gwynedd).

More than two dozen Welsh Saint Valentine's Day poems have survived from the eighteenth century. Few perceptible changes can be detected in the observance of the custom during this century and an abundance of romantic poems continued to be written. The tunes noted for their performance are 'Amaryllis', 'Bryniau'r Werddon', 'Cast away Care', 'Charity Mistress', 'Follow my Fancy', 'Ffarwel Trefaldwyn', 'Garway', 'King's Round', 'Leave Land', 'Let Mary Live Long', 'The Lord Monk's March *or* Ymdaith Mwngc', 'Milking Pail', 'Spanish Minuet' and 'Ymdaith Newydd *or* New March'.

With the exception of three poems, it is notable that the eighteenth-century Welsh Valentine songs and poems survived in north Wales: Harlech, Trawsfynydd, Y Bala and the Berwyn Mountains, Gwyddelwern, Llanymawddwy, Caernarfon, Llanddeiniolen, Llanllyfni, Beddgelert, Trefriw, Llangadwaladr/Ruabon, Cwm Llywenog in the upper reaches of Llanarmon Dyffryn Ceiriog parish, Bryneglwys, Nantglyn, Prion, Llangwm, Bwlch-y-ddâr near Llanrhaeadr-ym-Mochnant; in short, across Gwynedd, Conwy, Denbighshire, Wrexham County and the northern tip of Powys. The three exceptions were collected from the Cardigan area, from Cynwyl Elfed and from Clydach in the Vale of Neath.

By the close of the eighteenth century exchanging gifts had gradually been replaced by the exchange of written letters and other handmade tokens of affection, and this in turn was being replaced by printed messages on Valentine cards by the beginning of the nineteenth century.

As regards the design and beauty of Valentine cards the nineteenth century has been referred to as the golden era of Valentines, in particular the years 1840–60.[186] Between 1860 and 1880 when trade was at its best, 'the public spent a quarter of a million pounds annually upon valentines … [and] at least 5,000 people, mostly girls and women, were employed in valentine factories, at wages ranging 10s to 18s per week'.[187]

Verses (sentimental and vinegar) were written in cards (pretty and vulgar) and sent to the recipients for a variety of reasons and at no little cost. J.J. of Bronygadfa (just over the Welsh border, near Oswestry) describes how two of his acquaintances, William Lee and 'old Thomas Corbett, the wooden-legged pensioner', made and sold Valentine cards 'for the then reasonable sum of half-a-crown each, but which would now, I should think, be worth to a curiosity dealer at least ten times that amount'.[188] The old man was a poet as well as an artist. The *pennill telyn*, a stanza of folk poetry to be sung to harp accompaniment, was very popular. Longer poems were sung to tunes such as 'Belle Isle March' and 'See the Building'; lesser known tunes include 'Y Folantein', 'Follow my Fancy' and 'Young Watkin's Delight'. No tune is proposed for the performance of several nineteenth-century Saint Valentine's Day offerings, suggesting that more and more poems were sent by post or, given that most romantic relationships were pursued within walking distance of the couple's home, hand delivered in person by the sender, left on the doorstep or pushed under the door, rather than being material for vocal deliveries. A poem from the Cardigan area makes use of at least three different stanza forms, thereby making the process of choosing a tune/tunes a more difficult task.

In contrast to eighteenth-century Saint Valentine's Day poems, nineteenth-century survivors have been collected from a wide geographical location. There are extant songs and poems from eighteenth-century bastions such as Gwynedd, the historic Uwchaled Rural District (now part of the district of Colwyn) and from Llanrhaeadr-ym-Mochant, Llanbryn-mair and Welshpool in Powys; but a high proportion of nineteenth-century poems have been collected in

Ceredigion, specifically from Tal-y-bont, the Trefenter and Mynydd Bach area, Bronnant, Cardigan, two poems from the parish of Llanwenog and at least six from the parish of Llandysul. Glamorgan is represented by William Thomas Rees 'Alaw Ddu' who was born in Pont-rhyd-y-fen, and by D.P.D. of Aberdare in the Cynon Valley area of Rhondda Cynon Taf.

Several nineteenth-century Welsh poems written for Saint Valentine's Day are not love greetings or even satirical communications between potential lovers. A poem from the Llanrwst–Trefriw area in the Conwy Valley greets a child, possibly on his birthday. Another poem greets John Pritchard Parry, Melbourne, Australia, formerly of Nanmor, Beddgelert, but displays none of the marks of the Saint Valentine's Day ritual. Similarly two poems from Llangernyw in Conwy form part of a poetic debate on teetotalism, John Williams writing in support of abstinence and Dewi Havhesp arguing against. Saint Valentine's Day poems also ventured into the realms of the literary novel. A couplet originally written by Evan Evans 'Ieuan Glan Geirionydd' is used as a Valentine greeting in the novel *Y Ddau Efell neu Llanllonydd* (The Twins or Llanllonydd) by Isaac Foulkes. In the novel *Gŵr y Dolau: neu Ffordd y Troseddwr* (The Gentleman of Dolau: or The Way of the Criminal) by W. Llewelyn Williams (born in Brownhill, Llansadwrn in the Tywi Valley in Carmarthenshire), Robert Williams the tailor writes four Valentine stanzas on behalf of William Rowlands, the local curate, to send to Gladys Bowen, stanzas which she duly responds to with five Valentine stanzas of her own, and by returning the card that had cost the curate half a crown.

This contextual change indicated that the Valentine ritual was soon to enter into a different phase. Its tremendous popularity as a courtship ritual was in decline and by the turn of the twentieth century the custom of sending Welsh Saint Valentine's Day cards was almost obsolete. Journalists in local newspapers mourned its passing and commented unfavourably on the growth of the Christmas card industry. Two poems have survived from the twentieth century, both products of a competition held in 1996 and 1997 primarily to promote the Post Office and shop in Waunfawr, Aberystwyth in mid Wales: greeting a loved one was incidental. Again prompted primarily by reasons other than love, the twenty-first century has produced to date two Saint Valentine's Day *englynion*, both written at a creative writing class in *cynghanedd*.

A small proportion of the Welsh population has abandoned the cause of Saint Valentine and turned towards the native-born Dwynwen with whom to share matters of the heart. Greetings on Saint Dwynwen's Day, 25 January, were popular particularly in the 1970s, but the practice has not fired the Welsh imagination as did the production of Valentine songs and poems: 'Dwynwen is still unknown to many, if not most, in Wales outside Welsh-speaking culture.'[189]

As for red hearts and roses, no doubt they are here to stay. Across the centuries, from the single damask rose cited by Edward Morris in his seventeenth-century *cywydd* to Margaret Wyn, to the eighteenth-century description of Elisabeth Williams's beauty and intoxicating fragrance as a veritable rose of Sharon, to the nineteenth-century rose-clad cards sent by John Owen expressing his constant desire for Eleanor, red roses (and other suggestive flowers such as forget-me-nots) remain the go-to flowers for romantics in every age. The heart too has been appropriated to demonstrate idealized love. In the words of Charles Lamb:

> In these little visual interpretations, no emblem is as common as the heart, – that little three-cornered exponent of all our hopes and fears, – the bestuck and bleeding heart; it is twisted and tortured into more allegories and affectations than an opera hat.[190]

The ambitious and self-consciously fashionable young people (and old) of today have less time for sentimental love poetry and card sending than did their grandfathers and grandmothers, and for the time being it appears that an important slice of Welsh love-history has come to an end. And yet, with whispers of silk and lace back at the height of fashion, it is not impossible that we will witness once again the laudable custom of writing Welsh love poetry for Saint Valentine's Day at the heart of Welsh lovemaking.

Notes

1   Anita Brookner, *A Misalliance* (London: Cape, 1986), p. 5.

2   F. L. Cross and E. A. Livingstone (eds), *The Oxford Dictionary of the Christian Church* (Oxford: Oxford University Press, 2005; third edn rev.), p. 1687.

3   *New Catholic Encyclopaedia* (New York: McGraw-Hill, 1967–96), 14 (1967), p. 517.

4   Known originally as *Februa*, Latin for 'purifications' or 'purgings', or *Februatus*.

5   *Encyclopaedia Britannica* online at *https://www.britannica.com/topic/ Lupercalia* (accessed 6 January 2018).

6   For example, see Alban Butler, *Lives of the Fathers, Martyrs and Other Principal Saints* (London, 1756–9), s.v. February 14.

7   The Gregorian Calendar used in Britain today was adopted in the United Kingdom in September 1752 to replace the historic Julian Calendar, see further B. Blackburn and L. Holford-Strevens, *The Oxford Companion to the Year* (Oxford: Oxford University Press, 2003, repr. with corrections); D. Feeney, *Caesar's Calendar: Ancient Time and the Beginnings of History* (Berkeley and London: University of California Press, c.2007); S. Stern, *Calendars in Antiquity: Empires, States and Societies* (Oxford: Oxford University Press, 2012).

8   Jack B. Oruch, 'St Valentine, Chaucer, and Spring in February', *Speculum*, 56 (1981), 565.

9   Larry D. Benson (ed.), *The Riverside Chaucer* (Oxford: Oxford University Press, 2008), p. 389, lines 309–22.

10   Benson (ed.), *The Riverside Chaucer*, p. 394, lines 683–6.

11   Derek Pearsall, *John Lydgate* (London: Routledge and Kegan Paul, 1970), p. 97.

12   'Valentine's day love letter, February 1477', British Library [Online]. Available at: *http://www.bl.uk/learning/timeline/item126579.html* (accessed 20 March 2018).

13   See the 'Nuremberg Chronicle' [Online]. Available at: Cambridge Digital Library, University of Cambridge, *http://cudl.lib.cam.ac.uk/view/PR-INC-00000-A-00007-00002-00888/1* (accessed 20 March 2018). See further Christoph Reske, *Die Produktion der Schedelschen Weltchronik in Nürnberg/The Production of Schedel's Nuremberg Chronicle*, Mainzer Studien zur Buchwissenschaft, 10 (Wiesbaden: Harrassowitz, 2000); Adrian Wilson assisted by Joyce Lancaster Wilson, *The Making of the Nuremberg Chronicle* (Amsterdam: A. Asher, 1976).

14   *New Catholic Encyclopaedia*, 10, p. 933: 'in the New Testament the palm was connected with martyrdom (Apocrypha 7.9) and was used

to decorate grave-markers and tombs in the catacombs as a sign of the triumphal death of the martyr ... On mosaics and on sarcophagi it usually stands for paradise, and Christ is frequently portrayed amid palms in heaven.'

15   Martin Crampin, 'Gwydr Lliw yng Nghymru/Stained Glass in Wales', *http://stainedglass.llgc.org.uk/object/1796* (accessed 2 February 2017).

16   Trefor M. Owen, *Welsh Folk Customs* (Cardiff: National Museum of Wales/Welsh Folk Museum, 1974), p. 156.

17   One of the twenty-four established metres of Welsh poetry; it features heptasyllabic lines set in rhyming couplets, with full *cynghanedd* (a complex form of consonance) in each line.

18   Poem 1 'Cywydd i Mrs Margaret Wyn o Gwm Ein i ofyn Valentine i David Davies' [A *Cywydd* to Mrs Margaret Wyn of Cwm Ein to request a Valentine for David Davies].

19   Poem 2 'I ddiolch am rodd Valentine' [In gratitude for a Valentine gift].

20   Later, in 1852, William Roberts 'Nefydd' (1813–72) refers to 'yr hen ddefod ddiniwed a phoblogaidd: sef y "tynnu Valentine"' [the old and harmless popular custom: that is the 'drawing of a Valentine'], see W. Roberts, *Crefydd yr Oesoedd Tywyll* [The Religion of the Dark Ages] (Caerfyrddin: A. Williams, 1852), p. 62.

21   Poem 1.45–8.

22   Robert Latham and William Mathews (eds), *The Diary of Samuel Pepys* (London: HarperCollins, 1995), vol. 2 (1661), p. 36. The Pepys diary was housed at Magdalene College Library, Cambridge, until 1825, when the cipher was cracked by John Smith, and later edited by Richard Lord Braybrooke.

23   Poem 1.49–54.

24   Elis Lewis, *Ystyriaethau Drexelivs ar Dragywyddoldeb* [The Reflections of Drexelivs concerning Eternity] ([Oxford], 1661), p. 83; see also Geraint Bowen, 'Ystyriaethau Drexelivs ar Dragywyddoldeb, Elis Lewis, Rhydychen, 1661' [The Reflections of Drexelivs concerning Eternity, Elis Lewis, Oxford, 1661], *Journal of the Welsh Bibliographical Society*, 8/2 (July 1955), 81–3. The reflections of the Jesuit writer Jeremias Drexelius or Drechsel (1581–1638) were translated from Latin first into English by Dr R. Winterton and subsequently into Welsh by Elis Lewis of Llwyngwern, Penllyn in Gwynedd, and printed in Oxford by Henry Hall for Richard Davies. Since there was no printing press in Wales at this time most Welsh books were printed in London or on the Continent; Oxford was not easily accessible from Wales. Compositors both in England and on the Continent found Welsh orthography very difficult, which accounts for the inaccuracies.

25   Poem 1.67–9.

26   Poem 1.76–8.

27   Robert Wynne was a 'Clerk in Holy Orders, Vicar of Cerrig y druidion, Co. Denbigh, 1679, who died 26 December, 1696', see Thomas Allen Glenn (ed.), *The Family of Griffith of Garn and Plasnewydd in the County of Denbigh, as Registered in the College of Arms from the Beginning of the XIth Century* (London: Harrison and Sons, 1934), p. 259.

28   Latham and Mathews (eds), *The Diary of Samuel Pepys*, vol. 2 (1661), p. 40.

29   Latham and Mathews (eds), *The Diary of Samuel Pepys*, vol. 8 (1667), p. 65.

30   Latham and Mathews (eds), *The Diary of Samuel Pepys*, vol. 8 (1667), p. 62.

31   Latham and Mathews (eds), *The Diary of Samuel Pepys*, vol. 8 (1667), pp. 65–6.

32   Latham and Mathews (eds), *The Diary of Samuel Pepys*, vol. 9 (1668–9), pp. 67–8.

33   Latham and Mathews (eds), *The Diary of Samuel Pepys*, vol. 8 (1667), p. 86.

34   Violet A. Wlock, *Valentines* (York: Castle Museum, York for York Corporation, 1979), p. 5, records the following custom on 14 February: 'In Dorsetshire … the maids would hang up in the kitchen a bunch of such fresh flowers as they could obtain so early in the year, neatly suspended by a true lover's knot of blue riband. Among these early love flowers were the hyacinth, narcissus, primrose, polyanthus, and yellow crocus which was sometimes called Hymen's torch and the Flower of St. Valentine.'

35   The Song of Solomon 4:12–16.

36   The *tri thrawiad* metre 'first appears in the sixteenth century among the anonymous love poems found in the manuscripts of that period … *Cynghanedd* is always found in the last few syllables of the second and fourth line of each stanza', Thomas Parry (ed.), *The Oxford Book of Welsh Verse* (Oxford: Oxford University Press, 1962), p. 552.

37   Poem 2.7–8.

38   Compare 'tair sir Gwynedd' (the three counties of Gwynedd), a reference to the old kingdom of Gwynedd in 'Marwnad Syr Siôn Pilstwn' (Elegy to Sir John Puleston), a poem by Siôn Brwynog of Llanfflewyn in Anglesey dated 1551, see Gwilym H. Jones, 'Gweithiau Siôn Brwynog' [The Works of Siôn Brwynog], a typescript submitted to the National Eisteddfod of Wales held at Holyhead in 1927, NLW 11987E, p. 221; the *cywydd* is not included in Rosemarie Kerr, 'Cywyddau Siôn Brwynog' [The *cywyddau* of Siôn Brwynog] (unpublished MA thesis, University of Wales [Bangor], 1960).

39 It may be significant that the character representing Queen Elizabeth I was called Gloriana in Edmund Spenser's *Faerie Queene*, and that the pet name for the young woman in this poem is El.

40 Poem 2.17–18.

41 Poem 2.13–15.

42 Poem 3.4.

43 Parry, *The Oxford Book*, pp. 551–2.

44 Parry, *The Oxford Book*, p. 552.

45 On Hafod Ysbyty, Ffestiniog, Gwynedd, see G. J. Williams, *Hanes Plwyf Ffestiniog* [The History of the Parish of Ffestiniog] (Wrexham: Hughes and Son, 1882), pp. 54–5; Gruffydd Aled Williams, 'Edmwnd Prys ac Ardudwy', *The National Library of Wales Journal*, 22 (1981–2), 282–303 (in particular 286–90); J. Beverley Smith and Llinos Beverley Smith, *History of Merioneth, volume II: The Middle Ages* (Cardiff: University of Wales Press on behalf of the Merioneth Historical and Record Society, 2001), p. 450; 'North West Wales Dendrochronology Project: Dating Old Welsh Houses', *http://datingoldwelshhouses.co.uk/library/Hhistory/HHHafod-Ysbyty.pdf* (accessed 20 March 2018); *The Royal Commission on the Ancient and Historical Monuments in Wales and Monmouthshire: County of Merioneth*, 6 (London: HMSO, 1921), p. 31. The 1623 Rent Roll for Ardudwy refers to Humffrey David Lloyd paying rent for Havod Spyttu (3s. 4d) and for Llettu Wilim (0s. 8d), suggesting he was an owner-occupier; also Humff' David Lloyd paid rent for Gamallt and Llyn y Gamallt (0s. 2d) and for Gors and Llynnie Havod Spyttu (0s. 2d), see Rhian Parry, 'An Ardudwy Crown Rental of 1623', *Journal of the Merioneth Historical and Record Society*, 15 (2009), 384.

46 For the will of Jonet William, widow of Humphrey Lloyd of Hafod Ysbyty, see the wills of the Bangor diocese kept at the National Library of Wales, Bangor 1710/37. Most of her property was left to her daughter, Catherine Lloyd, who married Pierce Owen in 1711; they were tenants in Hafod Ysbyty.

47 On 'Consêt Arglwydd Straenee' see 'Hoffter Arglwydd Strain' in John Parry (Ruabon) and Evan Williams, *Antient British Music; or, a collection of tunes, never before published, which are retained by the Cambro-Britons* (London: Mickleborough, 1742), p. 3.

48 John Parry, 'To the Editor of the Cambro-Briton', *The Cambro-Briton*, 2 (London: John Limbird, 1821), p. 170.

49 The ballad was published by Dafydd Jones of Trefriw at the beginning of his anthology of poems entitled *Blodeu-gerdd Cymry* [An Anthology of Welsh Poems] (Amwythig: Stafford Prys, 1779; first edition 1759); and reprinted (with notes and a translation into English) in T. Gwynn Jones, 'Welsh Song Writing', *Journal of the Welsh Folk Song Society*, 2 (1914–25),

139–51, and in particular the section entitled 'An old ballad printed at the beginning of the Blodeugerdd (1756)', 148–51; it is further discussed in Daniel Huws, 'Gwisgo Merched â Mesurau'/'Dressing Women in Tunes', in Sally Harper and Wyn Thomas (eds), *Cynheiliaid y Gân: Ysgrifau i anrhydeddu Phyllis Kinney a Meredydd Evans/Bearers of Song: Essays in honour of Phyllis Kinney and Meredydd Evans* (Cardiff: University of Wales Press, 2007), pp. 180–8 with Appendices on pp. 153–79.

50   Meredydd Evans and Phyllis Kinney, 'Dauganmlwyddiant John Parry Ddall' [The Bicentenary of Blind John Parry], *Y Casglwr* [The Collector], 17 (1982), 9.

51   Huws, 'Gwisgo Merched â Mesurau', p. 169; see 'Stanes Morris', in Jeremy Barlow (ed.), *The Complete Country Dance Tunes from* Playford's Dancing Master (1651–ca.1728) (London: Faber Music Limited, 1985), p. 36 (tune 97).

52   Cardiff 4.156, ff. 232ʳ–3ᵛ.

53   Poem 7.

54   See, for example, Ann Marie Rasmussen, 'Fathers to Think Back Through: The Medieval German Mother-Daughter and Father-Son Conduct poems known as *Die Winsbeckin* and *Der Winsbecke*', in Kathleen Ashley and Robert L. A. Clark (eds), *Medieval Conduct* (Minneapolis: University of Minnesota Press, 2001), pp. 106–34.

55   Poem 7.25–9.

56   The Book of Joshua in the Old Testament, chapter 24.

57   Poem 7.42–3.

58   Poem 7.46–8.

59   Poem 18.31–3.

60   Poem 30.11–24.

61   Poem 29; for the dialogue poem genre see Dafydd Glyn Jones, 'Hawl ac Ateb' [Question and Answer], *Efrydiau Athronyddol* [Philosophical Studies], 57 (1994), 27–49; for the *cywydd llatai* (love-messenger *cywyddau*) see Arthur Howard Williams, 'Adar yng Ngwaith y Cywyddwyr' [Birds in the Work of the Cywyddwyr] (unpublished PhD thesis, Aberystwyth University, Aberystwyth, 2014), in particular chapter 4 which discusses birds as messengers and advisers.

62   Judging by the handwriting and the scribe's inconsistent orthographical practices, the manuscript was written by an individual with little formal education.

63   Dafydd ap Gwilym, the medieval Welsh poet born *c*.1320, is regarded as one of the greatest medieval poets of Europe. His poems to 'Yr Eos' [The Nightingale] and to 'Yr Eos a'r Frân' [The Nightingale and the Crow] are discussed in Williams, 'Adar yng Ngwaith y Cywyddwyr', 342–59. See also 'Cywyddau i adar fel negeswyr' [*Cywyddau* to birds as messengers],

in Bleddyn Owen Huws and A. Cynfael Lake (eds), Genres *y Cywydd* (Aberystwyth: Bleddyn Owen Huws and A. Cynfael Lake, 2016), pp. 201–26.

64 See, for example, poem 17.5–6 by Ioan Siencyn: 'Damweiniodd imi'n gynnar | Wrth lot, yn wir, eich enw pur' [It befell me [to obtain] promptly | By lot, in truth, your pure name].

65 NLW 1062B, 43.

66 Poem 15.9–16.

67 NLW 1062B, 43.

68 Poem 14.10–13.

69 Poem 27.9–10.

70 Poem 18.40–2.

71 Poem 21.8.

72 Poem 17.38–40.

73 Poem 24.31–3.

74 For utilizing hair in a ritual performance to see into the romantic future and foreseeing a life partner see John Jones 'Myrddin Fardd', *Llên Gwerin Sir Gaernarfon* [The Folklore of Caernarvonshire] (Caernarfon: Cwmni y Cyhoeddwyr Cymreig, Swyddfa Cymru, [1908]), p. 149: 'Dwy ferch ifaingc eisteddant i fyny mewn ystafell wrth dân, ar eu penau eu hunain, rhwng deuddeg ag un o'r gloch y bore, heb siarad dim â'u gilydd; a hwy a dorant y naill oddiar ben y llall flewyn am bob blwydd o'u hoedran, ac a'u rhoddant mewn llian cri gyda pheth o'r llysieuyn a elwir "gwir gariad", a llosged pob un ef ar ei phen ei hun, gan ddywedyd yn isel y geiriau hyn: 'Rwy'n offrwm y gwir aberth yma i'r hwn sydd fwyaf gwerthfawr yn fy ngolwg, ac yn erchi iti ddyfod yrwan ag ymddangos o'm blaen. Ac ar y gair fe ymddengys eu cariadau i bob un yn rhodio o amgylch yr ystafell, eithr ni wel y naill gariad y llall.' ('Two young girls sit up in a room beside a fire, by themselves, between twelve and one o'clock in the morning, without speaking to each other at all; and they cut, the one from the other's head, a hair for every year of their lives, and put them in a fresh cloth together with a little of the herb which is called "true love", and let each one burn it on her own, while saying the following words quietly: I offer this true sacrifice to the one who is most precious in my sight, and I charge thee now to appear before me. And with that their lovers appear to each one walking around the room, but the one doesn't see the other's lover.') The herb true-love is first mentioned in the herbal of John Gerard (1545–1612): Marcus Woodward (ed.), *Gerard's Herbal: The History of Plants* (London: Studio Editions, 1994), pp. 101–3; see plate 1.

75 Poem 11.19, 23–4.

76 Poem 3.7–8.

77   Poem 1.76.

78   Aled Rhys Wiliam (ed.), *Llyfr Iorwerth* [The Book of Iorwerth] (Caerdydd: Gwasg Prifysgol Cymru, 1960), §p. 50, lines 2–3; §p. 80, line 18; §p. 111, lines 19, 23, 28, 30, 42; §p. 116, line 9. This group of eight manuscripts, named after the lawyer and possible compiler Iorwerth ap Madog, may reflect the laws of Gwynedd during the reign of Llywelyn ap Iorwerth *c.*1194–1240 and Llywelyn ap Gruffudd 1246–82; see Cyfraith Hywel [Online]. Available at: *http://cyfraith-hywel.cymru.ac.uk/en/index.php* (accessed 22 March 2018).

79   Poem 5.9–12.

80   Poem 13.20–6.

81   Poem 16.17–18.

82   Poem 16.31–8, 41–2.

83   'House of Commons Select Committee On Administration of Justice in Wales', *Parliamentary Papers*, 2 (1820), 7.

84   Over 80 of his poems are preserved in NLW 346B, dated between 1768 and 1786.

85   Poem 33.9–12.

86   Poem 25.15–18.

87   Poem 11.1–6.

88   Poem 26.13–15.

89   Poem 19.1–7. Trefor M. Owen places this poem in the seventeenth century: 'a poem by an anonymous author of the same period [as Edward Morris, Perthi-llwydion (1633?–1689)]', see Owen, *Welsh Folk Customs*, p. 152.

90   Poem 24.10–12.

91   Poem 30.30–41.

92   Poem 6.11–14; Cwrtmawr 128A, 210–11 attributes the poem to Siôn Ellis, the harpist, adding the proviso 'eraill a ddywedant nad e' oedd yr awdur' [others say that he was not the author].

93   Brinley Rees, *Dulliau'r Canu Rhydd 1500–1650* [The Forms of Free-verse Poems] (Caerdydd: Gwasg Prifysgol Cymru, 1952).

94   For Huw Morys see poem 4.2; for Jonathan Hughes see poem 24.1; for Rees Lloyd see poem 28.21; for John Rees see poem 37.14; for Ellis Rowland see poem 9.11, 21, 34; for anonymous poets see poems 20.2, 27.3, 32.15.

95   Poem 9.3, 29.

96   Poem 10.3.

97   Poem 22.14; poem 27.1.

98   Poem 24.16.

99   Poem 5.9.

100   Poem 9.

101 For Huw Morys see poem 4.5; for Arthur Jones see poem 18.36.

102 Poem 28.33.

103 Poem 28.7.

104 The Book of Genesis 12:11, 14.

105 Thomas Charles, *Geiriadur Ysgrythyrol* [Scriptural Dictionary] (Wrexham: Hughes and Son, 1892), p. 799.

106 Poem 28.23.

107 Christ said of himself, 'I am the rose of Sharon, and the lily of the valleys', The Song of Solomon 2:1.

108 The Book of Genesis 29:17.

109 The Gospel according to Saint Luke 10:38–42.

110 Iago ab Dewi, 'Selection of Welsh Poetry', *Y Cymmrodor, the Magazine of the Honourable Society of Cymmrodorion*, 9 (1888), 12.

111 ab Dewi, 'Selection', 8–11.

112 Roger Cyffin also wrote poetry on topical themes, for example, 'a cywydd written in judgment on the Gunpowder Plot of 1605 and in praise of King James I', see *The Dictionary of Welsh Biography down to 1940* (London: The Honourable Society of Cymmrodorion, 1959), p. 89 and online at: *http://yba.llgc.org.uk/en/s-CYFF-ROG-1587.html* (accessed 22 March 2018).

113 The Book of Genesis 2:21–5.

114 Poem 4.32.

115 Poem 19.8.

116 Poem 11.21.

117 Poem 30.61.

118 See J. Lloyd-Jones, *Geirfa Barddoniaeth Gynnar* [Vocabulary of Early Poetry] (Caerdydd: Gwasg Prifysgol Cymru, 1931–63), p. 247.

119 S. Baring-Gould and J. Fisher, *The Lives of the British Saints*, 4 vols (London: The Honourable Society of Cymmrodorion, 1907–13), 2, p. 241.

120 Baring-Gould and Fisher, *The Lives of the British Saints*, 2, p. 242.

121 Poem 23.16.

122 Translated by *A Dictionary of the Welsh Language* as 'peasant poet, (uneducated) country poet', see *http://geiriadur.ac.uk/gpc/gpc.html* (accessed 23 March 2018), s.v. 'bardd'.

123 Poem 38, dated 1850 in NLW 23692A, f. 13[r].

124 John Jenkins's brother, Joseph Jenkins of Trecefel, Tregaron, gained notoriety as the 'Welsh Swagman' when he left home after nightfall on 8 December 1868, headed for Australia in a bid to escape debts of six hundred pounds, alcoholism, the antagonism of his family and his disreputable past. See further William Evans (ed.), *Diary of a Welsh Swagman, 1869–1894* (South Melbourne: Macmillan Company of Australia, 1975);

Bethan Phillips, *Rhwng dau fyd: y swagman o Geredigion* [Between two worlds: the swagman from Ceredigion] (Aberystwyth: Cymdeithas Lyfrau Ceredigion, 1998); Bethan Phillips, *Pity the Swagman: The Australian Odyssey of a Victorian Diarist* (Aberystwyth: Cymdeithas Lyfrau Ceredigion, 2001).

125   Twr y Dderi, 'Nodion o Geredigion' [Notes from Ceredigion], *Llais y Wlad* [Country Voice], 25 February 1876, 7.

126   Quoted in Catrin Stevens, *Arferion Caru* [Courting Customs] (Llandysul: Gwasg Gomer, 1977), p. 84.

127   The Book of Genesis 31:49.

128   Diana Cooper and Norman Battershill, *Victorian Sentimental Jewellery* (Newton Abbot: David and Charles, 1972), p. 64.

129   Poem 32.14–17.

130   'Anghofio Hen Arfer' [Neglecting an Old Custom], *The Cambrian News and Merionethshire Standard*, 21 February 1919, 6.

131   Poem 31.3–4.

132   Poem 37.

133   See further Owen, *Welsh Folk Customs*, pp. 156–8; Ruth Webb Lee, *A History of Valentines* (London: Studio Publications, 1952).

134   Owen, *Welsh Folk Customs*, p. 157.

135   'The Festival of St. Valentine', *The North Wales Chronicle*, 17 February 1877, 3.

136   D. G. Williams, 'Casgliad o Lên Gwerin Sir Gaerfyrddin' [A Compilation of Carmarthenshire Folklore], in E. Vincent Evans (ed.), *Transactions of the National Eisteddfod of Wales Llanelly, 1895* (London: National Eisteddfod Association, 1898), p. 357.

137   Marie Trevelyan, *Folk-lore and Folk-Stories of Wales* (London: Elliot Stock, 1909), p. 244; she further notes: 'Dreams of St. Valentine's Eve were supposed to be fateful. A child born on Valentine's Day would have many lovers. The farmers said a calf born on St. Valentine's Day was of no use for breeding purposes. If hens were set to hatch on Valentine's Day, all the eggs would be rotten.' (p. 245).

138   Jini Jôns, 'Sisial Godre'r Berwyn' [Whisperings at the Foot of the Berwyn], *Llangollen Advertiser, Denbighshire, Merionethshire and North Wales Journal*, 20 February 1914, 6.

139   Mary Russell Mitford, 'The Two Valentines', in *Our Village: Sketches of Rural Character and Scenery* [Online]. Available at: *https://books.google.co.uk/ books?id=Fow7AAAAYAAJ&pg=PA505&dq=wooings+begun+on+the+ Fourteenth+of+February&hl=en&sa=X&ved=0ahUKEwiSx4Xcyl7aAhX EL1AKHfFeBPYQ6AEIKTAA#v=onepage&q=wooings%20begun%20 on%20the%20Fourteenth%20of%20February&f=false* (accessed 26 May 2017).

140 Quoted in Frank Staff, *The Valentine & its Origins* (London: Lutterworth Press, 1969), pp. 44–5.

141 David Vincent, *Literacy and Popular Culture: England 1750–1914* (Cambridge: Cambridge University Press, 1989), p. 44.

142 *Evening Express*, 19 February 1895, 2.

143 Glasgow University Library Special Collections Department [Online]. Available at: *http://special.lib.gla.ac.uk/exhibns/month/feb2002* (accessed 5 April 2017).

144 Staff, *The Valentine*, p. 66.

145 Owen, *Welsh Folk Customs*, p. 158.

146 SFAWC 14.159.271.

147 Annebella Pollen, '"The Valentine has fallen upon evil days": Mocking Victorian valentines and the ambivalent laughter of the carnivalesque', *Early Popular Visual Culture*, 12 (2014), 152, available online at: *http://www.tandfonline.com/doi/abs/10.1080/17460654.2014.924212?journalCode=repv20*, DOI: 10.1080/17460654.2014.924212.

148 Poem 61.

149 Poem 57.

150 Poem 48.25–32.

151 Poem 48.21–4.

152 Rhys Dafydd, 'Rhys Dafydd Sy'n Deyd' [It is Rhys Dafydd who proclaims], *Y Clorianydd* [The Arbiter], 25 February 1904, 3.

153 William Thomas Rees 'Alaw Ddu' (1838–1904) was born in Pwll-y-glaw near Pont-rhyd-y-fen in Glamorganshire; see further Rhidian Griffiths, 'Alaw Ddu: o'r pwll at y gân' [From the coalmine to song], *Y Casglwr* [The Collector], 35 (1988), 3.

154 Poem 49.17–22.

155 Betsan Jones, 'Betsan Jones ar Bobol a Phethau (Gyni Hi ei Hunan)' [Betsan Jones on People and Places (By She Herself)], *Y Clorianydd* [The Arbiter], 17 February 1910, 3.

156 Poem 54.12.

157 Poem 46; Twr y Dderi, 'Nodion o Geredigion', 7.

158 Poem 47; Twr y Dderi, 'Nodion o Geredigion', 7.

159 Jôns, 'Sisial', 6.

160 Anonymous, 'Sant Falantein', *Tarian y Gweithiwr* [The Worker's Shield], 13 February 1896, 5.

161 Poem 35.33–40.

162 Poem 59.1–4.

163 For similar Valentines that 'could be between 15–65 shillings each, according to one stationer's advertisement of 1875', see T. Chapman, 'Valentines for Presentation', advertisement, *The Graphic*, 6 February 1875, 143, quoted in Alice Crossley, 'Paper Love: Valentines in Victorian

Culture', in Helen Kingstone and Kate Lister (eds), *Paraphernalia! Victorian Objects* (London: Routledge, 2018), e-book chapter 12, n. 15.

164 Poem 50; [Robert Williams], *Gwaith Barddonol Trebor Mai* [The Poetical Works of Trebor Mai] (Liverpool: I. Foulkes, 1883). In the biography, Robert Williams explains his pseudonym: 'Nid yw TREBOR MAI yn ddim ond "I am Robert" o chwith' (TREBOR MAI is merely 'I am Robert' read backwards), p. v. The volume is reviewed in *Y Traethodydd* [The Essayist] (January 1884), 132.

165 Fabian's Bay, 'Good Templarism', *The Cambrian*, 12 July 1872, 8 [Online]. Available at: *http://newspapers.library.wales/view/3331460/3331468/69/templarism* (accessed 6 December 2017).

166 Obituary, *The North Wales Weekly News*, 19 March 1909, 12: 'We regret to record the death of Mr. John Williams, or better known by his bardic name – "Llenor o'r Llwyni," at the ripe age of 82 years.'

167 Poems 51, 52.

168 See Huw Walters, 'Cerddi ymddiddan ynghylch ymfudo i Awstralia' [Dialogue Poems regarding emigrating to Australia], *The National Library of Wales Journal*, 31 (winter 2000), 381–400; Rhiannon Ifans, *Awstralia, Gwlad yr Aur: Teithiau i Awstralia drwy lygad y baledwyr Cymraeg* [Australia, Land of Gold: Journeys to Australia through the eyes of the Welsh ballad writers] (Aberystwyth, Cymdeithas Lyfrau Ceredigion, 2008).

169 Poem 53.9–16.

170 'Dygwyl Falentein', *Y Cymro* [The Welshman], 18 February 1897, 5.

171 'St. Valentine's Day', *Evening Express*, 15 February 1900, 4.

172 Andronicus, 'Nodion Cartrefol' [Homely Notes], *Y Genedl Gymreig* [The Welsh Nation], 17 February 1892, 5.

173 Jones, 'Myrddin Fardd', p. 245.

174 Mrs Kate Davies, in a manuscript held in the St Fagans National Museum of History's archives and quoted in Owen, *Welsh Folk Customs*, p. 155.

175 Jones, 'Betsan Jones ar Bobol a Phethau', 3.

176 'Digwyddiadau yr Wythnos: Cartrefol' [The Week's Events: Domestic], *Baner ac Amserau Cymru* [Liverpool, and North and South Wales general advertiser], 26 December 1906, 8.

177 John Emyr (ed.), *Lewis Valentine, Dyddiadur Milwr a Gweithiau Eraill* [A Soldier's Diary and other works] (Llandysul: Gomer, 1988), p. 13.

178 Emyr (ed.), *Dyddiadur Milwr*, p. 41.

179 The Lewis Valentine diaries and correspondence are held at the National Library of Wales; for a selection of papers relating to the First World War see its *Cymru 1914* website, *http://cymru1914.org/cy* (accessed 26 March 2018). See further D. Densil Morgan, *Cedyrn Canrif: Crefydd a Chymdeithas yng Nghymru'r Ugeinfed Ganrif* [The Mighty of the Century:

Religion and Society in twentieth-century Wales] (Caerdydd: Gwasg Prifys-gol Cymru, 2001), in particular pp. 68–104; Arwel Vittle, *Valentine: Cofiant i Lewis Valentine* [Valentine: A Biography of Lewis Valentine] (Talybont: Y Lolfa, 2006).

180 Siôn T. Jobbins, *The Phenomenon of Welshness or 'How many aircraft carriers would an independent Wales need?'* (Llanrwst: Gwasg Carreg Gwalch, 2011), pp. 41–7.

181 Poem 66.

182 Poem 67.

183 For the series see the note to Poem 67.

184 Poem 69.

185 Poem 68.

186 Owen, *Welsh Folk Customs*, p. 157.

187 Fflur Morse, 'Be my Valentine: Victorian Comic Valentines', 9 August 2018, Amgueddfa Blog: Amgueddfa Cymru – National Museum Wales, *https://museum.wales/blog/2016-02-09/Be-My-Valentine-Victorian-Comic-Valentines/* (accessed 3 April 2017).

188 J.J., Bronygadfa, 'Ancient Valentines', *Bye-gones*, 26 December 1894, 508.

189 Jobbins, *The Phenomenon of Welshness*, p. 46.

190 Charles Lamb, 'Valentine's Day', *The Essays of Elia*, first published in book form in 1823, available online at Project Gutenberg *www.gutenberg.org/files/10343/10343.txt* (accessed 20 March 2018).

Figure 1: *St Valentine, stained glass by Glantawe Studios, designed by Colwyn Morris, 1994, St Mary's Church, Swansea; Photo © Martin Crampin.*

Figure 2: *Handmade Valentine from Llanbryn-mair in Powys;* © *National Museum of Wales.*

Figure 3: *Comic Valentine;*
© *National Museum of Wales.*

Figure 4: *'Guess who sends this': Valentine card sent*
by John Owen to Eleanor Pritchard;
by kind permission of Miss Mair Jenkins.

Figure 5: 'Yours for ever': padded and perfumed
Valentine card sent by John Owen to Eleanor Pritchard;
by kind permission of Miss Mair Jenkins.

Figure 6: *Valentine card envelope addressed to Miss Elinor Pritchard; by kind permission of Miss Mair Jenkins.*

Figure 7: *Valentine card envelope addressed to Miss E. Pritchiard; by kind permission of Miss Mair Jenkins.*

Figure 8: *'I'll be constant & true': Valentine card sent by John Owen to Eleanor Pritchard; by kind permission of Miss Mair Jenkins.*

Figure 9: *Message on the printed centre panel of 'I'll be constant & true' reads 'Let us be happy together'; by kind permission of Miss Mair Jenkins.*

Figure 10: *Inscription on 'I'll be constant & true';
by kind permission of Miss Mair Jenkins.*

Figure 11: *'Constancy': Valentine card sent by John Owen to Eleanor Pritchard; by kind permission of Miss Mair Jenkins.*

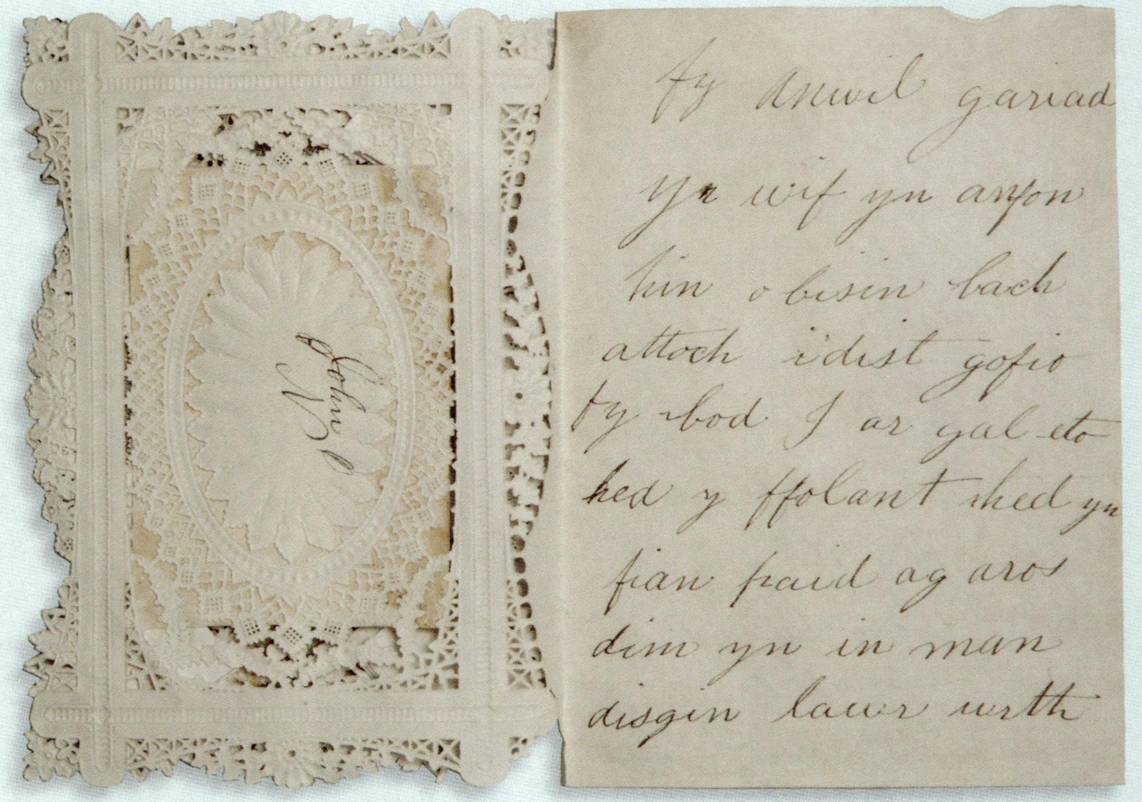

Figure 12: *Inscription on 'Constancy';*
by kind permission of Miss Mair Jenkins.

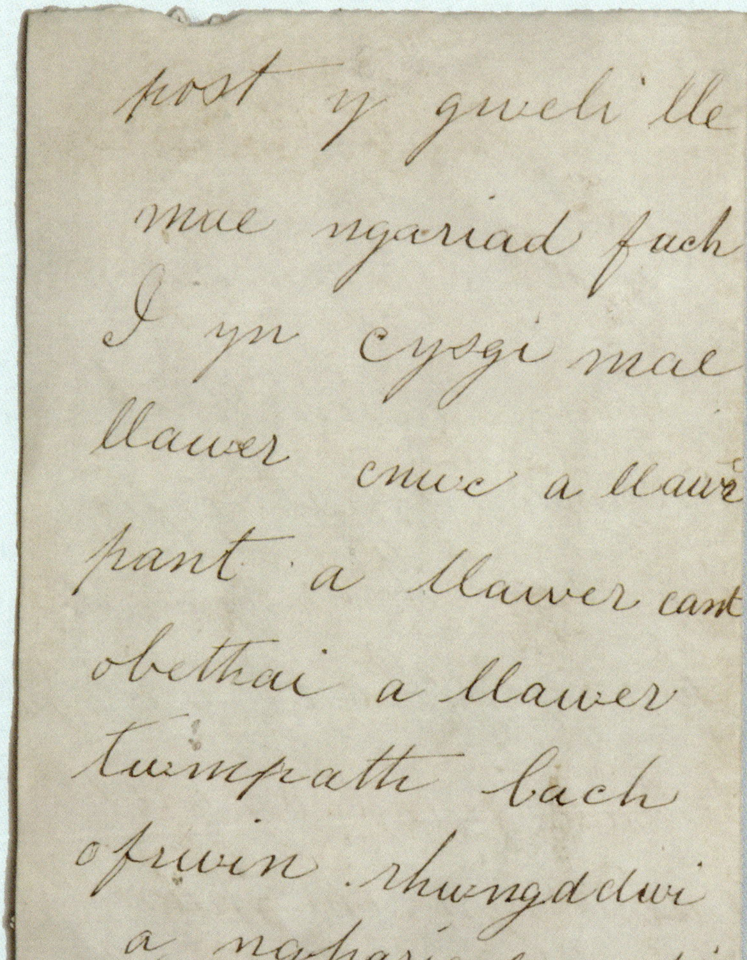

post y gweli 'lle
mae nghariad fach
I yn cysgi mae
llawer cnuc a llawr
pant a llawer cant
obethai a llawer
twmpath bach
o frwin rhwng ddwi
a nghariad ar hin
brid hin yn fir oddi
wrth eich anwil ganiad

Figure 13: *Inscription on 'Constancy' continued;*
by kind permission of Miss Mair Jenkins.

Figure 14: *'Ever the same': Valentine card sent by John Owen to Eleanor Pritchard; by kind permission of Miss Mair Jenkins.*

Figure 15 (above): *Inscription on 'Ever the same'; by kind permission of Miss Mair Jenkins.*

Figure 16 (left): *Inscription on 'Ever the same' continued; by kind permission of Miss Mair Jenkins.*

Figure 17: *'Affections Offering': Valentine card sent by John Owen to Eleanor Pritchard; by kind permission of Miss Mair Jenkins.*

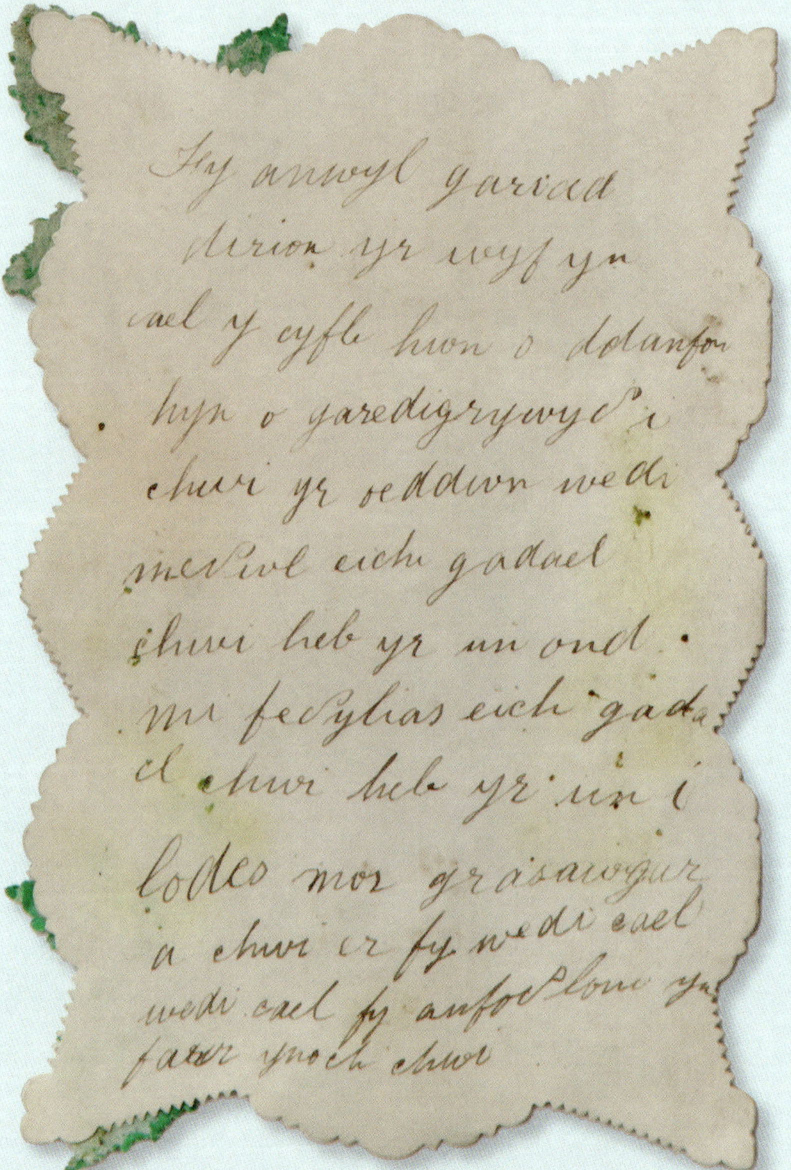
Fy anwyl gariad
dirion yr wyf yn
cael y cyfle hwn o ddanfon
hyn o garedigrwydd i
chwi yr oeddwn wedi
meddwl eich gadael
chwi heb yr un ond
mi feddyliais eich gada-
el chwi heb yr un i
loddeo mor grasawgur
a chwi er fy wedi cael
wedi cael fy anfodlono yn
fater ynoch chwi

Figure 18: *Inscription on 'Affections Offering'; by kind permission of Miss Mair Jenkins.*

Tunes

Amaryllis

Belle Isle March

Bryniau'r Werddon

Charity Mistress *or* Elusenni Meistres

Difyrrwch Gwŷr Emlyn

Diniweidrwydd

Fenyw Fwyn

Y Folantein

Hud y Frwynen

King's Round *or* Iechyd o Gylch

Leave Land *or* Gadael Tir

Let Mary Live Long *or* Hir Oes i Fair

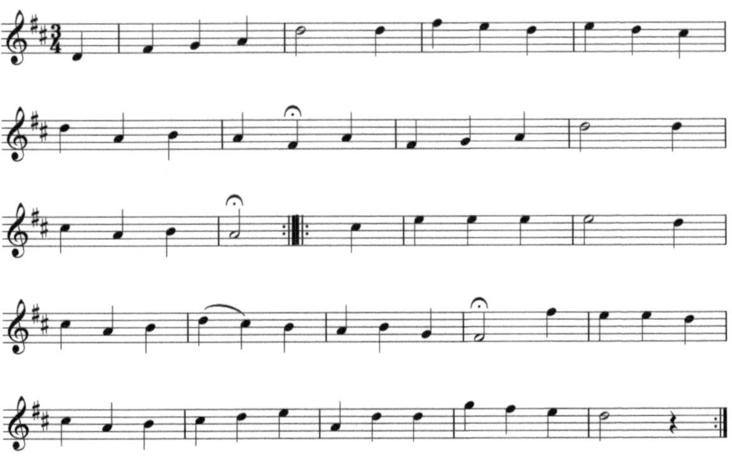

The Lord Monk's March *or* Ymdaith Mwngc

Milking Pail

See the Building *or* Gwêl yr Adeilad

Spanish Minuet

Stanes Morris

Sunselia

Synnwyr Solomon

Welsh Valentine Songs and Poems

1   Cywydd i Mrs Margaret Wyn o Gwm Ein i ofyn
    Valentine i David Davies

     Mae un ardd, am ddawn urddas,
     Yn llawn o glod fel llwyn glas,
     Ail i Eden oleudeg
4   Yw'r llwyn a dw', a'r lliw'n deg;
     Bryniau gwiw, heb rew na gwynt,
     Yn flodau nefawl ydynt,
     Ac un pwysi gwyn peiswyrdd
8   Ymwisg â mawl ymysg myrdd;
     Pêr ei arogl, pur euraidd,
     Blodeuog wir enwog wraidd;
     Marged Wyn, mawr gadwyni,
12   Meini claer i'w mwnwgl hi,
     Ebrill gwawn, briallu gwŷdd,
     Meillionen, mwy llawenydd,
     Llygaid dydd, llu ced diddos,
16   Daw mwsg o'r un damasg ros,
     Sirianen sy aur eneth,
     Lliw'r saffrwm ei blaenglwm bleth;
     Gwaedoliaeth a gydeiliodd
20   Â glendid pryd, rhwyddfyd rhodd;
     Trwy ddoniau natur ddynol,
     Didwn air, nid ydyw'n ôl;
     Dw' gwiwlwys, diau galwn
24   Dyrchafiad y tyfiad hwn,
     Y cyrraedd hon, cu rwyddhau,
     Ddawn gras, dda enwog risiau,
     A chyflawnder, hoywder hawl,
28   Hoff rad doniau ffortunawl.
     Ufudd was wy', foddau serch,
     Câr i hon, ceir ei hannerch,
     Câr gwael wyf, cywir goel aeth,
32   Mor ddedwydd mawredd odiaeth.
     F'enaid oedd fy nedwyddwch,
     Godi 'mhen llawen o'r llwch;
     Bachgen wy' heb och gen i,
36   E dywynnodd daioni,

1   A *Cywydd* to Mrs Margaret Wyn of Cwm Ein to request
a Valentine for David Davies

      There is one garden, for [its] gift of dignity,
      That is full of praise like a green grove,
      Comparable with Eden fair and beautiful
4   Is the grove that is cultivated, and the colour is fair of appearance;
      Fine hills, without ice or wind,
      They are heavenly blossoms,
      And [there is] one white posy with a green mantle [of leaves]
8   That is clothed in [particular] praise among ten thousand;
      Sweet its perfume, pure golden,
      Blossoming [and] truly illustrious rootstock;
      Margaret Wynne, long chains
12   [And] shining gems [hang] about her neck,
      April gossamer, forest primroses,
      Clover, greater joy,
      Daisies, a host [of them] in a generous gift,
16   Musk emanates from the one damask rose,
      A cherry is this excellent girl,
      Her plait, knotted at the front, is the colour of saffron;
      Lineage has interweaved
20   With beauty of countenance, gift of happiness;
      On account of the gifts of human nature,
      True word, she is not found wanting;
      One of precious and comely cultivation, I would doubtless call for
24   The exaltation of this bloom,
      That there should reach this [woman], lovingly easing the way,
      The gift of grace, good [and] illustrious steps [of promotion],
      And fullness, elegant right,
28   Of choice [and] generous fortunate blessings.
      I am a humble young man, means of love,
      Her dear one, it is permitted to greet her,
      I am a poor companion, pang of true faith,
32   How felicitous is excellent greatness.
      My beloved was my bliss,
      To lift my joyful head from the dust;
      I am a boy without sighs,
36   Goodness has shined,

Arafa' pwyll, ar fab bach
O'i fawr awydd foreach;
Bore gwanwyn, brig einioes,
40   Gyfan fydd a gofia'n f'oes;
Obaith codiad, byth cadwa'
Yn ŵyl y dydd annwyl da,
Uchelwyl iawn, lawn o les,
44   Fawr a gwledd fy arglwyddes;
Y pedwerydd dydd, diau,
Wir adde' clod, ar ddeg clau
O Chwefror oedd a chyfri,
48   Ddwyn mawr ddaioni i mi.
Honno ei gwir henw y ges,
Lleuad doniau, lle tynnes
Valentine, foliant hynod,
52   Clo des dawn, clau destun clod,
Foesgarwch, o fysg eraill,
I gyd o'r llaw, gado'r lleill;
Damweiniodd, mi a'i dymunes,
56   Dan fy llaw, dyna fy lles;
Papur oedd, pob rhai wyddant,
Di-wael gwych a dalai gant;
Mynnwn gael, am uniawn go'
60   Yr awron ei oreuro
Ag aur tawdd, all hawdd wellhau
Y lithr yn ei lythrennau.
Pan wybûm pa enw o barch
64   Y gefais i i'w gyfarch
Neidiais, fael hirgais, fel hydd,
Awr lân, o wir lawenydd;
Gwasgu y wnawn, yn llawn lles,
68   Henw'r fun hon i'r fynwes,
A'i gusanu, gais hynod,
Gwn o barch ac un ei bod,
Ac ar 'y mhen gwiw rym hawl,
72   Ffafr ydy' hoff hyfrydawl;
Gwell gen i, a henwi hon,
Yno ei chyrredd na choron;

Gentlest of temperament, on a dear young man
Out of his earlier great desire;
A spring morning, at the height of life,
40 That will I remember in its entirety all my life;
Hope of advancement, I will forever keep it
A feast day, the dear [and] good day,
A fitting high festival, highly beneficial,
44 Of importance, and my lady's feast;
The fourth day, doubtless,
Sincerely acknowledging praise, on ten swiftly
Of February it was by count,
48 That brought me great goodness.
She, her very name I received,
Moon of talents, as I drew [the name of my]
Valentine, exceptional praise,
52 Knot of warm moral virtue, ready subject of praise,
Refinement, from among others,
Entirely by hand, leaving the others behind;
It happened, I wished it,
56 [That the Valentine came] to my hand, that was to my gain;
It was a paper, everyone knows [this],
Excellent, splendid, that it would be worthwhile for a hundred
  [to obtain];
I insist upon the right, for righteous recollection,
60 This moment to gild it
With molten gold, that can easily improve
The fluency of its letters.
When I learned whose name, out of respect,
64 I had received to greet,
I leaped, prince with the far-reaching quest, like a stag,
Holy hour, out of true joy;
I would press, with abounding profit,
68 This woman's name to the bosom,
And kiss it, excellent request,
I know her essence, out of respect and in agreement,
And upon my head, by right of excellent authority,
72 It is a choice [and] delightful favour;
On naming this [woman] I would prefer,
Over obtaining a crown, to attain her there;

Hwylio mawredd helm urddas,
76 Ruban gwyn ar ben ei gwas,
Lliw a wisga i'n 'wyllysgar,
Lliw hon pob calon a'i câr.
O caf einioes, cof iawnwedd,
80 Ennyd o febyd i fedd,
Nid â i'm pen, na dim pall,
Yn hen ŵr, un henw arall.
Cynta' un cawd daioni,
84 Was go sâl y wisgais i,
A di-gudd y digwyddo
Doeth o ferch diwaetha' fo,
A'i maddeuant, buddiant byd,
88 Am y rhyfyg mawr hefyd.

Edward Morris (?1633–89)

Sources
Cardiff 4.10, 875–6
Gwenllian Jones, 'Bywyd a Gwaith Edward Morris Perthi Llwydion' [The Life and Works of Edward Morris Perthi Llwydion] (unpublished MA thesis, University of Wales [Aberystwyth], 1941), 256–7

Variant readings
Line 12 yw'[i] mwnwgl (Jones, 'Bywyd a Gwaith Edward Morris')
Line 15 llu(g)ed diddos (Jones, 'Bywyd a Gwaith Edward Morris')

Date
Seventeenth century.

Locality
The poet, Edward Morris (?1633–89), lived in Perthi Llwydion, Cerrigydrudion, in the historical county of Denbighshire in north Wales, now Conwy.

As preparation for the majesty of a crown of dignity,
76 A white ribbon on her young man's head,
A colour that I will readily wear,
Every heart adores the colour of this woman['s complexion].
If I am given life, well-formed recollection,
80 A short time from infancy to grave,
There will not enter my head, and that without ceasing,
As an old man, any other name.
First of all, goodness was obtained,
84 Quite insignificant young man, I was adorned [with her name]
And it will manifestly happen,
Wise young woman, he will be [the] last [to wear her name],
And her forgiveness, prosperity of [this] neighbourhood,
88 Also for the great presumption.

Edward Morris (?1633–89)

Note
Edward Morris writes on behalf of David Davies requesting that Mrs Margaret Wynne should be his Valentine. Margaret Wynne of Cwm Main, 'daughter of Captain Evan Lloyd of Plas Duon, in the parish of Llanwnog in Arwystli' in the historical county of Montgomeryshire, now Powys, was married to Robert Wynne, the local vicar; he was 'parson of Caer y Drudion in 1679, *ob.* 26th Dec. 1696', see J. Y. W. Lloyd, *The History of the Princes, the Lords Marcher and the Ancient Nobility of Powys Fadog and the Ancient Lords of Arwystli, Cedewen and Meirionydd*, 6 vols (London: T. Richards, 1881–7), 6, p. 80. The marriage settlement was dated 2 March 1656[–7], and they had two sons (Evan, heir of Robert born about 1663, and John), see Thomas Allen Glenn (ed.), *The Family of Griffith of Garn and Plasnewydd in the County of Denbigh, as Registered in the College of Arms from the Beginning of the XIth Century* (London: Harrison and Sons, 1934), p. 259.

Measure
Cywydd.

2   I ddiolch am rodd Valentine

Y liwgar olygus, gain seren gysurus,
Lon, heini, lân, hoenus a dawnus ar dw',
Mi fydda, mae'n fuddiol, ['n] eich cofio yn wastadol,
4   Bun weddol, dda, foesol, ddifasw.

Rwy' tan rwymedigeth, yn ôl fy ngwybodeth,
I ddiolch yn heleth, wych odieth, i chwi
Am ddangos mor weddedd eich cariad helaethedd
8   Trwy fwynedd, ddiomedd dda i mi.

Chwychwi yw'r garedica, fwyn, weddedd fun wiwdda
A'r helaeth wawr haela, hawddgara, deg wedd,
Hyfrydwch y frodir a seren y Teirsir
12   Ac eglur, dda feinir addfwynedd.

El eurwych, El ara', El glirwen, ail Gloria,
El rasol, ail Rosa, chwi roesoch, main dw',
Rodd imi, 'n ôl 'r amod, mewn wllys da, parod
16   Yn Valentine hynod, dan henw.

Er mwyn eich gwir gofio mi gadwa nhw er gwirio
Y rhodd tra parhao, er clirio ar eich clod,
A gweddus yw imi roi diolch amdani
20   I chwi, y fun heini, fwyn, hynod.

Rhof ganwaith ar gynnydd, da goelion digelwydd,
Ddiolch i chwi beunydd, lon beunes, lle bwyf,
A'ch clod yn ddiogan a fydd yn ei [d]datgan
24   Yn ddiddan, lliw'r wylan, lle'r elwyf.

Edward Morris (?1633–89)

2   In gratitude for a Valentine gift

The fair in appearance, beautiful [one], handsome joyous star,
Happy, vivacious, pretty, spirited, and blessed in form,
I will remember you constantly, it is fitting,
4   Beautiful of countenance, good, high-principled young woman,
        devoid of wantonness.

I am under [great] obligation, in accordance with my conversance
        [with this custom],
To give copious thanks to you, exceptionally splendid [one],
For manifesting in such a becoming way your abundant love
8   By means of your tender, ungrudging goodness towards me.

You are the most generous [of women], fair, modest, good and
        worthy young woman
And the magnanimous, most generous dawn, most amiable, of
        comely countenance,
Delight of the region and star of the three counties
12   And an illustrious, gracious, gentle young woman.

Beautiful and excellent El, patient El, bright and blessed El,
        comparable with Gloria,
El full of grace, comparable with Rosa, you have given me, slim
        of build,
A gift, in accordance with the promise, with eager good will
16   An excellent Valentine, by name.

In order to remember you truly I will keep them so that I can attest to
The gift for its duration, so that your praise is made clear,
And it is seemly that I should give thanks for it
20   To you, vivacious, courteous, excellent lady.

I will thank you a hundred times and more, good [and] true beliefs,
Daily, happy lady, wherever I may be,
And I will declare irreproachable praise for you
24   With delight, [one with a complexion] the colour of the seagull,
        wherever I go.

Edward Morris (?1633–89)

Sources
NLW 9B, 192
Hugh Hughes (ed.), *Barddoniaeth Edward Morris Perthi Llwydion* [The poems of Edward Morris Perthi Llwydion] (Liverpool: Isaac Foulkes, 1902), pp. 49–50
Jones, 'Bywyd a Gwaith Edward Morris', 378

Variant readings
Line 13 Glora (NLW 9B, 192)
Line 23 datgan (NLW 9B, 192)

Date
Seventeenth century.

Locality

The poet, Edward Morris (?1633–89), lived in Perthi Llwydion, Cerrigydrudion, in the historical county of Denbighshire in north Wales, now Conwy.

Measure

Tri thrawiad sengl; the song can be sung to 'Gadael Tir y ffordd hwyaf'; for 'Leave Land' or 'Gadael Tir y ffordd hwyaf' see Phyllis Kinney, 'The Tunes of the Welsh Christmas Carols (II)', *Canu Gwerin (Folk Song)* [hereafter *CG*], 12 (1989), 11–13; Phyllis Kinney and Meredydd Evans (eds), *Hen Alawon (Carolau a Cherddi)* [Old Tunes (Carols and Poems)] (n.p.: Welsh Folk Song Society in association with the National Museum of Wales (Welsh Folk Museum), 1993), number 42.

3   Dechre dau bennill Valendine ar 'Sunselia'

Y gangen ddi-gudd, lon, beraidd, lawn budd,
Bur, frigog, odidog a gwridog ei grudd,
Drych yn y dre a lloer ym mhob lle,
4   Gwedd seren siriolwen, A geinwen ac E;
Gwisgo rwy y rhain er mwyn eich corff cain
Sydd loywach a phurach, eglurach na'r glain;
Eich enw, gwawr wen, fel blodau pêr bren,
8   G'leuni heb drueni yw fy mhwysi yn fy mhen.

Mi fynna 'n fy lein, lân deg Falendein,
I dreio'ch caredigrwydd, gwir sicrwydd yw'r sein;
Eich tegwch eich hun yn anad yr un
12   Yr ydw yn ei ddewis, llewyrchus ei llun,
Ac oni cha i chwi, hoff rosyn, yn ffri,
Caf docyn cyn Clame, diame ydwy' i.
Mi a'i gwisga bob dydd tra bo chwi â'ch llaw 'n rhydd
16   I gofio'ch hawddgarwch, difyrrwch da fydd.

Huw Morys (1622–1709)

Sources
Cwrtmawr 225B, 48
W[alter] D[avies] (ed.), *Eos Ceiriog, sef Casgliad o Bêr Ganiadau Huw Morus* [Eos Ceiriog, that is a Collection of the Sweet Songs of Huw Morus], 1 (Wrexham: I. Painter, 1823), p. 121

Variant readings
Title: Dau benill i Ferch ieuanc, ar Wyl VALENTINE (D[avies], *Eos Ceiriog*, p. 121)
Line 8 fy mhwsi ar fy (D[avies], *Eos Ceiriog*, p. 121)
Line 9 Y fi a lyna 'n (D[avies], *Eos Ceiriog*, p. 121)
Line 15 llawn'n (Cwrtmawr 225B, 48)
The author is not named in Cwrtmawr 225B.

3   The commencement of two Valentine stanzas on 'Sunselia'

    The unconcealed bough, happy, sweet, filled with blessings,
    Pure, prosperous, radiant and rosy-cheeked,
    A vision in the town and a moon in every place,
4   [With the] countenance of a joyful white star, a splendidly pure
        A and E;
    I wear these [letters] in honour of your fine figure
    Which is brighter and purer, more brilliant than the jewel;
    Your name, white dawn, is like the blossom of a fragrant tree,
8   My posies on my head are uninterrupted light.

    In my line [of poetry], virtuous beautiful Valentine, I wish to
    Test your generosity, it is the sign of true conviction;
    It is your own beauty in preference to any other
12   That I choose, [one of] flourishing appearance,
    And if I do not obtain you freely, beloved rose,
    I have no doubt that I will obtain a token before Mayday.
    I will wear this daily while your hand is free
16   To bear in mind your amiability, it will be [my] good pleasure.

Huw Morys (1622–1709)

Date
Seventeenth century; Cwrtmawr 225B, however, is dated 1775–80.

Locality
The poet, Huw Morys (1622–1709), also known by his bardic name 'Eos
Ceiriog' [the nightingale of Ceiriog], was from Hafodgynfor in the parish
of Llangollen, Denbighshire, but spent the greater part of his long life at
Pontymeibion in the parish of Llansilin in Powys, about six miles west
of Oswestry.

Note
Verses written for A.E.

Measure
For 'Sunselia' see Kinney and Evans, *Hen Alawon*, number 46.

4   Dechre [cerdd Valendine] ar 'Sunselia'

Y gu eneth gain, a'r goleuni glain,
Benodol bun wiwdlws, lliw Fenws, ael fain,
Eich tegwch a'ch dawn, rhy loyw a rhy lawn,
4   A'm gyrrodd, dan gurio, i dramwy'n drwm iawn;
Ciwpid a'i gwnae, fe fu arno fai,
Na wnaethai ar gariad na throiad na thrai;
Os serch a hir sai', fel llwydrew fis Mai,
8   Mi dodda yn y diwedd, modd rhyfedd, medd rhai.

Fy llygaid fy hun, a'm clustiau'n gytûn,
A wnaethon gam hwythau, bu beiau ar bob un!
Am graffu ar eich lliw, y winwydden wiw,
12   A gwrando'ch ymadrodd a'm brathodd i'm briw,
Rwy'n diodde ac yn dwyn pur gariad heb gŵyn
Oblegid fod glendid yn f'erlid i'n fwyn;
Ni fuasai dan f'ais na thrymder na thrais
16   Pe buaswn heb weled na chlywed eich llais.

Caredigrwydd rwydd radd mewn cwlwm a'm cadd,
Rwy'n ofni mai cariad i'm lleuad a'm lladd;
Os tegwch a'm dwg i'r ddaear ddi-wg
20   Fe fydd i chwi ogan a'i ddarogan yn ddrwg;
Ystyriwch mewn pryd mai gwagedd i gyd
Yw cyfoeth, hudoliaeth, bywoliaeth y byd;
Llarieiddiach, lliw'r ôd, i fyw ac i fod
24   Yw twymyn ffyddlonddyn na cherlyn na chod.

Dyn wyf fi dan iâ, ni wn i beth a wnaf
Am wres a chynhesrwydd, rhywiogrwydd yr haf;
Chwychwi a'm hiachâ, os dyfn wllys da,
28   O'ch tyner glaearwch, hawddgarwch a gaf;
Mi a fyddaf, fy lloer, diana' a di-oer,
Yn llon ac yn llawen fel c'lomen mewn cloer;
Mwy mawredd i mi eich hardd wyneb chwi,
32   Liw Efa, na lifin mawr frenin a'i fri.

4   The commencement [of a Valentine poem] on 'Sunselia'

The beloved, beautiful young woman, and the light of a jewel,
Appointed young woman, worthy and beautiful, [with a
      complexion] the colour of Venus, [and a] slender eyebrow,
Your beauty and your gifts, too bright and too generous of measure,
4   Has caused me, languishing, to walk very slowly;
It is Cupid who is responsible, he is at fault
For not having turned back or ebbed [the tide] of love;
If love remains long, as does the hoarfrost of the month of May,
8   Some say it will eventually dissolve, by strange means.

My own eyes, and my ears in agreement,
They too have inflicted an injury upon [me], each one is at fault!
For observing closely your complexion, the noble vine,
12   And listening to your utterances has pierced me sorely,
I suffer and bear a pure love without complaint
Because purity tenderly pursues me;
There would not be in my breast sorrow or violent [passion]
16   Had I not seen [you] or heard your voice.

Love, in ready degree, has tied me in a knot,
I fear that love for my moon will kill me;
If beauty carries me to the kindly grave
20   You will be reproached and its foreboding will be evil;
Contemplate in good time that all is vanity,
All the world's riches, charm, livelihoods;
More genial, [one with a complexion] the colour of the snow, for
      life and existence
24   Is the passion of a loyal man, than a churl or a pouch[ful of money].

I am a man of ice, I know not what I will do
For the heat and warmth [and] mildness of the summer;
You can restore me to health, if [your] good will demands,
28   In your gentle kindness I will find favour;
I shall be, my moon, ardent and without blemish,
Cheerful and joyous as a dove in a dovecote;
Of more excellence to me is your beautiful face,
32   [One with a complexion] the colour of Eve, than the livelihood
      and prestige of a great king.

Canmoliaeth a gewch os chwi a drugarhewch,
Rhoi purdeb am burdeb mewn undeb a wnewch;
Rhowch i mi serch lefn, drych afiaeth, drachefn,
36 A chariad am gariad didroiad da'i drefn;
Wel, dyna'r tri pheth, ni phlyg teg ei phleth,
I gynnal diddanwch, difyrrwch di-feth;
Gwell i barhau yw dwy galon glau
40 Na dwyfil o bunnau yn dyrau rhwng dau.

Dymunwn cyn hir, wen seren y sir,
O waelod cydwybod gael gwybod y gwir –
A oes fodd i mi, mun, eich cael wrth fy nghlun,
44 Y wiwloer ddiwelw, ar fy helw fy hun?
S gynnes, os ca', wawr ddydd ar awr dda,
Iawn ddywedyd, rwy'n ddedwydd, yn ufudd a wna;
'Meillionen y lles yn goflaid a ges,
48 Lân ethol wenithen, sef t'wysen y tes.'

Huw Morys (1622–1709)

Sources
Cwrtmawr 225B, 44–5
D[avies], *Eos Ceiriog*, pp. 122–4

Variant readings
Title: Arall (D[avies], *Eos Ceiriog*, p. 122)
Line 2 liw (D[avies], *Eos Ceiriog*, p. 122)
Line 4 dramwyo (D[avies], *Eos Ceiriog*, p. 122)
Line 8 Mi a (D[avies], *Eos Ceiriog*, p. 122)
Line 15 na thrallod na thrais (D[avies], *Eos Ceiriog*, p. 122)
Line 37 na phlyg (D[avies], *Eos Ceiriog*, p. 122)
Line 43 i mi'r fun (D[avies], *Eos Ceiriog*, p. 122)
Line 45 y wawr (D[avies], *Eos Ceiriog*, p. 122)

You will be praised if you act compassionately,
You will give purity for purity in unity;
Give me gently flowing love, vision of joy, once more,
36   And love for undeviating love in perfect harmony;
Well, those are the three things, the one with the beautiful plait
      of hair will not compromise on,
Necessary to maintain comfort, unerring pleasure;
To continue [together], it is better to have two true hearts
40   Than two thousand pounds in mounds between two [people].

Before long I wish, blessed star of the county,
Upon my conscience, to know the truth –
Is it possible for me, young woman, to have you by my side,
44   Noble moon that is without paleness, in my possession?
Warm S, if I may, excellent hour of dawn,
Speak in truth, I am blessed, I will do so faithfully:
'I have received, to embrace, the clover of beneficence,
48   A pure, chosen grain of wheat, that is, the ear of corn in the heat
      of the sun.

Huw Morys (1622–1709)

Date
Seventeenth century; Cwrtmawr 225B, however, is dated 1775–80.

Locality
See poem 3, *Locality*.

Note
Verses written for 'S', see line 45.

Measure
For 'Sunselia' see Kinney and Evans, *Hen Alawon*, number 46.

5   Penillion Malandein neu Valentine

Lliw heulwen gynhesol, bêr gannwyll gynhyrchiol
A drefnodd Duw nefol nod reiol ar dro'd,
Ei hil, am haelioni, yn ôl ei rhieni,
4   Ni fedra i mo'u henwi yn eu hynod.

Eich enw, y fun fwynedd, a dynnes, nod iawnedd,
Yr ewig arafedd, hoff iredd ei phart,
Rwy'n rhoddi fy ngobeth fod imi or'chafieth
8   Oherwydd sein odieth Siân Edwart.

Blode gwlad Troea, yn ddigysgod mi a'ch gwisga,
Dewises y lana', hawddgara' wrth ei grudd;
Chwi wyddoch y gyfreth am hyn o wasaneth,
12   Mae imi daladigeth yn digwydd.

Myfi a lawenes yr awr y dewises
Y dduwies, hardd beunes, fwyn gynnes ei gwedd;
Dywyd pob cwmni o'ch achos, lloer wisgi,
16   Mai 'mhen i fydd pwysi'r cwmpasedd.

Dienw (?Huw Morys (1622–1709))

Sources
Cwrtmawr 231A, 35
Cwrtmawr 225B, 35–6

Variant readings
Line 1 heulen (Cwrtmawr 225B, 35)
Line 7 ngobeth im orchafieth (Cwrtmawr 231A, 35)

Date
Not noted, but a note by Dafydd Marpole in Cwrtmawr 225, 86, attributes Cwrtmawr 231A, a manuscript entitled 'Gwaith H. Morys a Roger Jones', to the last quarter of the seventeenth century. Cwrtmawr 225B

5   Malandein or Valentine stanzas

Countenance of warm sunshine, sweet flourishing candle
Whom [the] heavenly God predestined, royal purpose,
Her lineage, for generosity, with regard to her parents,
4   I am unable to express its excellence.

Gentle woman, I have drawn your name, righteous intention,
Graceful doe, beloved [and] thriving in her role,
I place my hope that there is a privilege [ahead] for me
8   On account of the exceptional sign of Siân Edwart.

The most superior in the land of Troy, I will wear you[r name
        openly and] without shadow,
I have chosen the most beautiful, most amiable by [the blush of]
        her cheek;
You are acquainted with the custom as regards this duty,
12   A remuneration is to be made to me.

I became joyful the [very] hour I chose
The goddess, beautiful lady, gentle [and] warm of countenance;
Every company says it is because of you, animated moon,
16   That my head will be encompassed with posies.

Anonymous (possibly Huw Morys (1622–1709))

was copied between 1775 and 1780, and this song was transcribed from
Cwrtmawr 231A.

Locality
Not noted. If the author is Huw Morys (1622–1709), see poem 3, *Locality*.

Note
The poem was written for Siân Edwart.

Measure
Tri thrawiad sengl; the song can be sung to 'Gadael Tir y ffordd hwyaf';
for 'Leave Land' or 'Gadael Tir y ffordd hwyaf' see Kinney, 'Tunes (II)',
11–13; Kinney and Evans, *Hen Alawon*, number 42.

6   I ofyn Valandine i Jonett Willm, sef gwedi,
      gwraig Humphre Lloyd o Hafod 'Sbyty
      ar 'Consêt Arglwydd Straenee'

      Eglur seren glaerwen glir,
      Goleuwen, sad, goleuni y shir,
      Yr ydw i yn danfon yn ddi-wad
4   Er anrhydedd i'th fawrhad
      Heb geisio gwad o gariad gwir,
      A dyma'r achos, teg ei gwawr,
      A wnaeth i mi ysgrifennu i lawr:
8   Yn Valandine digwyddais gael
      Yr hyn beth ni wela i'n wael.
      Daioni a mael dy enw mawr,
      Sioned wyd y seined wych,
12   Lliw distrych ar y don,
      Williams eilwaith helaeth wyd,
      Lloer annwyl, deg ei bron.
      A minnau sydd, liw mynwes ôd,
16   Y ffordd y rhodie i tan y rhod,
      Mewn cyfan iaith yn cofio'r nod,
      Bydd hawddgar, ddisglair don.
      Rwy felly dan dy enw cain,
20   Fun gynnil, fain ei gwasg,
      Mi brofa rodio tref a llan
      I'th wisgo tan y Pasg
      A thi gei fawl iawn hawl yn hy
24   A llawenydd ym mhob llu;
      Dyro a fynnych, feinir gu,
      Nid oes ond hynny o'm tasg.

      Siôn Ellis y Telyniwr a'i gwnaeth medd rhai, eraill a ddywedant
      nad e' oedd yr awdwr.

6   Requesting a Valentine from Janet William, later
the wife of Humphrey Lloyd of Hafod Ysbyty
on 'Lord Strain's Delight'

Brilliant star, radiant [and] clear,
Of fair complexion, steadfast, light of the county,
I send [greetings] without denial
4   In honour of your exaltation
Without attempting to deny true love,
And this is the reason, beautiful of mien,
That caused me to write:
8   It happened that I drew [your name] as a Valentine
Something I do not consider to be a poor [thing].
Your great name is goodness and gain,
Sioned you are the noble signet,
12   [One with a complexion] the colour of white-crested waves at sea,
Williams you are repeatedly generous,
Cherished moon, fair of breast.
And I, [one with a complexion] the colour of a swell of snow,
16   As regards the manner in which I walk under the heavens,
With fine language I remember the appointed time,
Be amiable, bright wave.
I am therefore under [the authority of] your beautiful name,
20   Accomplished young woman, slender of waist,
I will experience walking in town and village
To wear you[r name] until Easter
And you will be praised, rightful entitlement, with boldness
24   And obtain joy in every assembly;
Give whatever you please, beloved young woman,
That is all there is to my task.

*John Ellis the Harpist wrote it according to some, others say that
he was not the author.*

Source
Cwrtmawr 128A, 210–11

Date
Undated poem in a manuscript dated 1738.

Locality
The poem was written on behalf of Humphrey Lloyd (d.1702) of Hafod Ysbyty, not far from Beddau Gwŷr Ardudwy, Ffestiniog, Gwynedd, and was copied into a manuscript from the Trawsfynydd district.

Measure
For 'Consêt Arglwydd Straenee' see 'Hoffter Arglwydd Strain' in John Parry (Ruabon) and Evan Williams, *Antient British Music; or, a collection of tunes, never before published, which are retained by the Cambro-Britons* (London: Mickleborough, 1742), p. 3; John Parry, 'To the Editor of the Cambro-Briton', *The Cambro-Briton*, 2 (London: John Limbird, 1821), 170. But it is difficult to see how any version of this tune offered by John Parry in *Antient British Music* is suitable. 'Stanes Morris' might be more appropriate, see Jeremy Barlow (ed.), *The Complete Country Dance Tunes from* Playford's Dancing Master (1651–ca.1728) (London: Faber Music Limited, 1985), p. 36 (tune 97).

7 Carol y Valentine

Harri:
 'Nos da i'r fwyalch, ddifalch ddawn,
 Swydd bron haul, sydd brynhawn
 Hyd y gwŷdd, gwinwydd gwawn,
4 Llon o nwyf, yn llunio'n iawn
 Llawenydd llawngar lles.'

Mwyalchen:
 'Mi wna fy rhan, yn ôl fy rhyw,
 Yn anad un, yn enw Duw.
8 Yr adar bach, yr ydw i'n byw!
 Cana i yn llafar claear, clyw,
 Yfory od yw hi des.
 Pam, Harri, mor ddifri mae'r ddwyfron?
12 Cais blethu neu nyddu newyddion.
 Oni wyddost beth a'i gwnaeth
 Ni chei mwy na chŵyn na maeth
 Rhyw 'ffeiriedyn, ffrityn ffraeth,
16 Ar amod hwn a rwymai'n gaeth,
 Ni feddai saeth i serch.
 Nid prudd-der, maith arfer, mo'th orfod,
 Daw amser â llawnder ollyngdod.'

20 Harri:
 'Och! i'r byd, penyd pwys!
 Â'i ofalon dewrion dwys
 Y gwrie'r maen, wâr geirie mwys;
 Hynny a'm gyr i dan y gwys
24 Nid gwaith un feindlws ferch.'

Mwyalchen:
 'Estyn dim nid elli ar d'oes,
 Na wna yn fyrrach, leiach loes,
 Gad ti hynny i'r Gŵr a'th roes,
28 A ddioddefodd ar y groes
 I safio dy einioes di.'

Harri:
 'Dy eirie doeth a dery yn da;
 Heno, yn wir, hynny a wna
32 Yn gadarn gyda Josua.'

7   Valentine Carol

Harri: 'Good evening to the blackbird, [with the] diffident gift
               [of song],
         [Whose] role [is performed] on a slope facing the sun,
               [and] is of an afternoon
         In the trees, gossamer vines,
4   One of joyful vigour, verily composing
         Happiness that is complete profit.'

Blackbird: 'I will fulfil my part, in accordance with my species,
             In preference to all, in the name of God.
8   The little birds, I am alive!
             I will sing loudly [and] pleasantly, take note,
             Tomorrow if it is sunny and warm.
             Why, Harri, is the heart so cheerless?
12   Make an attempt to interweave or compose tidings.
             If you do not know what caused it
             You will obtain henceforth neither the sympathy nor
                   nurture
             Of some priestling, glib good-for-nothing,
16   With the stipulation that he tie [men] captive
             [Since] he would not possess a love arrow [himself].
             Your defeat is not a long-lasting experience of sorrow,
             Time will bring full deliverance.'

20   Harri: 'Woe to the world, burden of torment!
              With its troubles, mighty [and] sombre,
              It makes manly the precious stone [fig. *leader*], civilized
                    gentle words;
              It is that which sends me to my grave,
24   Not the work of any slender and pretty young woman.'

Blackbird: 'You cannot add anything to your lifespan,
             Do not make it shorter, or less painful,
             Leave that to the One who made you,
28   Who suffered on the cross
             To save your life.'

Harri: 'Your wise words strike a good [note];
         This evening, indeed, I will do that
32   Steadfastly with Joshua.'

Mwyalchen: 'Er dawn, yn rhwydd edifarha
                Yn gyntaf, rhwydda rhi;
                Gad ymaith bob artaith cybydd-dra,
36   Nid mwy o drawseirie a drysora;
                Ni roes fy Nuw imi'n fy nerth
                Na chŵys na chod, sorod serth,
                Ond hel i bigo o lawer perth
40   Oddi yma i'r fedwen geinwen gerth
                I ganu yn brydferth bryd.'

Harri: 'Dy gyngor, maith ordor, a'th eirda,
                Fwyalchen d[d]u gefen, a gofia.
44   Hi aeth yn nos, agos yw,
                Ffarwél i'r llwyd, cywira o'r lliw,
                A ddoi di 'r ha i goed y rhiw,
                Nyni ein dau, i ganu i'n Duw
48   O byddwn ni byw yn y byd?'

Dienw

Sources
NLW 11990A, 54–6
NLW 9B, 193–4
Cwrtmawr 171D, 128–9

Variant readings
Line 48 fyw yn diwedd y Bŷd (NLW 9B, 194); byw yn diwedd y byd
(Cwrtmawr 171D, 129)

Date
This undated poem copied into NLW 11990A is partly in the hand of
Rees Roberts, whose name appears under the dates 1685 and 1689,
other parts date from the eighteenth century; NLW 9B, 193–4 was copied
between 1736 and 1755; Cwrtmawr 171D was copied in 1902.

Blackbird: 'For blessing, with readiness repent
            First of all, most generous king;
            Leave behind all pangs of miserliness,
36   I will not gratify any more cross words;
            My God gave me in my life
            Neither furrow nor pouch, foul dregs,
            But to pick and to peck from several hedges
40   Between here and the splendidly pure [and] wonderful
                birch grove
            [And] to sing in beautiful comeliness.'

Harri: 'Your advice, ambitious command, and your good word,
            Black-backed blackbird, I shall bear in mind.
44   Night has come, it is close by,
            Farewell to the russet [bird], most honest and upright
                one of this hue,
            Will you come in summertime to the wooded slope,
            We two, to sing to our God
48   If we are [still] alive in the world?'

Anonymous

Locality
NLW 9B is in the hand of Dafydd Jones 'Dewi Fardd' (?1708–85) of
Trefriw, near Llanrwst, in the upper Conwy Valley, north Wales. Several
owners of NLW 11990A also lived in the Trefriw area.

Note
The poem is untitled in NLW 11990A, but in NLW 9B the title 'Carol y
Valentine' (Valentine Carol) was added by a later hand, and this title
was copied into Cwrtmawr 171D. Edward Morris, Perthi Llwydion, is the
author of the two poems that precede this poem in NLW 9B, and another
of his poems follows this Valentine carol. It would be unwise to attribute
this poem to him with no attestation of authorship. However, it bears
the marks of the seventeenth century and on this premise the poem is
placed with the seventeenth-century poems.

Measure
Not noted.

8   Dau bennill i ofyn calennig am Falandein

Hyd atoch, lloer gellweirus, afieithus foddus fun,
Nef annwyl, bryd Tuana, llawena, llonna ei llun:
Rwy'n danfon, trwy lawenydd, yn siwr oherwydd serch,
4   I'ch annerch, main ei chanol, synhwyrol, foddol ferch;
Darllenwch chwithe'r llythyr ar eglur gywir gân,
Na bydded gas y gennad, fy nghariad, leuad lân.

[A] nesu wnaeth y nosweth, fun eiddil, gynnil, gain,
8   Fe ddaeth y dygwyl weithian i dynnu'r Falandein.
[Fe ro]ddodd imi heddiw eich iawnedd enw chwi
[O blit]h llaweroedd eraill, fwyn ddidwyll gannwyll gu;
[Er mwyn ei]ch gwisgo, gwenfron, loer hinon o liw'r ha',
12   [Rhowch chwithau] imi'n hwylus ystôr o'ch 'wyllys da.

E.W.

Source
NLW 431B, 28

Date
The manuscript, written from both ends, dates from the seventeenth
century, with later additions; the first fifty-two pages were written by
Robert Parry in the mid-seventeenth century, but p. 28 on which the
Valentine stanzas are recorded is a later addition.

8   Two stanzas requesting a Valentine gift

Unto you, mischievous moon, merry [and] modest young woman,
Dear heaven, countenance of Tuana, most joyful, most cheerful in
        manner:
I send, in joy, confident on account of affection,
4   To greet you, slender of waist, sagacious, seemly young woman;
Read the letter [written] in [the form of a] plain sincere song,
Let not the message be disagreeable, my love, beautiful moon.

And the evening has drawn near, slender young woman,
        accomplished, beautiful,
8   The feast day is now come [on which] to draw the Valentine.
[It] gave me today your righteous name
[From among] many others, gentle, guileless, precious candle;
[So that I may] wear you[r name], white-breasted lady, [clear] moon
        of fair weather [with a complexion] the colour of the summer,
12   [Give thou] to me readily an abundance of your good will.

E.W.

Locality
Y Bala, Gwynedd, possibly; the manuscript has been in the possession
of John Lloyd of Bala.

Measure
This poem can be sung to 'Bryniau'r Werddon', see Kinney and Evans,
Hen Alawon, number 45, by repeating the second couplet.

9   Cerdd ar 'Cast Away Care' i ofyn Valentine

    Y perl gwyn, purloyw gannaid,
    Ddynes waredd ddawnus euraid,
    Aeres Helen wiwras haeledd,
4   O blaid gweiniaid, blodau Gwynedd,
    Can croeso i'r haul gwresog olwynog i'r wlad,
    Tydi ydi gwir gynnyrch a llewyrch gwellhad;
    Dy ddyfod di adre o'th gaerau maith gudd,
8   Diryfedd oedd weled cyn deced y dydd,
    Fel seren gysurol foreuol fawr wen
    Awrorau wir eurwych yn entrych y nen.

    Venus ydwyd, fwyn osodiad,
12   Dewis coron duwies cariad;
    Call iawn ffyniant gwell na Ffenics,
    A mwyn eneth fel maen onics;
    Homer yn ddiau pe byddai fe byw
16   Fe eiliai dy foliant a'th haeddiant maith yw;
    A Virgil heb amau 'sgrifennai er dy fwyn
    Ac Orffiws benfelyn a'i delyn ar dwyn;
    Ped fai y naw Musies a'u maswedd yn ffri,
20   Gwir amod, ymgrymen' a chanen' i chwi.

    Ped fase Fenws, duwies fwynedd,
    Mars a Juno mor sidanedd,
    Er pwyso eu rhan ni buasai'r rheini
24   I'm tyb ac ateb tebyg iti,
    A barn gydwybodol dda reiol i roi
    A thithau'n bedwaredd, hoff waredd, heb ffoi;
    Cwest gonest i'w gynnal am afal, fy mun,
28   Ceisiesit ti'r treial ar afal er un,
    Er Helen wawr hylwydd, deg arwydd di-gêl,
    Na glendid deg eraill, di gerit ti'r bêl.

9   A poem on 'Cast Away Care' requesting a Valentine

The white pearl, shining [and] radiant,
Gentle, gifted, illustrious woman,
Heiress of Helen, of gracious generosity,
4   In favour of the weak, the most superior in Gwynedd,
A hundredfold welcome to the warm wheel of sun to the land,
You are the true fruit and radiance of excellence;
Your homecoming from your long hidden fortresses,
8   It was unsurprising to see how fair the day,
Similar to a comforting, large [and] clear morning star,
A truly [and] excellently resplendent Aurora at the zenith of the
        celestial sphere.

You are Venus, of gentle bearing,
12   Choice crown of the goddess of love;
Extremely astute increase, excelling that of Phoenix,
And a gentle girl similar to an onyx stone;
Homer doubtlessly if he were alive
16   Would fashion your praise, and your merit is extensive;
And Virgil without doubt would write [a poem] for your
        [name's] sake
And golden-haired Orpheus and his harp [would make music]
        openly;
Were the nine Muses and their levity to stand unimpeded,
20   Sincere promise, they would bow and sing your praises.

Were Venus, gentle goddess,
Mars and Juno so silken,
Even though they evaluated their contribution, they would not be,
24   In my estimation and answer, like unto you,
And to give a conscientious opinion of good rule
You would be fourth, favourite love, with no escape;
If an honest trial for an apple were held, my sweetheart,
28   You would enter the contest for [the] apple, in spite of whosoever,
In spite of Helen of the winning appearance, of [the] fine [and]
        unconcealed mark [of loveliness],
Or the beauty of ten more, you would win the [golden] ball.

Rwy'n gwisgo'n loyw d'enw dinam
32 O lwyr alwad, Lowry William,
A balch gen i, gwawr sidanbleth,
Fenws onest, fy ngwasaniaeth;
Hyn ydyw fy mwriad, trwy gennad i'ch gwas:
36 O'ch llaw wych alluog fawr enwog o ras
Y peth a ewyllysioch neu fynnoch, y fun,
A roddi'n ddigyffro o'ch eiddo chwi'ch hun;
Cewch felys ganmoliaeth o buriaith y bardd
40 A chlod, y fun alawnt, pan wneloch chi o'n hardd.

Ellis Rowland (c.1650–c.1730)

Source
Cerddi Bangor 2 (3)

Ballad sheet reading
Line 31 gwisgi'n

Date
Not noted; Ellis Rowland's dates are *c.*1650–*c.*1730; the ballad sheet was printed in Shrewsbury by John Rhydderch for the seller, Owen Williams. John Rhydderch was a printer in Shrewsbury 1715–33, therefore the printing of this Valentine song can be dated to the period 1715–30, but not necessarily its date of composition.

Locality
Not noted; Ellis Rowland was a native of Harlech, and wrote poems to persons connected with Ardudwy in the historical county of Merionethshire, now Gwynedd.

I wear, openly, your unblemished name
32 In accordance with an unqualified invitation, Lowry William,
And I am proud, dawn of the silken plait,
Honest Venus, of my office;
This is my intention, if you grant your servant permission:
36 From your excellent able hand that is greatly renowned for its
graciousness
That what you will or desire, sweetheart,
You should give, without stir, from your own possession;
You will receive sweet praise in the pure language of the poet
40 And honour, gallant lady, when you cause him to become
handsome.

Ellis Rowland (c.1650–c.1730)

Note
Verses requesting a Valentine's gift from the hand of Lowry William
(line 32).

Measure
For 'Cast Away Care' or 'Bwrw Gofid Ymaith' see Edward Jones, *Musical and Poetical Relicks of the Welsh Bards preserved by tradition, and authentic manuscripts, from remote antiquity, never before published*, 2 (London: printed by A. Strahan for the author, 1794), p. 175; digitized by the National Library of Wales. It is difficult to see how the version of this tune offered by Edward Jones is suitable.

10   Pennill o fawl i ferch ar y mesur a elwir 'Milking Pail'

Derbyniwch, leuad lon, naturiol freiniol fron,
Y g'lomen, glod, ichwi mae'n bod, gain hynod, y gân hon;
Yn Falentein heb fael, ail Helen, heulwen hael,
4 Digwydde i'm rhan, blodeuyn pob man, eich enw gwiwlan gael.
O fysg y teg, da fri di-freg, fun landeg hoywdeg hy,
Eich cael a wnawn, deuliw'r gwawn, a'ch llewyrch llawn,
Wenynen iawn, oreuddawn gyflawn gu.
8 Gwybyddwch, fwyn, dan gofio 'nghwyn, mai fi sy yn dwyn y dasg
Drwy wisgo yn glyd o flaen un o'r byd mewn cariad cyd
Eich enw o hyd fel penyd tan y Pasg.

Dienw

Sources
Cardiff 3.68, 95
Cardiff 2.14, 68

Variant readings
Title: pennill i'w falentein (Cardiff 2.14, 68)
Line 3 Yn ffalentein heb ffael, ail Elan haelwen hael (Cardiff 3.68, 95)
Line 5 O fysg deg (Cardiff 3.68, 95)
Line 8 Ow! byddwch fwyn tan gofio cwyn un mab sy'n dwyn y dasg
(Cardiff 2.14, 68)
Line 9 Drwy wisgo yn glyd eich henw o hyd mewn cariad cyd (Cardiff
2.14, 68)
Line 10 O flaen un o'r hyd fel penud tan y Pasg (Cardiff 2.14, 68)

10 A stanza in praise of a woman on the measure known
    as 'Milking Pail'

Receive, joyful moon, gentle privileged heart,
The dove, praise, this song exists in your honour, exceedingly
        beautiful [one];
As a Valentine without profit, comparable with Helen, riotous
        sunshine,
4   It befell me, the most superior in all places, to obtain your worthy
        and pure name.
From among the fair, good [and] guileless [one] of high esteem,
        beautiful, light-hearted and lovely, brave young woman,
I would obtain you, twice as fair as gossamer, and your abounding
        radiance,
Righteous bee, supreme gift [and] totally beloved one.
8   Know, gentle one, remembering my plaint, that it is I who
        performs this duty
By wearing comfortably, in the presence of any one in the world,
        in a love of one accord,
Your name constantly as a penance [imposed by love] until Easter.

Anonymous

Date
Not noted, but Cardiff 2.14 was copied between 1720 and 1736 – most
of its contents copied between 1720 and 1724; Cardiff 3.68 was copied
between 1730 and 1740.

Locality
Not noted; Cardiff 2.14 was copied by William Rowland of Hendy, Llan-
faglan, near Caernarfon; Cardiff 3.68 was copied by Robert Thomas,
Carneddi, Beddgelert, Gwynedd, between 1730 and 1735 and the
additions copied by William Griffith of Drws-y-coed near Beddgelert,
Gwynedd, *c*.1740.

Measure
For 'Milking Pail' see Claude M. Simpson, *The British Broadside Ballad
and its Music* (New Brunswick: Rutgers University Press, 1966), p. 492.

11   I ofyn Falandein

J ac A, heulwen ha', hoyw wen serchog,
Yw f'angyles enwog, E ac N, walches wen,
A ga' dros ben hawddgarwch byd;
4   F ac O, drefnus dro, drwyadl ei 'madroddion,
Lana erioed a welson, U, L, K, *vowels* da,
Galonnog o'r lawena i gyd.
Eich enw chwi ddae' i mi o ddeg,
8   Yn Falandein mae'r ddalen deg,
Na ruswch yn rhoi rhodd, mae'n hawdd rhyngu 'modd
Mewn bydol fodd, wybodol ferch;
Wrth wisgo'r naw llythyren gain
12   Synnu rwy'n cydseinio y rhain
Wrth gofio eich pryd glân dan iraidd frig mân,
Eurlwys eirian sidan serch;
Rwy'n gwybod, cyn dyfod i bennod y Pasg,
16   Fy rhiain fwyn, eglur, y bwriwch eich tasg,
Nid rhaid imi enwi dim ichwi, fy mun,
Y peth a fo gweddol chwi a'i gwyddoch eich hun:
Cael un o'ch gwallt chwi i'w roi ar 'y mhen i
20   Er mendio fy mri, lliw ewyn y lli,
Mi fyddwn mor llon ag oedd Absalon,
Hyfrydwch i'w fron, ar doriad y dydd,
Ac yna bydd hardd i'ch weled eich bardd
24   A'i gorun fel gardd, ei galon a chwardd,
Oherwydd fy mod yn mynd tan eich nod,
I ddatgan eich clod mae 'nhafod yn rhydd.

Dafydd Jones (?1708–85)

11   Requesting a Valentine

J and A, summer sunshine, cheerful [and] affectionate young
    woman,
Is my renowned angel, E and N, blessed noble woman,
That I will take, over and above the world's loveliness;
4   F and O [in their] correct order, eloquent her expression,
The fairest that we ever saw, U, L, K, good vowels,
The most sincere of all the most delightful [women].
I obtained your name from [among] ten,
8   The pretty sheet of paper is a Valentine,
Do not rush to bestow a gift, it is easy to please me
In a secular manner, wise young woman;
As I wear the nine beautiful letters [of your name]
12   I am amazed as I speak these [letters] in harmony
As I bring to mind your beautiful countenance below fresh,
    fine hair,
Golden, beautiful, radiant, silken love;
I know, before the Easter period arrives,
16   My gentle [and] illustrious young woman, that you will fulfil
    your duty,
I do not have to specify to you any [gift], my sweetheart,
You know for yourself what is fitting:
To have one lock of your hair to place on my head
20   In order to improve my esteem, [one with a complexion] the
    colour of the crest of a wave,
I would be as happy as Absalom,
Joy to his heart, at the break of day,
And then it will be comely for you to see your poet
24   With the crown of his head like a garden, his heart will be merry,
Because I become under obligation to you
My tongue is free to proclaim your praise.

Dafydd Jones (?1708–85)

Sources

NLW 9B, 15–16

NLW 21738B, 22v

Cwrtmawr 128A, 208–9

Dafydd Jones, *Blodeu-gerdd Cymry* [An Anthology of Welsh Poems] (Amwythig: Stafford Prys, 1759), pp. 192–3

Variant readings

Line 2 walched (Cwrtmawr 128A, 208)

Line 3 Ac E dros ben (NLW 9B, 15; Jones, *Blodeu-gerdd Cymry*, p. 192)

Line 5 dda (NLW 9B, 15; NLW 21738B, 22ᵛ)

Line 9 mae'n hawdd rhannu y modd (NLW 9B, 15; Cwrtmawr 128A, 208)

Line 13 Gan gofio (NLW 9B, 15)

Line 14 aurlwys Irlan (Cwrtmawr 128A, 208)

Line 18 a gweddol (Cwrtmawr 128A, 208)

Line 19 roi yn y mhen i (Cwrtmawr 128A, 208)

Line 20 fo mendiau fy mri (Cwrtmawr 128A, 208)

Line 21 Ni fyddwn (NLW 9B, 15)

Line 22 Hyfrydwch y fron (NLW 9B, 15; Cwrtmawr 128A, 208)

Date

Not noted, but NLW 9B was compiled between 1736 and 1755; Cwrtmawr 128A was transcribed in 1738; NLW 21738B was copied 1789–1803.

Locality

Not noted, but the poet is Dafydd Jones 'Dewi Fardd' (?1708–85) of Trefriw, near Llanrwst, in the upper Conwy Valley, north Wales.

Note

A Valentine song written to greet Jane Foulk.

Measure

The tune 'Ymdaith Mwngc' or 'The Monk's March' is derived from a seventeenth-century country dance tune, see Phyllis Kinney, *Welsh Traditional Music* (Cardiff: University of Wales Press in association with Cymdeithas Alawon Gwerin Cymru, 2011), pp. 62, 232; for the tune see Edward Jones, *Musical and Poetical Relicks of the Welsh Bards preserved by tradition, and authentic manuscripts, from remote antiquity, never before published*, 1 (London: printed for the author, 1784), p. 67, made suitable by halving the notes in the first sentence; 'The Lord Monk's March', in Barlow (ed.), *The Complete Country Dance Tunes*, p. 44 (tune 151). The tune is named after General George Monck (1st duke of Albemarle, 1608–70), an officer in the Cromwellian army, later a key figure in the restoration of Charles II.

12 Dau bennill Malamteim

    Glana beunes, glain y bonadd,
    Dda, dwys haeladd, gymra hawl,
    Trawych lodes, drych gweledydd,
4   Lliwod moelydd, lleuad mawl;
    Duw gynirad, degan eurad,
    Medd y wledd, bun lwysedd lun,
    Dewr o foliant ydi drefoledd bloda,
8   'Merod bloda, mowrion breichia
    A wnaeth rhinwedd mwya a'i thrin;
    Iachus eneth, ei chusanu,
    Gla' waun, ar goron a'r gwin,
12 Gwell na siwgur holl na seigiau,
    Goelbur, owchus gowlad imi,
    Blys i mi, na blas ei min.

    Lloer ireiddwen, wiwlon, lywaeth,
16 Gannwyll afiaith, gain ei llun,
    Wiwlan, hoyw, o galon helaeth,
    Fwyn lyfodraeth, fun aur lun;
    Tegan tegwch, harddwch urddol,
20 Gywir reiol, fel dyna'r sein;
    Gwas gwych iawn, rwy'n gwisgo'ch enw,
    Grefydd groyw, loyw lein:
    Meddyliwch, gwenfron, lunieiddlon lili,
24 Gywir gyflawni eich ffansi, rhag ffein;
    Parliament mwyndar sydd yn barnu,
    Gyfraith mabiath meibion Gymru,
    Gofiwch dalu Malamdeim!

Dienw (?Cadwaladr Morus)

12   Two Valentine stanzas

Most beautiful lady, jewel of the nobility,
Good, of intense generosity, of most estimable authority,
Exceedingly magnificent young woman, a vision to the beholder,
4   [One with a complexion] of snow-coloured summits, moon
        of praise;
One visited by God, precious loved one,
Mead of the banquet, a young woman of beautiful appearance,
She who is the most superior in the city is mightily praised,
8   Empress [over the] finest, one of generous support
Who wrought and handled the greatest virtue;
Favourable young woman, to kiss her,
Wilderness of [love]sickness, [is better] than a crown and the wine,
12   Better than all sugars or dishes [of food],
Pure of faith, my passionate loved one,
My excessive desire, is the taste of her lip.

Fresh and radiant moon, gentle and cheerful, tractable,
16   Candle of gaiety, beautiful in appearance,
Worthy and pure, vivacious, generous of heart,
Gentle in guidance, young woman of excellent aspect,
A favourite with regard to fairness of appearance, noble beauty,
20   Sincere, regal, even as that is the sign;
An exceedingly magnificent young man, I wear your name,
Pure religion, [in a] polished line [of poetry]:
Consider, white-breasted young woman, graceful and joyous lily,
24   [How] to accurately fulfil your fancy, for fear that [you are
        penalized with] a fine;
[The] parliament of pleasure has decreed,
Law of frivolity of the young men of Wales,
Take heed to pay [your] Valentine [gift]!

Anonymous (probably Cadwaladr Morus)

Source
Peniarth 244B, 91

Manuscript readings
Line 5 gin niriad
Line 6 wedd; *medd y wedd* could be translated 'in the like manner of mead', but *medd y wledd* 'mead of the banquet' seems more appropriate; this intoxicating drink, produced locally, symbolized sustenance in the work of medieval Welsh poets; see further Marged Haycock, *'Where Cider Ends, there Ale begins to Reign': Drink in Medieval Welsh Poetry* (Cambridge: Cambridge University Press, 1999).
Line 25 Balmamand; the reading has been changed to *Parliament* in accordance with the corresponding line in poem 13.

Date
Not noted; the manuscript is dated *c*.1735.

Locality

The manuscript is entitled 'The Book of Richard Wiliam, clochydd Llan Llyvni', suggesting that the poem was collected in the Llanllyfni district, Gwynedd.

Note

This anonymous poem was probably written by Cadwaladr Morus, compare lines 15–27 with poem 13 by Cadwaladr Morus. There has been some confusion in the arrangement of the lines with the result that stanza one has 14 lines and stanza two has 13 lines.

Measure

'ar hud y fedlemas newydd' is noted at the end of the poem; no tune bearing that name was found in the collections. It is possible that the copyist refers to 'Hud y Frwynen', see J. Lloyd Williams, 'The Earlier Collections of Traditional Welsh Melodies', *Journal of the Welsh Folk Song Society*, 3 (1930–41), 14, made suitable by repeating one line in the melody.

13   I ofyn Falentein ar 'Diniweidrwydd'

Gwawr oleugu, gwâr olygon,
Gangen hoywfron, hyfryd yw,
Feingan, fwyngu, fun rywiogedd,
4   Glain egluredd, arafedd ryw,
Seren siriol, nefol, nwyfus,
Riain barchus, hoenus, hael,
Mi ges eich enw, ar gais ni chwyna,
8   Blodau'r dyrfa, mwya mael:
Gellwch, gwenfron, lunieiddlon lili,
Hardd gyflawni ffansi, rhag ffael;
Nid wy'n tasgu, glendid Cymru
12   Ond y byddoch i'w chwenychu,
Feingan, fwyngu, fain ei hael.

Lloer oleuwen, lliw aur lywaeth,
Gannwyll afiaith, gain ei llun,
16   Wiwlan, hoywlan, galon helaeth
Drwy lywodraeth, feinaur lun,
Tegan tegwch, harddwch urddol,
O ryw reiol, dyna'r sein;
20   Gwas gwych iawn, rwy'n gwisgo'ch enw,
Cri air croyw, loyw lein:
Ceisiwch, gwenfron, lunieiddlon lili,
Lwyr gyflawni ffansi, rhag ffein;
24   Parliament mwyngu sydd yn barnu,
Cyfraith mabiaeth meibion Cymru,
Y dylech dalu eich Falendein!

Cadwaladr Morus

13   Requesting a Valentine on 'Diniweidrwydd'

Beautiful and beloved [young woman as pretty as] dawn, [with]
    tender eyes,
Girl of the cheerful heart, it is delightful,
Slender and fair [of complexion], tender and beloved, noble
    young woman,
4   Brilliant jewel, of a gentle nature,
Joyful star, heavenly, passionate,
Esteemed, lively, generous young woman,
That I obtained your name, immediately I do not complain,
8   Choicest of the multitude, greatest benefit:
You have power, white-breasted young woman, graceful and
    joyous lily,
To nobly fulfil a fancy, lest [you are accused of] negligence;
I do not impose a task [upon you], beauty of Wales,
12   Save that which is in accordance with your wish,
Slender and fair [of complexion], tender and beloved, slender
    of eyebrow.

Fair-complexioned moon, golden-coloured tress[es],
Candle of gaiety, beautiful in appearance,
16   Worthy and pure, vivacious, generous of heart
In guidance, of slender and excellent aspect,
A favourite with regard to fairness of appearance, noble beauty,
Of regal lineage, that is the sign;
20   An exceedingly magnificent young man, I wear your name,
A word of sweet entreaty, [in a] polished line [of poetry]:
Attempt, white-breasted young woman, graceful and joyous lily,
To wholly fulfil a fancy, for fear that [you are penalized with]
    a fine;
24   [The] tender and amiable parliament has decreed,
Law of frivolity of the young men of Wales,
That you should pay your Valentine [gift]!

Cadwaladr Morus

Sources
NLW 9B, 15
Cwrtmawr 128A, 209–10
Cwrtmawr 171D, 31

Variant readings
Line 9 Ceisiwch gwenfron (NLW 9B, 15; Cwrtmawr 171D, 31)
Line 10 Lwyr gyflawni (NLW 9B, 15; Cwrtmawr 171D, 31)
Line 12 ond a fyddo chwi (Cwrtmawr 171D, 31)
Line 14 oleulan (NLW 9B, 15; Cwrtmawr 171D, 31)
Line 19 siriol (NLW 9B, 15; Cwrtmawr 171D, 31)
Line 22 loywlon Lili (NLW 9B, 15; Cwrtmawr 171D, 31)
Line 23 wir gyflowni (NLW 9B, 15; Cwrtmawr 171D, 31)

Date
Not noted; NLW 9B was compiled between 1736 and 1755; Cwrtmawr
128A was transcribed in 1738; Cwrtmawr 171D was transcribed in 1902.

Locality

Not noted, but NLW 9B was copied by Dafydd Jones 'Dewi Fardd' of Trefriw, and Cwrtmawr 128A was compiled in the Trawsfynydd area.

Note

In NLW 9B, 15 the poem is attributed, in a different hand, to Cadwaladr Morus; the second stanza of this song is an edited version of the second stanza of the anonymous poem 12; compare also 13.9–10 with 13.22–3.

Measure

In NLW 9B, 15, the poem is entitled *I ofyn Valentine ar y Dini-weidrwydd &*, followed by the note *(ne yn hytrach conset ar* [   ]*)*. For 'Diniweidrwydd' see Phyllis Kinney, 'The Tunes of the Welsh Christmas Carols (I)', *CG*, 11 (1988), 46–7; Kinney and Evans, *Hen Alawon*, number 36; it is possible to sing this Valentine song to 'Diniweidrwydd' provided that line 12 of each stanza is sung on a repeat of the notes for line 11.

14 I ofyn Malandein ar 'Charity Mistress'

Derbyniwch gen i ganiad,
    Hoff rediad ffri,
    I'ch annerch chwi,
4 I ddangos fy ewyllysgarwch –
    Am hyn na fernwch fi.
Yr awen fach a rewodd
    A dylodd dawn llawenydd llawn;
8 Gwell gennych na goganu
    Bardynu yn barod iawn.
I wisgo eich enw gwastad
    Rwy'n gofyn cennad, clywch y cwyn,
12 A hyn o dasg dan ddyddie'r Pasg,
    Y ganaid feinwasg fwyn,
Nid er mael na phower
    Ond o bleser mwynder maith;
16 Gwnewch chwithe â mi, lliw ewyn lli,
    A fynnoch gwedi'r gwaith.

Richard Thomas

Sources
NLW 9B, 16
Cwrtmawr 128A, 391
Cwrtmawr 171D, 31

Variant reading
Title: yr unrhyw etto; ar Charity Meistres (NLW 9B, 16)

Date
Undated: NLW 9B was compiled in 1736–55, Cwrtmawr 128A in 1738 and Cwrtmawr 171D was copied in 1902.

Locality
Not noted: the poem was copied into NLW 9B by Dafydd Jones 'Dewi Fardd' of Trefriw, near Llanrwst, in the upper Conwy Valley, north Wales;

14 Requesting a Valentine on 'Charity Mistress'

Accept from me a song,
　　A praiseworthy [and] fluid run [of music],
　　To greet you,
4　To show my good will –
　　Do not judge me for this.
The poor muse is frozen
　　And the gift of [bringing about] abounding joy has lost its
　　　　brightness;
8　Rather than mock you prefer
　　To pardon swiftly.
To wear your agreeable name
　　I ask permission, heed the plea,
12　And this task [I will undertake] until the days of Easter,
　　The radiant, slim-waisted, gentle one,
Not for gain or power
　　But out of pleasure [and] great tenderness [of heart];
16　Do you unto me, [one with a complexion] the colour of the crest
　　　　of a wave,
　　As you will following this deed.

Richard Thomas

the title of Cwrtmawr 128A is 'Llyfr Ofer Gerddi Margaret Davies 1738' (A Book of Frivolous Poems by Margaret Davies 1738), a manuscript written by Margaret Davies of Coetgae-du, Trawsfynydd in Gwynedd; Cwrtmawr 171D was copied by J. H. Davies from manuscript and printed sources, notably NLW 9B.

Note
In NLW 9B, 16 the poem is attributed, in a different hand, to Richard Thomas; in Cwrtmawr 128A, 391 to Dic Thomas; and in Cwrtmawr 171D the poem is attributed to Richard Thomas.

Measure
The tune title has been crossed out in NLW 9B, 16. For the tune 'Charity Mistress' (a corruption of the tune title 'Gerard's Mistress') see Kinney, 'Tunes (I)', 43–4; 'Elusenni Meistres', in Kinney and Evans, *Hen Alawon*, number 26.

15 Dechre penillion Valentine ar y mesur a elwir 'Amaryllis'

Hyd atoch, g'lomen glaerwen glir,
Hardd fynyglwen, seren sir,
O'm geirie yn awr rwy'n gyrru yn wir
4   I'th annerch, feinir fwynedd,
Hyn o anerchion, swynion sein,
Wirfelys lein orfoledd:
Cael ateb gweddol siriol serch,
8   Iawn gymwys ferch, nac omedd.

Eich enw llon a ddaeth i'm llaw,
Hawddgara' bun, yn un o naw
Ymysg ifienctid trefnid traw,
12   Hardd fenyw hylaw, hwylus;
Yn tynnu Falentine gytûn,
Gwawr radol, fun gariadus,
Y fi fu heno, blode ha,
16   Rwy'n leicio, yn fwya lwcus.

Rhowch chithe gennad, leuad lon,
O'ch hael, naturiol, freiniol fron,
Bun wisgi hardd, i wisgo hon,
20   Glain, dirion union eneth;
Gair a dd'wedych, drydrych don,
Eill roddi i feibion fabieth,
A'th bur olygon gloywon glân
24   A'm daliodd dan hudolieth.

Richard David

Source
NLW 312D, 70

Date
Not noted; NLW 312D was copied early in the eighteenth century.

Locality
Not noted; the manuscript is in the hand of the poem's author, Richard David of Llanymawddwy.

15 The commencement of Valentine stanzas on the
measure known as 'Amaryllis'

Unto you, bright, pure white dove,
Beautiful white-necked one, star of the county,
In words I now send in truth
4   To greet you, tender young woman,
These salutations, a sign of blessings,
Sincerely blissful line[s] of joy:
[That I may] receive an answer of pleasant [and] cheerful affection,
8   Exceedingly becoming young woman, do not refuse.

Your happy name came into my hand,
Most pleasant young woman, one of nine
From among [the names of] the young people arrayed there,
12   Beautiful, skilful [and] friendly woman;
In drawing [the name of] an agreeable Valentine,
Gracious dawn, loving young woman,
It was I who was this evening, choicest [one] of summer,
16   I am so pleased, the most lucky.

Grant permission, joyous moon,
From a generous, gentle, noble heart,
Beautiful [and] animated young woman, to wear it,
20   Jewel, gentle girl of integrity;
[The] word you speak, sea wave of exceptional appearance,
Is able to confer on men a frivolousness,
And your pure, clear bright eyes
24   Have bewitched me.

Richard David

Measure

For 'Amaryllis' see Simpson, *The British Broadside Ballad*, pp. 17–18;
Barlow (ed.), *The Complete Country Dance Tunes*, p. 47 (tune 165). On
its popoularity in England for the singing of mocking songs, see Harold
Love, 'That Satyrical Tune of "Amarillis"', *Early Music*, 35/1 (1 February
2007), 39–48.

16 Cwynfan merch a dalodd Valantein

Gwrandewch! Rwy'n bwriadu
I ddweud am y Bradwr,
Rwy'n ochain yn gethin
4   O waith y Rhagrithiwr;
Myfi oedd yr hogen
O glomen! i ymglymu
Mewn oes ddiangherydd
8   A Rhys yn fy ngharu:
Ymeilio, ceseilio, cusanu'n gysonol,
A'i freichiau'n ganghennau
O gwmpas fy nghanol;
12   Enethod diwegi, myfi ni thebygwn
Fod un ferch a basodd
Yn well ei chondisiwn.

Rhys ym mis Chwefrol,
16   Rhagrithiol fu'r weithred,
A roes i mi Valant
Oedd galant ei gweled;
A minnau, oherwydd
20   Fod Rhys yn fy ngharu,
Yn brwysgo'n y dalaith
Mewn osgedd ei dalu;
Mi wariais fy arian,
24   Mi brynais, o fawredd,
Werth grôt o ardyson
Heb lid na digasedd;
Â'm dwy law fy hunan,
28   Trwy gariad digerydd,
Y darfu imi eu stofi
A'u rhoi nhw i Rys Dafydd.

Pan cas e'r gardyson
32   O gwmpas ei goesau
Fe drows arna' ei gefen,
Gu feinwen, gwae finnau:
Merch arall a'i hudodd
36   Ac yntau yn anwadal,

16   The plaint of a woman who paid a Valentine

Listen! I intend
To speak of the Betrayer,
I sigh heavily
4   On account of the Dissembler;
I was the young girl,
Oh pigeon[-brain]! to tie myself up
In an unmerciful age
8   And [to have] Rhys loving me:
Joining together, embracing, kissing constantly,
And his arms like branches
About my waist;
12   Sensible girls, I would not imagine
That any girl who passed by
Is in a better condition [than myself].

Rhys, during the month of February,
16   It was an act of hypocrisy,
Gave me a Valentine [gift]
That was a splendid sight [to behold];
And I, because
20   Rhys loved me,
Had become intoxicated in the district
And was inclined to pay him [a Valentine gift];
I spent my money,
24   I bought, out of pride,
A groat's worth of garters
Without anger or love;
With my own two hands,
28   Out of blameless love,
I knitted them
And gave them to Rhys Dafydd.

As soon as he placed the garters
32   About his legs
He turned his back on me,
Loving, fair-complexioned slim one, woe is me:
Another girl charmed him
36   And he was fickle,

Am dorri ei addewid
Fe ddaw arno ddial.
'Doedd hithau'r ferch felen
40   Ond coegen rhy eger;
Myfi yn ei drwsio
A hi['n] mynd â'i bleser;
Rwy'n weddw ddigydmar:
44   Wrth rodio yn y goedwig
Och! ganwaith i'm geni
Na chawn arno gynnig!

Dewch ataf, erdolwyn,
48   Swyddogion y dalaith,
Mi fynna'n o gyfrwys
I roi arno gyfraith:
Amdan y gardyson
52   Mi dodaf e chwysu
A'i feddiant heb gwestiwn
Fydd raid iddo gosti:
Ni thraid i mi ochain,
56   Mae'r gyfraith o'm hochor
Mewn troeon unionffel
A'r treial yn Henffor:
Gwell fusai'r cystowci,
60   Gwir heini ydyw'r hanes,
Fy nghymryd i'n dirion,
Fwyn, burion gydmares.

John Jenkin 'Ioan Siencyn' (1716–96)

Sources
NLW 19B, 328–30
Elizabeth Gloria Roberts, 'Bywyd a Gwaith Ioan Siencyn (1716–1796)'
[The Life and Works of Ioan Siencyn (1716–1796)] (unpublished MA
thesis, University of Wales [Aberystwyth], 1984), 409–10

Date
1743.

For breaking his promise
Revenge will come upon him.
And she, the blonde girl, was nothing
40 But a forward coquette;
I clothing him
And she receiving his sensual gratification;
I am an unpartnered widow:
44 As I walk in the forest
Woe is me my birth a hundred times
That I am not offered a chance on him!

Come to me, I pray,
48 Officers of the province,
I insist with all cunning
Upon putting the law on him:
Concerning the garters
52 I will cause him to break sweat
And the value of his estate, without question,
He will have to evaluate:
I do not need to sigh,
56 The law is on my side
With regard to incidents which were clearly [perpetrated] with
        wiliness
And the trial is to be held in Hereford:
It would have been better for that churl,
60 The story is a truly spirited one,
To have taken me [as his] tender,
Gentle, most perfect partner.

John Jenkin 'Ioan Siencyn' (1716–96)

Locality
According to the note below the poem, 'Siôn Siencin y Bardd bach ai cant
ar ddeisyfiad Thomas Lewis o Bant Hwdog, 1743' [John Jenkin the young
Poet wrote this at the request of Thomas Lewis of Pant Hwdog, 1743']; Pant
Hwdog is in Cynwyl Elfed, Carmarthenshire. The poem is written in the
first person singular, in the persona of the woman disappointed in love.

Measure
No tune is noted.

17 Pennill a ddanfonodd y prydydd mewn Valantine i'w
    gariad, a'i wraig yn ôl hynny, ar 'Spanish Minuet'

F'anwylyd hyfryd hafaidd
Yn syw heb sen, derbyniwch, gwen,
Fy llythyr, meinir fwynaidd
4   I'ch mawredd bonedd ben;
Damweiniodd imi'n gynnar
Wrth lot, yn wir, eich enw pur
Yn ôl f'ewyllys hawddgar,
8   Fy meinwar glaear glir;
Am hynny'n awr mi ddoda' lawr
Eich enw gweddus, deuliw'r wawr,
Mewn Valantine ddewisol,
12   Nid er mwyn tâl o fawrion fael
Ond geirwir gariad gwrol,
Dymunol gen i gael.
Chwi wyddoch chwi, 'r ddyn braf ei bri,
16   Pa beth yn hawdd a'm boddia i:
Cael arwydd cu o'ch cariad.
Trwy obaith llawn o'r cyd y cawn
Gydoesi trwy ddewisiad,
20   Fy nghariad deg ei dawn.

Mae coed y maes yn deilio
A'r hediaid glân, o fawr i fân
Fel tannau pêr yn tiwnio,
24   Ymliwio maent hwy'n lân;
Mae pob rhyw edn hawddgar
Yn canu'n glyd, mor fawr ei fryd,
Yn gydnerth am ei gydmar
28   Dros wyneb daear fyd.
A finnau sy'r ddyn ffraethaidd ffri
'N dra diwyd yn eich dewis chwi
Fod i myfi'n gydmares
32   O waith fy mod o dan fy nod
I'th wylio er y'th weles,
Cei gen i gynnes glod.

17 A stanza the poet sent in a Valentine to his sweetheart,
and his wife after that, on 'Spanish Minuet'

My lovely summery sweetheart,
Splendid [and] without censure, accept, blessed one,
My letter, gentle young woman,
4   Into your magnificent noble life;
It befell me [to obtain] promptly
By lot, in truth, your pure name,
In accordance with my affable pleasure,
8   My slender and cultivated one, gentle and pure;
For that reason I now place
Your glorious name, one who is twice as fair as the dawn,
In a choice Valentine,
12   Not for a payment of great gain
But in order to procure a sincere, strong love
That is delightful for me to receive.
You know, greatly esteemed young woman,
16   What will readily please me:
To obtain a dear sign of your love [towards me].
In sincere hope that out of this union we are allowed to
Live together from choice,
20   My love [who has] outstanding gifts.

The trees of the field wax green with leafage
And the spruce birds, large and small,
Are singing like sweet [harp] strings,
24   They expostulate with vigour;
Every kind of affable bird
Is singing happily, so generous his nature,
Robustly for his mate
28   Across the face of the earth.
And I am the readily eloquent man
Who is most diligent in choosing you
To be my partner
32   Because I am under obligation
To wait in hope for you since I [first] saw you,
I will give you warm praise.

F'anwylyd bur, mae'n wir fy mod
36   Yn caru'ch gwedd, trwy gleuwedd glod,
      Liw'r manod, hynod hanes:
      K. R., rwyf fi'n dy ddewis di
      Fod i myfi'n gydmares,
40   Fy nuwies gynnes, gu.

John Jenkin 'Ioan Siencyn' (1716–96)

Sources
NLW 19B, 209–11
John Howell (ed.), *Blodau Dyfed* [Flowers of Dyfed] (Caerfyrddin: J. Evans, 1824), pp. 397–9
William Hughes Griffiths (ed.), *Diliau'r Awen; sef, Crynodeb o waith Awenyddol y Diweddar Ardderchog Brydydd Evan Thomas Rhys, o Lanarth, Ceredigion (...) ac eraill* [Honeycombs of the Muse; that is a compendium of literary works by the late great poet Evan Thomas Rhys of Llanarth, Ceredigion (...) and others] (Aberystwyth: D. Jenkins, 1842), pp. 189–90
Roberts, 'Bywyd a Gwaith Ioan Siencyn', 343

Variant reading
Line 8 Fy meinwar galiar glir (NLW 19B, 210)

My pure darling [one], it is true that I
36 Love your countenance, through urgent praise,
One who has a complexion the colour of fine snow, excellent
          report:
K. R., I choose you
To be my partner,
40 My warm, dear goddess.

John Jenkin 'Ioan Siencyn' (1716–96)

Date
Not noted; the manuscript into which the poem was copied is dated
1752–93; the author's dates are 1716–96.

Locality
Not noted; John Jenkin came from Cardigan, and the manuscript was
copied in the Cardigan area in south-west Wales.

Measure
For 'Spanish Minuet' see the Ifor Ceri manuscript 'Melus-seiniau Cymru',
NLW 1940Ai, f. 117ʳ⁻ᵛ.

18   Dechre y 3dd gerdd o fawl i ferch, ar 'Ffarwel
      Trefaldwyn'

      Cywir galon, teg add'wydion, clyw anerchion, cwynion cân,
      Serch a ffansi sydd yn peri imi dy hoffi yn lili lân;
      Ni fedra i eto mo'ch anghofio mewn darfwriad, ond myfyrio
4   A synfeddylio yn ddi-les o'r dolur gur a garies,
      Ail angyles gynnes gu.
      I draethu eich mawl a'ch mawrglod a'ch rhinwedd peredd
            parod
      Fe red 'y nhafod, rydwi yn hy;
8   Tryma cerydd ydyw cariad i roi 'madawiad, trawiad trist,
      Ni ddichon aur nac arian giwrio pe ceid yn costio lloned cist
      Ond efo chwi, goleuni glanweth, y mae rhagorol ffisigwrieth;
      Dowch yn berffeth burffydd a rhowch add'wydion dedwydd
12   Dorri cystudd dwyrudd dyn;
      [Er] maint yw lliwied llawer rhowch, drwy fendith, fwynder,
      [Gyfo]ed tyner, yn gytûn.

      Er bod gweithredoedd gwag, athrodion anian lownion yn y
            wlad,
16   [Fe d]daw caredigrwydd a chynhesrwydd lle mynno yr Arglwydd,
            dedwydd Dad,
      [Wyll]is Duw ac wyllys dynes, geirie hynod, gore hanes,
      Er gwaetha males milen ymlaen yr â ei dynghedf[en]
      I dorri absen cynnen cas,
20   A'r sawl a roed i ymewino ni ddichon dyn mo'u rhwystro,
      Duw i'w llwyddo a roddo ras.
      Mae'n rhaid i minne ddiodde yn ddiddig i waith tafode, droe
            drwg,
      Drwy anialwch a distyrwch (dyma degwch!) Duw a'm dwg;
24   Ni ches i yn wir er bod yn angall erioed y gair o redeg arall
      Ac rwyf i yn diball dybio na wnewch chi ar undyn wrando
      Fytho yn rhuo beio byth;
      Wrth gadw eich cwmni llawen ni chlywes i erioed air absen,
28   Yr hawddgar gangen, seren syth.

18 The commencement of a third poem in praise of a
woman, on 'Ffarwel Trefaldwyn'

Loyal heart, [woman of] sincere promises, hear greetings, plaints
in song,
Love and fancy cause me to delight in you, pure lily;
I cannot yet forget you by intent, but [must] contemplate
4   And muse unprofitably on the pang of anguish that I carried,
One who is comparable with a beloved affectionate angel.
To express your praise and your exceeding renown and your
fragrant, ready virtue
My tongue will run, I am bold;
8   Love is a most severe chiding which causes a parting, sad stroke,
No gold or silver could cure [it] even though provided at the cost
of a cofferful,
But with you, pure light, there is excellent medicine;
Come in perfect true faith and make blessed promises
12 To end the affliction of face [suffered by] a man;
Even though the reproach of many is so great bestow, with a
blessing, gentleness,
Tender [companion], with amity.

Even though there are senseless deeds [and] slanders of an
abounding nature in the land,
16 Kindness and affection will come where the Lord wills, blessed Father,
[The will] of God and the will of a woman, notable words, the
best in history,
In spite of cruel malice his destiny will advance
In order to ruin slander, hateful discord,
20 And those who were appointed to strive [to this end] no man can
possibly stop them,
God will give his blessing so that they may succeed.
I must endure with composure the work of tongues, ill turns,
Through wilderness and contempt (what fairness!) God will bear me;
24 Truly, even though I am foolish, I have never been accused of
ousting another
And I will unfailingly hold the opinion that you will not listen to
anyone
Who would be forever censuring loudly;
While keeping your happy company I never heard one slanderous
word,
28 Amiable young woman, honest star.

Clywch fy nghyffes, f'annwyl feistres, gair a lunies gore lein,
Ni wnewch, gobeithio, ychwaith mo'r digio ei manwl diwnio
    Malandein;
Canol Chwefror, trysor trwsiad, mae pob aderyn rydwi'n dirnad
32   Dangos cariad cywir i ga'lyn rheol natur,
    Bawb yn ddifyr, bob yn ddau;
    Rwy finne yn cwyno caniad, fel clomen ddof ymddifad,
    Am bortreiad clymiad clau.
36   Rhag ofn Giwpid ollwng ergyd
    I ddwyn o'r byd y bywyd bach,
    I achub hoedel cyn rhoi ffárwel,
    Gwynfan uchel, gwna fi yn iach;
40   Petawn i berchen mil o bunne mi rown fy meddwl yr un modde,
    Am fod hyd ange yr dynged imi dy gael yn gowled,
    Coelia hyn o faled fer;
    Pei gallwn, hon a hennwn, llythrenne aur gosodwn,
44   Mwya garwn, M ac R.

Arthur Jones, clochydd Llangadwaladr (fl. *1743–56)*

Source
Sir John Williams's Ballad Collection, 168, 6–7, held at the National
Library of Wales, Aberystwyth

Date
Not noted; Arthur Jones, *fl.* 1743–56; the ballad sheet was printed in
Shrewsbury for the publisher Thomas Roberts during the eighteenth
century.

Locality
Arthur Jones is styled *clochydd* (bellringer or sexton) at Llangadwaladr
in Denbighshire, also sexton of Ruabon where he died.

Hear my confession, my dear sweetheart, a greeting that I
    composed, best line [of poetry],
You will not, I hope, take offence that it is a finely tuned Valentine;
In mid-February, richly attired, it is my understanding that each bird
32   Shows true love in accordance with the law of nature,
Each with pleasantness, two by two;
I mourn in song, like a tame dove that is orphaned,
For an image of a swift joining together.
36   Lest Cupid shoots an arrow
To take from the world the insignificant life [of mine],
To save [my] life before [I] bid farewell,
Loud lamentation, make me well;
40   If I possessed a thousand pounds I would [still] set my mind in
    the same way,
So that it were destined that I should have you in my embrace
    unto death,
Give credence to this short ballad;
If I were able, it is she I would name, I would set out in gold letters,
44   The one I love most, M and R.

Arthur Jones, sexton of Llangadwaladr (fl. 1743–56)

Note

Verses written for M.R.; J. H. Davies, *A Bibliography of Welsh Ballads Printed in the Eighteenth Century* (London: The Honourable Society of Cymmrodorion, 1910) refers to the poem by the title 'Cerdd o fawl i ferch megis i ofyn Falantine' [A poem of praise to a woman as if to request a Valentine].

Measure

'Ffarwel Trefaldwyn', a traditional Welsh air, 'seem[s] not to have survived', see Kinney, *Welsh Traditional Music*, p. 37.

19 I ofyn Falendein

Hyd atoch, hafedd gannwyll Gwynedd,
    Gore ei fonedd o Gaer i Fôn,
L E diledieth, W I diwenieth,
4   Ac S eilweth mewn sylwedd sôn,
I O diamhur, N E dan awyr,
    Ac S dda ei gysur mewn synnwyr sydd
Yn flode meibion, dwyrudd dirion,
8   Ail i Solomon ffyddlon ffydd;
Be cawn i 'newis yn yr ynys
I wneud y foddus liwus lein,
    Y chwi er hynny 'rwy i'w chwenychu,
12   O fil i'w dynnu'n Falendein.

Dienw

Sources
O. M. Edwards (ed.), *Beirdd y Berwyn 1700–1750* [The Poets of the Berwyn 1700–1750], Cyfres y Fil (Llanuwchllyn: Ab Owen, 1902), p. 78
E. G. Millward (ed.), *Blodeugerdd Barddas o Gerddi Rhydd y Ddeunawfed Ganrif* [The Barddas Anthology of Eighteenth-century Free-metre Poems] ([Abertawe]: Cyhoeddiadau Barddas, 1991), p. 312

Date
First half of the eighteenth century.

19   To request a Valentine

Unto you, summery light of Gwynedd,
    Of the best lineage from Chester to Anglesey,
Eloquent L E, sincere W I,
4   And S to speak of [you] again [as one] with substance,
Pure J O, N E beneath sky,
    And S of good comfort who is in every sense
The most superior of young men, two gentle cheeks,
8   Comparable with Solomon of loyal faith;
If I were given the choice of the island
To write to in a well-fashioned line of rich colour,
    Even so, it is you that I covet
12   Out of a thousand to draw as a Valentine.

Anonymous

Locality
The area of the Berwyn Mountains according to O. M. Edwards, roughly bounded by Corwen in the north-west and Bala in the south-west.

Measure
No tune is noted, but see 'Synnwyr Solomon', *Journal of the Welsh Folk Song Society* [hereafter *JWFSS*], 1 (1909–12), 89, made suitable by repeating the second half of the melody. Solomon is mentioned in line 8.

20   Pennill Malandein

> Hyd atoch, gwawr eurad, hardd leuad o lun,
> Yn fwynglau, fain funglws, ail Fenws yw'r fun,
> I'ch tynnu chwi yn weddus, mae f'wyllys i'n fawr,
> 4   Yn Falandein fwynedd, bun gwyredd ei gwawr.
> Er imi mewn papur, o ran cysur mwyn, cu,
> Gofio lliw'r manod, gwawr hynod, mor hy,
> Onid y'ch chwi'n bodloni, y lili wen lân,
> 8   Gobeithio na ddigiwch ond teflwch i'r tân.

Dienw

Source
NLW 9047A, 58ʳ

Date
Not noted; the other Valentine poem in this manuscript (an English
Valentine poem by the transcriber, Cadwaladr Davies, b.1704, and is for
Mrs Jane Jones, see appendix to poem 20) is dated 14 February 1749.

Locality
Not noted; the manuscript was transcribed by Cadwaladr Davies of
Gwyddelwern, which is approximately two miles north of Corwen in
Denbighshire in north Wales.

Measure
No tune is noted; 'Difyrrwch Gwŷr Emlyn' is suitable, see *JWFSS*, 3
(1930–41), 188, but there is nothing to link the tune with these stanzas.

20 A Valentine stanza

Unto you, golden dawn, of the appearance of a beautiful moon,
Gentle and sincere, slender [and] beautiful maiden, the young
    woman is comparable with Venus,
I am ardently desirous to draw you[r name] in a seemly manner
4   As a tender Valentine, young woman of waxen colour.
Although I, on paper, for the sake of gentle [and] loving comfort,
Remembered [the one with a complexion] the colour of fine snow,
    spectacular dawn, so boldly,
If you do not consent, the pure white lily,
8   I hope you will not take umbrage, but that you will throw [the
    paper] into the fire.

Anonymous

Appendix to poem 20

Mrs Jane Jones   February 14th 1749

True Heart of Gold true love of mine
I draw you for my valentine
Not for ones but for ever
Not for the Gift but for the Giver
Some draw valentine by Lot
Some draw them which they love not
I draw you which I love best
I choose you out of all the rest

Your Humble Servant
Cadwalader Davies (b.1704)

21   Mrs N-M:

Hyd atoch, siriol seren, tân 'glura ei chlod, sy bura'n bod,
Blodeuyn tirion tyrfa, chwychwi ydi rhedfa rhod,
Eich glendid sy'n disgleirio fel haul ar galch, 'y mun ddi-falch,
4   A'ch synnwyr sy'n rhagori a hwnnw yn peri parch,
A minne sydd mewn ffansi ffydd tan ddwe[u]d mai dedwydd
        ydyw'r dydd
Yr hities ar eich enw yn loyw lein yn Falandein,
N ac M yn rhywiogedd, mae rhinwedd ar y rhain,
8   I'ch gwisgo yn ffri trwy eich cennad chwi sy'n rhydda i'w gole,
        a mau imi;
Nid ydw i eich holi ond eich ewyllys da, lliw'r hinon ha,
Ond a fyddo hardd ei gwedd yn gymwys, nis gwn a ga'.

Edward Edwards

Source
NLW 1062B, 43

Manuscript reading
Line 10 ond afytha hardd a gwedd

Date
1757.

21   Mrs N-M:

Unto you, joyful star, a fire of most eminent praise, [and] who is
    the purest in existence,
[In the estimation of] a multitude you are the most superior one
    [and so] gentle, you are the channel of the wheel [of Fortune],
Your beauty shines like the sun on lime, my demure young woman,
4   And your wisdom excels and creates respect,
And I am in [a state of] faith's fancy declaring that it was a
    felicitous day
When I hit upon your name, in a burnished line, as a Valentine,
N and M of noble lineage, there is virtue in these [letters],
8   To wear you[r name] freely with your permission is most generous
    and with her knowledge, and is in my possession;
I do not claim you only your good pleasure, [one with a
    complexion] the colour of the summer sunshine,
But will the one who is beautiful of countenance be equitable,
    I do not know whether I will gain [her].

Edward Edwards

Locality
Not noted, nor is the location of the compilation of the manuscript noted.

Note
A Valentine poem for Mrs N. M.

Measure
No tune is noted.

22 Dechre pennill Falandein ar y mesur a elwir 'Gwêl yr Adeilad'

Rwy'n gofyn, Elsbeth haelwych,
Hardd gangen lawen lewych,
   Gyrrwch gennad
4 I wisgo yr leinie, yr loywedd,
A wnaed i chwi, fun iredd,
   Ddiferedd fwriad,
Mewn lein i'ch tynnu yn Falandein;
8   Rhaid rhoi, lliw'r hinon,
   Ofer 'ddewidion
O waith prydyddion, im roddion am y rhein,
   Caned gynt iaith Gomer
12   Yn ofer lawer lein;
Mae'ch gwawr ar dir yn wir yn awr
   Fel Elen deca'
   A Rachel w'cha,
16 Prydferthwch Martha, Susanna, loywa' ar lawr,
A'ch penpryd, loer wawr lariedd, sy yn pasio mawredd mawr.

Dienw

Source
NLW 4697A, 27

Date
Not noted; the manuscript was compiled between 1758 and 1765 and this poem was transcribed on 21 February 1760.

22 The commencement of a Valentine stanza on the
    measure known as 'Gwêl yr Adeilad'

I request, generous and excellent Elsbeth,
Beautiful bough [of] joyous lustre,
        That you give permission
4   To wear the lines, bright one,
Composed for you, thriving young woman,
        One of uncensorable intention,
In a line [written] to draw you[r name] as a Valentine;
8   One must offer, [one with a complexion] the colour of the
            sunshine,
        Vain promises
Composed by poets, to me gifts [in recompense] for these [lines],
        Formerly there was sung [in] the language of Gomer
12   Many lines in vain;
Your appearance on earth is now truly
        Similar to that of loveliest Elen,
        And the most splendid Rachel,
16   The beauty of Martha, Susannah, the brightest on earth,
And your countenance, moon of gentle brightness, excels great
        magnificence.

Anonymous

Locality
Not noted; the manuscript was transcribed by Robert Evans, Syrior,
Llandrillo-yn-Edeirnion, in the historical county of Merionethshire, now
Gwynedd.

Measure
For the tune 'Gwêl yr Adeilad' or 'See the Building' see Kinney, 'Tunes
(I)', 34–5; Kinney and Evans, *Hen Alawon*, number 16.

23   Dechre dau bennill Falandein i'w canu ar 'Garway'

Y fwyngu feingan, ddiddan, ddiddwl
Addfain fyddo, addfwyn feddwl;
Swydd a chanad rwy'n chwennych
4   Sef, cario eich enw, y fenyw, yn fynych
Yn Falandein o *line* a lunies,
Yn hon mae, meindw, eich enw a'ch hanes;
Mi a'ch mola beunydd byth arbennig
8   Fel gwas da yng ngwaed a gostyngedig:
Y fun gariadus, fwyn, garedig,
Rhowch chwi yn rhwyddedd fwynedd fenig.

Gabriel Evans, y fun lefen,
12   Sy'n eich cyfarch chwi yn eich cefen;
Wrth glywed cym'in yn eich ca'mol
Amdanoch Mary rwy' yn ymorol;
Na wnewch yn f'erbyn, y fun fawrbarch,
16   Harch im ddygiad, lleuad Llywarch,
Rhowch yn llesol a wyllysiwch,
Rhowch yn fwyn y peth a fynnoch,
Mi dd'weuda finne byth tra byddoch
20   Bob daioni o'r dawn amdanoch.

Thomas Lewis o Gwm Llywenog

Source
NLW 4697A, 151–2

Date
The poem was copied on 6 January 1761.

Locality
Cwm Llywenog in the upper reaches of Llanarmon Dyffryn Ceiriog parish,
on the Berwyn Mountains, an isolated area of moorland, Denbighshire;

23 The commencement of two Valentine stanzas to be
    sung to 'Garway'

The dear and gentle, slender and pale-complexioned one,
     engaging, intelligent,
She is slender, of gentle thought;
I covet a task and permission [to perform it]
4   That is, to carry your name, young woman, frequently
As a Valentine in a poem that I have composed,
Your name and your story is in it, slender one;
I will praise you daily [and] forever, matchless one,
8   Being a young man of good pedigree, and humble:
The loving young woman, gentle, kind,
Give a pair of gloves freely and obligingly.

Gabriel Evans, the refined young woman,
12   Is greeting you in your prime;
Hearing so many praising you
I [too] seek you, Mary;
Do not take against me, the greatly respected young woman,
16   Grant me a taking away, moon of Llywarch,
Give with beneficence what you have a mind to,
Give with tenderness what you will,
I will proclaim all the days of your life
20   About you, concerning every graciousness of gift.

Thomas Lewis of Cwm Llywenog

Cwm Llywenog does not appear in the Archif Melville Richards Place-
name Database.

Note
The poem was composed on behalf of Gabriel Evans to be sent to Mary.

Measure
'Garway' is the noted tune title, but no tune of that name was found in
the collections.

24 Dechre pedwar pennill Malandein ar fesur a elwir
'Cyfarfod Da' ne 'Well Met Brother Will'

    At Fenws deg, fwyn, gain, addfwyn, gyneddfol,
    Wenithen wen ethol, wych weddol ei chŵyn,
    Lliw'r ewyn a'r od,
4   Malandein deg yw f'anrheg i'r feinir,
    Llai annerch ni welir drwy'r teirsir ar ddeg,
    Ferch liwdeg ei chlod.
    Er lleied yw hon, Jane Lewis wen, lon,
8   Mae purder eich bron yn ffyddlon i'w 'mgleddu
    Gan imi ryfygu yn llwyr dynnu lliw'r don.
    Un Evans wyf, clywch, o garmon oer guwch,
    Nid oes un wlad uwch, ces goruwch cwr Lloeger
12   Fy magu yng Nghwm Eger dan lawer o luwch.

    Wrth ddallt fod eich bron deg, union yn gynnes
    O gariad ac eurwres y tynnes i at hon,
    Lliw'r hinon, lloer hardd;
16   Llawenydd pob lle yw Troea portreiad,
    Eich tegwch a'ch dygiad mewn gwlad ac mewn tre
    Fel geme mewn gardd;
    I'r gangen dan go', aur frigog o'r fro,
20   Mawl rywiog a ro', ei heiddo mewn haeddiad,
    Ni cheir un fwy 'i chariad yn dŵad dan do;
    Yr ewig hael ryw a llonwych ei lliw,
    Chwi wyddoch fy mriw, nid ydyw ond ffoledd
24   Im siarad gormodedd o wagedd, ni wiw.

    Os cennad a ga', mi'ch gwisga'n gyhoeddus
    O burchwant yn barchus a'm dewis waith da,
    Cysona ydyw'r swydd;

24 The commencement of four Valentine stanzas on a
    measure known as 'Cyfarfod Da' or 'Well Met Brother Will'

To fair Venus, amiable, beautiful, gentle, of a fine disposition,
Excellent grain of wheat, pure, elect, magnificent, seemly in her
        condolence,
[One with a complexion] the colour of the crest of a wave and of
        the snow,
4   My gift to the young woman is a fine Valentine,
Greetings to a more slender person will not be in evidence
        throughout the thirteen counties,
Young woman of comely honour.
Even though she is so small, blessed [and] joyous Jane Lewis,
8   The purity of your breast will loyally cherish him
Since I have presumed to attract utterly [one with a complexion]
        the colour of the wave.
I am Evans, listen, a lover with a cold frown,
There is no higher country, I was, above England's border,
12 Brought up in Cwm Eger under many snowdrifts.

On perceiving that your fair, honest breast is warm
With love and golden passion I was attracted to her,
[One with a complexion] the colour of the sunshine, beautiful moon;
16 The joy of all places is the portrait of one [who is comparable with
        Helen] of Troy,
Your beauty and your deportment in town and country
Are like gems in a garden;
To the golden-haired bough of this neighbourhood, assuredly
20 I give generous praise, that is her just desert,
None with a greater love will enter under a roof;
Graceful doe of noble lineage and one who is splendid and joyful
        of countenance,
You know my pain, it is but folly
24 For me to speak an excess of vanity, it avails nothing.

If I obtain your permission, I will wear you[r name] in public
Out of a pure desire, with respect, and this is my chosen blessed
        task,
Most agreeable office;

28 Caf gario'n ddi-rus gysurus feddylie
    Tra bo'ch yn fy llyfre, mewn llanne ac mewn llys
    Yn gofus i'n gŵydd.
    Eich enw da chwi fydd mowredd i mi
32 Dros ddeufis neu dri, y lili oleulan,
    Yng nghopa fy nghapan, nid bychan fy mri!
    Hawdd ichwi 'moddhau os byddwch mor glau
    Â'm ffyddlon goffáu; ni wela i'n rhy fychan
36 Pe cawn i o'ch min wynlan ond cusan neu ddau.

    Hen arfer y wlad a'i bwriad, heb eiriach,
    Cyfrannu cyfrinach, os hwyrach lesâd,
    O'i tyniad a'i tasg;
40 O Falandein Ŵyl bydd disgwyl ac edrych
    Am fwyniant yn fynych yn haelwych i hwyl
    Cyn perwyl y Pasg.
    A minne'r un modd, 'run clefyd a'm clodd
44 A 'mryd yma ymrôdd, fe flysiodd fy mhleser
    Fwy weled eich purder na'r hyder i'r rhodd.
    Y feinir ddi-feth, hoff, lân, teg ei phleth,
    Ni symiai mo'r dreth i'r eneth aur anian:
48 Meddyliwch am Evan fab Evan am beth.

Jonathan Hughes (1721–1805)

Source
Cwrtmawr 41B, i, 109

Date
1767.

Locality
The poem was written by Jonathan Hughes on behalf of Evan
Evans, Cwm Eger, Bryneglwys in the southern part of Denbighshire

28 I can carry, without hesitation, pleasant thoughts
    While you are in my good books, in church and state [you will be]
    Remembered in our presence.
    Your good name will be my greatness
32 Over two or three months, the pure bright lily,
    On the crown of my cap, I shall not be of little esteem!
    It is easy for you to please me if you are swift enough
    To remember me with loyalty; I do not perceive it too small a thing
36 Were I to receive from your pure shining lip a kiss or two.

    It is an old custom of the land, and its design, without stinting,
    Is to share a secret, and possibly an advantage,
    From the drawing [of a name] and its task;
40 From Valentine's Festival onwards there will be an expectancy
            and a looking out
    For frequent pleasure, liberally wanting merry-making
    Before the purposes of Easter.
    And I do likewise, it is the same ailment that has overcome me
44 And my desire is devoted to this, my pleasure was an excessive
            longing [for you],
    More from seeing your purity than from confidence in the gift.
    Unerring young woman, beloved, pure, beautiful her plait [of hair],
    I would not estimate the cost of the gift for the golden-natured
            young woman:
48 Think of Evan son of Evan for a little while.

Jonathan Hughes (1721–1805)

(six miles north of Corwen) to be sent to Jane Lewis, Ty'n-y-rhos, Bryneglwys.

Measure

Jonathan Hughes is the only poet to use the titles 'Cyfarfod Da' or 'Well Met brother Will' to this measure. In Simpson, *The British Broadside Ballad*, pp. 437–8, the tune is entitled 'Let Mary Live Long', and in John Owen, Dwyran's collection 'Hir Oes i Fair'; for 'Hir Oes i Fair' see Kinney, 'Tunes (II)', 17–18; Kinney and Evans, *Hen Alawon*, number 1.

25   Dau bennill Malentein i'w canu ar 'King's Round'

Bun fain, gain, gu, harddwch tegwch tŷ,
Rwy'n gyrru drwy bur gariad
Hon yma, pura peth, fel trin neu godi treth,
4   Y sidan bleth osodiad,
Sef, Malandein a lunies
I'w cofio chwi, fy angyles,
Neu wisgi beunes ymysg bonedd;
8   Gobeithio, hardd ei dwyfron,
Na byddwch ddim anfodlon,
Fun liwdeg, union flode Gwynedd.

Ni bydd dydd y dasg ond ympirio cyn y Pasg,
12   Lliw blode damasg, feinwasg fwynedd,
A'm galw i'r fan y boch, lliw rhosyn gwyn ne goch,
A rhoddi, gwyddoch, rhodd fo gweddedd;
Fel hyn **MA**e henw'r lodes
16   Fwyneiddia e**RI**oed a weles,
Mi a'i sgrifennes, gynnes gannwyll,
MOR gymw**YS** hwylus haela
I gofio eich tad yn nesa,
20   Mae hynny ddweuda ei henw'n ddidwyll.

Hugh Jones (?1700–82)

Source
Cwrtmawr 41B, i, 136

Date
12 February 1768.

Locality
Not noted; the poet's home was in Llangwm in Conwy County, close
to the borders with Denbighshire; the manuscript was written in the
Llansilin/Llanrhaeadr-ym-Mochnant area in Powys.

Note
Stanzas for Mari Morys.

25 Two Valentine stanzas to be sung on 'King's Round'

Slender, fair, beloved young woman, [the] beauty [and] fineness
    of [any] home,
I send out of pure love
This here, purest object, similar to handling or levying a tax,
4   [One with] the demeanour of the silk plait,
That is, a Valentine that I composed
To remind you, my angel,
Or an animated lady among the gentry;
8   I hope, beautiful heart,
That you will not be unwilling,
Young woman of fair countenance, honest, the most superior
    in the land of Gwynedd.

The day appointed for the task will appear before Easter,
12   [One with a complexion] the colour of damask flowers,
    slender-waisted gentleness,
And to call me to the place where you will be, [one with a
    complexion] the colour of a white or red rose,
And give, you know [this], a gift that is appropriate;
This is the **MA**iden's name,
16   Fai**R**est that **I** ever saw,
I wrote it down, affectionate candle,
MOst proper, f**R**iendl**Y**, most generou**S**,
To remember your father['s name] next,
20   The one who declares her name is sincere.

Hugh Jones (?1700–82)

Measure

For 'King's Round' see 'Iechyd o gylch neu King's Round' in the collection
'Melus-Seiniau Cymru', made by John Jenkins 'Ifor Ceri' in 1817–25, which
is NLW 1940A, f. 91ʳ, available online at: *https://viewer.library.wales/46*
55107#?c=0&m=0&s=0&cv=181&xywh=869%2C34%2C2845%2C2951
(accessed 23 November 2017); see also Daniel Huws, 'Melus-Seiniau
Cymru', *CG*, 8 (1985), 32–50, and Daniel Huws, 'Melus-Seiniau Cymru:
Atodiadau', *CG*, 9 (1986), 47–57. 'King's Round' is also known as 'Iechyd
Ogylch' in Dafydd Jones's anthology of poems entitled *Blodeu-gerdd
Cymry* (Amwythig: Stafford Prys, 1779; first edition 1759), p. xxvii.

26 Pennill i'w roddi mewn Valentine

At fy nghares, geinwen gynnes,
Hardd beunes, lodes lân,
I chwi, meinir, mi ddymunwn,
4   Pe medrwn, gyrrwn gân.
Y ddoeth, synhwyrol, foddol fun,
Yn ofni Duw a pharchu dyn,
Yn medru gwiwddoeth 'madrodd gweddol,
8   A llesol iawn ei llun;
Mi rof eich enw, rwyf i'ch annerch,
Ar lannerch fach o lein,
Os medra'u gosod, 'madrodd cyson,
12   Fel tirion Valentine.
Rhof R ac O, i ledio i lawr,
N, E, dwy A, rai gwycha'u gwawr,
Dwy S, a J, sy'n ola'n eilio,
16   'R ôl im fyfyrio'n fawr:
A dyna'r naw llythyren
Sy'n enw'r ffraethwen ffri,
Y sawl a'u 'drycho doed, ymdreched,
20   Dealled, enwed hi.
Rho'r naw llythyren hyn
'N bur gain ar bapur gwyn
I weld yn eglur enw cywir
24   Y feinir, bawb a fyn.
R'ych chwi, fy mun hawddgara,
Yn rhydda i enwi rhodd,
Fe fydd eich 'lusen, mi wn, yn llesol
28   A buddiol, wrth fy modd;
Rwy'n disgwyl bydd y dasg
Cyn pennod dydd y Pasg,
Bydd Duw a dynion yn gweld daioni
32   Mun wisgi, main o wasg.

John Thomas, Penffordd-wen (1757–1835)

26 A stanza to place in a Valentine

Unto my sweetheart, affectionate, beautiful woman,
Noble lady, pure young woman,
To you, tall and graceful one, I would desire,
4   If I were able, to send a poem.
The wise, sagacious, seemly young woman,
Fearing God and honouring man,
Able to speak worthy and wise, seemly words,
8   And very blessed of appearance;
I will place your name, I am to greet you,
On a little space on a line [of poetry],
If I am able to place it, faithful utterance,
12   As a tender Valentine.
First I will set down R and O,
N, E [and] two As, of most excellent hue,
Two Ss, and J, that interweave finally,
16   Following great musing on my part:
And those are the nine letters
Which form the name of the generous one who is pure and
      eloquent,
Those who want to look at them, come, strive,
20   Interpret, let her be named.
Place these nine letters
In purity and beauty on white paper
To see clearly the trustworthy name
24   Of the young woman whom all desire.
You, my most amiable young woman, are
Most free to name a gift,
Your charity, I know, will be salutary
28   And profitable, pleasing to me;
I intend that the task be accomplished
Before the period of Easter Day,
God and man will see goodness,
32   Animated young woman, slender of waist.

John Thomas, Penffordd-wen (1757–1835)

Sources

John Thomas, *Telyn Arian* [Silver Harp] (Llanrwst: J. Jones, 1857), p. 106

Rhiannon Ifans, '"O na bai fy mhen yn feipen ...": golwg eto ar y canu Ffolant' [O that my head were a turnip ... : a second look at Valentine songs], *CG*, 21 (1998), 27

Date

Not noted; the poet's dates are 1757–1835.

Locality
Not noted; the poet spent the greater part of his life in Penffordd-wen in the parish of Nantglyn, Denbighshire.

Note
A Valentine to Sara Jones.

Measure
No tune was noted.

27 Un pennill i'w ganu ar 'Farts mwngc', neu 'March Mounk'

Meinir lon, disglair don, ail i Elen, fwynedd feinwen,
Loywedd liw, rasol ryw, y seren syw, gysurus wedd,
Gwinllan gain, Fenws fain, bryd angyles, ddoniol ddynes,
4   Foddus fun, lariedd lun, yw hon ei hun a'i heini hedd;
Yn ddwys i chwi mi ddois â chân i ofyn cennad, leuad lân,
Wisgo lein o Falentein, cyfion fein, i'wch cofio'n siwr;
Os byddwch bodlon, hinon hardd, mi'i gwisga'n bur ag osgo bardd
8   O hyn dan y Pasg, y fun fain ei gwasg, yn llawen dasg, lliw
        ewyn dŵr;
Nid ydw i'n deisyfu er hynny un rhodd,
Ond chwennych eich cofio a'ch cyfarch bob modd,
Eich glendid fel glud, a'm bwriad o'r byd
12   I'r grafel oer grud, bun gwyredd ei phryd,
A'ch geirie mor ffraeth [ ]or cyfyng fodd caeth,
I'm cadarn iawn faeth, a'm codai yn fyw;
Ni fedra i rwy'n gwybod yn hynod, fun hael,
16   Roi mawl i chwi'n weddus air moddus er mael,
Ond dangos 'y mod mewn wllys, tan rhod,
I glymu i chwi glod a chael gwisgo nod
O'ch enw mwyn iawn, lloer gynnes, lliw'r gwawn,
20   Urddoledd ei dawn, ar ddelw gwedd Duw.

Dienw

27 One stanza to be sung to 'Marts mwngc', or
'March Mounk'

Joyous young woman, shining wave, comparable with Helen,
    gentle, slender and beautiful one,
Clear countenance, gracious lineage, the excellent star, cheerful in
    appearance,
Exquisite vineyard, slender Venus, with the appearance of an
    angel, gifted woman,
4   Pleasing young woman, mild of manner, is she herself and her
    active serenity;
Solemnly I have come to you with a song requesting permission,
    clear moon,
To wear a line of Valentine, righteous slender one, to remember
    you by with unfailing certainty;
If you are willing, beautiful sunshine, I will wear it sincerely taking
    the stance of a poet
8   From now until Easter, the slender-waisted young woman, a joyful
    task, [one with a complexion] the colour of sea foam;
In spite of that I do not request a gift,
I simply desire to remember you and to greet you by every means,
The intransigence of your comeliness, and my intention in this
    present world
12 Until I enter the cold cradle of the gravel [i.e. the grave], young
    woman of waxen countenance,
With your words so eloquent [...] in a straitened, restricted manner,
To me a powerful [and] meet sustenance, will resurrect me;
I know that I will not be able, with excellence, generous young
    woman,
16 To praise you in a fitting manner, courteous word, for [my own]
    gain,
But to show that I am ardently desirous, under the sun,
To compose a verse of praise for you and to be permitted to wear
    a sign
Of your very noble name, affectionate moon, [one with a
    complexion] the colour of gossamer,
20 So dignified her grace, in the image of the countenance of God.

Anonymous

Note

The pamphlet's contents list refers to this poem by the title:

> Pennill mwyn sain ar ddydd Valendine
> Ar fesur mwyn bwnc; ei henw 'March Mwnc'

> [A stanza of sweet sound on Valentine's day | On a measure
> pertaining to a pleasant matter; its title 'March Mwnc']

Source

Cerddi Bangor 1 (26)

Date

Not noted; the ballad sheet was printed in Shrewsbury by Thomas
Durston for the seller, William Jones, during the eighteenth century.

Thomas Durston published between 1711 and 1767; the date 1764 is handwritten on the ballad sheet.

Locality
Not noted.

Measure
The tune 'Ymdaith Mwngc' or 'The Monk's March' is derived from a seventeenth-century country dance tune, see Kinney, *Welsh Traditional Music*, pp. 62, 232; for the tune see Jones, *Musical and Poetical Relicks of the Welsh Bards*, 1, p. 67, made suitable by halving the notes in the first sentence; 'The Lord Monk's March', in Barlow (ed.), *The Complete Country Dance Tunes*, p. 44 (tune 151). The tune is named after General George Monck (1st duke of Albemarle, 1608–70), an officer in the Cromwellian army, later a key figure in the restoration of Charles II.

28 Dau bennill Malandein ar 'Follow my Fancy'

Hyd atoch, meinwen, seren siriol,
Y feindw gynnes, fwyndeg, unol,
Derbyniwch draserch annerch unol
4   Drwy gywir degwch yn garedigol:
Y fun garedig, eurfrig, irfron,
Ddifalch, weddol, fuddiol foddion,
Ail i Sara, lana linon,
8   Y feinael agwedd, fwyn olygon,
Â Malandein y mola i'n deg
Eich purdeg, fwyndeg feindw;
Rwy mewn llawenfyd hyfryd, hael,
12   Wych union, gael eich enw.
Yn fy llyfre a'm breinti[e] bri,
Y lili heini, hoenus,
Y fun hawddgara, deca ar dwyn,
16   Gu seren fwyn, gysurus,
Y chwi ydyw'r ddidwyll gannwyll goeth,
Rhieinddoeth wiwddoeth, wedded,
Y chwi ydyw'r glaerwen seren sir
20   A'r ddifyr feinir fwynedd,
Yr hawddgar Fenws burlwys bêr,
Eglurder fwynder feindw,
Hardd rosyn Saron, tirion, teg,
24   Hoff landeg eurdeg irdw.

O ran eich bod, gwawr hynod, heini,
Drwy bur gariad yn rhagori,
Mawr ei chaffael, rwy yn eich hoffi
28   Yn Falandein, dda lein oleuni.
Os rhowch chwi gennad, euraid aeres,
Pêr a mwynedd, pur ei mynwes,
I'ch gwisgo'n fwynlan, burlan, bierles,
32   Drwy bura cynnydd, fel yr amcanes,
E dwbwl W, mi dybia'n lân,
Yw'r fei[n]gan, ddiddan ddyddie;

28   Two Valentine stanzas on 'Follow my Fancy'

Unto you, slender and beautiful young woman, cheerful star,
Affectionate, gentle and fair, agreeable, slender one,
Accept the passion of a steadfast greeting
4   Kindly, by means of [your] true beauty [of character]:
The beloved, golden-haired young woman, young of heart,
Humble, beautiful of countenance, of fitting behaviour,
Comparable with Sarah, most beautiful ash tree,
8   In appearance the one with slender eyebrows, gentle eyes,
By means of a Valentine I will praise with favour
Your pure and pretty, gentle and fair, slender figure;
I am in a world of happiness, pleasant [and] generous,
12   Gallantly sincere, since acquiring your name.
In my books and my illustrious blessings,
The vivacious, light-hearted lily,
The most amiable young woman, most beautiful on earth,
16   Beloved, gentle, consoling star,
You are the sincere refined candle,
Worthy and wise, seemly [and] sagacious young woman,
You are the brilliantly radiant star of the county
20   And the enchanting, gentle young woman,
The amiable Venus, pure and beautiful, sweet,
Brightness [and] geniality, of slender figure,
A beautiful rose of Sharon, gentle, amiable,
24   Favourite, comely and fair, gloriously beautiful one [with the]
          young figure.

In respect of the fact that you, splendid vivacious dawn,
Excel with regard to pure love,
It is magnificent to have you, I delight in you
28   As a Valentine, light of good line.
If you give permission, golden heiress,
Sweet and gentle, one of pure heart,
To wear you[r name] affably [and] sincerely, peerless one,
32   Through purest gain, as I had intended,
E double W, I clearly assume
Is the slender and pale-complexioned one, happy days;

Y fun gariadus wiwlwys wen,
36   Siriolwen aelwen ole,
Ag osgo rhwydd mi wisga rhain
Drwy gywir sain gysonedd
Nes cael add'wydion, moddion mael,
40   Fod imi gael ymgeledd.
Hawdd ichwi, meinwen, rhyngu modd
Drwy bur gywirfodd arfer;
Nid wy'n chwenychu meddu 'ch mael,
44   Fy meindw, ond cael eich mwynder
Drwy serch a chariad, leuad lon,
Yn dirion, union, annwyl.
Ow! teg ei bron, mewn llon wellhad
48   Rhowch imi anrhegiad rhugl.

Rees Lloyd

Rees Lloyd a'i gwnaeth dros Richard Foulk o Fwlch-y-ddâr yn Falandein i Elisabeth Williams merch y Grin Hôl o ymyl Llan-fyllin yn y flwyddyn 1775

Source
Cwrtmawr 41B, i, 34

Manuscript readings
Line 13 breinti bri
Line 34 feigan

Date
1775.

Locality
The poem was written by Rees Lloyd, Nant Irwen, on behalf of Richard Foulk of Bwlch-y-ddâr near Llanrhaeadr-ym-Mochnant, on the boundary

The loving, precious and comely, blessed young woman,
36   Cheerful radiance, with a white brow,
With swift inclination I will wear these [letters]
With a sincere note of concord
Until I receive promises, means of gain,
40   That I will be provided for.
It is easy for you, slender and beautiful young woman, to please me
By means of a pure custom, correctly performed;
I do not covet your riches,
44   My slender one, but rather your tenderness
In affection and love, joyous moon,
Gently, sincerely, lovingly.
Oh! amiable of heart, for joyful recovery [to health]
48   Grant me a swift presentation [of a gift].

Rees Lloyd

Composed by Rees Lloyd for Richard Foulk of Bwlch-y-ddâr as
a Valentine for Elisabeth Williams daughter of Green Hall near
Llanfyllin in the year 1775

between Llangedwyn and Llanfechain, as a Valentine for Elisabeth Wil-
liams, the daughter of Green Hall on the outskirts of Llanfyllin, Powys.

Measure
The tune noted is 'Follow my Fancy', see J. Lloyd Williams Papers
AH1/36, f. 95ᵛ, at the National Library of Wales; Cass Meurig, *Alawon
John Thomas: a fiddler's tune book from eighteenth-century Wales* (Aber-
ystwyth: National Library of Wales, 2004), tune 371. Compare also 'Dilyn
Serch' in John Parry, *British Harmony, being a collection of antient
Welsh airs, the traditional remains of those originally sung by the bards
of Wales* (Ruabon and London: John Parry and P. Hodgson, 1781),
p. 9, tune number 4, a variant form of 'Follow my Fancy'. However, it is
unlikely that 'Follow my Fancy' can accommodate these stanzas.

29   [Di-deitl]

Yr eos dewrfost diddig,
Cenhadwr ffraeth arbennig,
Tegwawdydd mwyn, pruddlais ben,
4   Dydi yw Capten coedwig.

Ti'n hyn heb wneuthur taring,
Dy reso ni bydd cyfyng,
Os dau droso' i'n lawn ar led
8   Odd' yma hed, y rhid[d]ing.

Ac annerch, cyng[a]n barod,
Hoffe[dd enifer], mwyn huffe manod,
Llewndid tyrfa, glendid gwlad,
12   Ym mhob ymddygiad mawrglod.

Mi wn nad rhaid im yngan
Rhoi'n dy ben di ddatgan,
Y dwedi'n ffraeth wrth deg ei dawn
16   Fal pe bawn fy hunan.

A dweud wrth ddyn hoyw
Fy mod yn gwisgo'i henw
Yn Valentine, Gwen deg ei phryd,
20   Fal garland, nid yn salw.

Gwedi dyfod imi
Wrth lot ymysg y cwmpni
Fel na allwn, Gwen dda 'i chlod,
24   Ond rhoi hysbystod ichwi.

Os dyma'r gwir fod amser
Medd hen ddiarhebion mwynber,
Gwell o'r byd Gwen fawr ei gras
28   Na mynd i maes o'r arfer.

A thyma i chwi'r achosion
A wnaeth myfi mewn moddion
Yn hyn o waith rhyfygu ar neb
32   Na byddwn heb gyfeillion.

29   [Untitled]

      The genial nightingale, [with his] long boast [to potential mates],
      A matchlessly fluent messenger,
      A beautiful poet, wise-voiced ruler,
4   You are the Captain of the forest.

      You are thus without delay,
      Your welcome will not be ungenerous,
      If you will go far and wide on my behalf,
8   Fly away from here, the courageous one.

      And greet [in] eager song,
      [The delight of the company], gentle drift of fine snow,
      Most excellent in the multitude, comeliest in the country,
12   In every behaviour [she] is much praised.

      I know that I need not utter
      Or put into your head how to set forth [my message],
      That you will speak to the beautifully gifted one excellently
16   As if I were [speaking] myself.

      And tell [the] vivacious one
      That I wear her name
      As a Valentine, Gwen fair of countenance,
20   As a garland, and not shabbily.

      It had come to me
      By lot in the presence of the company
      So that I was unable, Gwen of goodly praise,
24   But to declare you[r name].

      As it is the truth that this occasion,
      According to old melodious proverbs,
      Is better for the world, Gwen of great grace,
28   Than to let the custom be forgotten.

      And here I give you the reasons
      That I decided upon by some means,
      In this deed I did not presume upon anyone
32   So that I should not be without friends.

Ac felly, pan y gweles
Eich enw, serchog dduwies,
Dyma obaith fore a hwyr
36 Nad metha'n llwyr fy neges.

Gan ddwedyd yn ddiragraith
Greso, fostben, unwaith;
Er ys dyddie, clywch, ar hyn
40 Fûm yn ei erfyn ganwaith.

Yn awr ydd wy', mewn llawngred,
Dan hwyl, yn hoffi'r weithred;
Am fy nhrafel, clywch yn syth,
44 Na cha' i fod byth ar golled.

Dos weithon, dyna nhrwbwl,
A rho fe'n llaw'r ddyn *faithful*
Trwy ddwyn fy annerch pur dros ben,
48 A gwneled Gwen 'i meddwl.

Dienw

Sources
The Penrice and Margam Estate Records, Literary Papers (no. A72) held
at the National Library of Wales, Aberystwyth
Ifans, 'Golwg eto ar y canu Ffolant', 30–2

Variant readings
Line 9 cyngen (Penrice and Margam)
Line 10 hoffe hinife mwin huffe manod (Penrice and Margam)

Date
The manuscript is undated, but is likely to date from the eighteenth
century.

And so, when I saw
Your name, charming goddess,
Here was hope morning and evening
36   That my message would not fail completely.

Saying once, without hypocrisy,
Welcome, boastful ruler;
For many days, take heed, concerning that
40   Which I have longed for a hundred times.

I am now, in full faith,
In good spirits, enjoying the task;
For my labours, hear [this] at once,
44   I shall never be at a loss.

Go henceforth, that is my difficulty,
And put it in the hands of the faithful one
By delivering my exceedingly pure greeting,
48   And let Gwen make up her own mind.

Anonymous

Locality
Not noted; however, Group A papers in the Penrice and Margam Collection are associated with Plas Dyffryn Clydach in the Vale of Neath in south Wales.

Note
The descriptive 'A Welsh song to a Valentine' appears alongside this anonymous poem; to judge from the handwriting and the orthographical practices, the manuscript may have been written by an individual with little formal education. 'Gwen' is a noun meaning 'fair maiden, pretty girl', and is also a personal name for a female.

Measure
Triban.

30 Penillion Malandein i'w canu ar 'Ymdaith Newydd'
neu 'New March'

Wrth arfer maith yrfa
Byw dyrfa bob dydd,
Hyn sydd o hen sail,
4   Nid oes un creadur
Yn bybyr heb ail;
Yn wryw a benyw
Rhoes Duw'r holl stôr
8   Trwy'r môr a'r tir maith
A'u natur i adnabod
A gwybod eu gwaith;
Wrth gwmwl naturieth
12   Mae ystyrieth mis du
Ond Valendine felys
Yn serchus iawn sy'
Ymlygu drwy'r wlad
16   Fod Gwanwyn yn gynnydd,
Hap hylwydd pob had;
Cnawd adar a physgod
Sy'n gwybod eu gwŷn,
20   Ac felly cyfeillach
Sydd olliach i ddyn;
Pob llun sy yn ei lle
Wrth dreifniad Rhaglunieth,
24   Iawn arfaeth y Ne'.

Y gair 'Valandine'
Sy'r *line*, arwydd-lun
O'r grym rywiog wraidd:
28   Cadernid a gallu
Sy'n trefnu lle traidd;
A m'fi, Peter Jones
O Brion, sy â'm bron
32   Yn hoffeiddlon goffáu
Hen arfer, hoen wirfodd,
A glymodd yn glau.

30 Valentine stanzas to be sung to 'Ymdaith Newydd'
    or 'New March'

In accordance with the habits of life's long course
[Lived] daily [by] a spirited crowd of people,
It is [clear] on ancient foundation
4   That there is not one creature
Who is peerlessly splendid;
Male and female,
God has presented the complete provision [of creatures]
8   Throughout the oceans and the vast earth,
Together with their natural [inclination] to identify
And comprehend their work;
It is by the [dark] clouds of nature
12 That the black month is reflected upon,
But sweet Valentine
Is with great passion
Making manifest throughout the land
16 That Spring is on the increase,
[With] propitious good fortune to every seed;
The flesh of birds and fish
Realizes its desire,
20 And therefore friendship
Is for man [also] conducive to health;
Every image is in its place
By the ordinance of Providence,
24 The just [eternal] purpose of Heaven.

The word 'Valentine'
Is the line, a symbol
Of the power [that is] of noble lineage:
28 Strength and might
Rule wherever it permeates;
And I, Peter Jones
Of Prion, do in my heart
32 Lovingly and joyfully call to mind
An old custom of voluntary passion
Which has swiftly tied together [in marriage].

      Chwychwi, Beti Rob[er]ts,
36 Yn bert sydd i'm bodd
      Yn Valandein dyner,
      Wir haelber ei rhodd.
      Drwy eich gwirfodd a'ch gwawr
40 Rwy' yn erfyn cynhorthwy
      Borth mwy'r Buarth Mawr.
      Yn fachgen, os ydw i
      Heb sadio fy mhleth,
44 Chwi glywsoch mai bachgen
      Fydd bachgen am beth,
      Nid meth i wneud mawl
      I chwi sy mewn oedran,
48 Myn Houw, mewn hawl.

      Am gymaint a glywes
      Neu sonies o serch
      Anwylfun [...]
52 Trwy gariad tra geirwir
      A chywir [...]
      Eich gwyso, awch gwasgar,
      Sydd hawddgar o hyd,
56 Mae'n hyfryd mwynhau
      Eich cennad a'ch cynnydd,
      Hoff ysty[...]
      Hen genedl ogonedd,
60 O fonedd y [...]
      Hil Cynfarch ap Meirion,
      Anrhegion iawn hy,
      Dda deulu, mewn dawn,
64 Llin rhywiog Llanrhaeadr
      Yw'r gair gore gawn;
      Beth bynnag fu'r bonedd
      Yn hoywedd cyn hyn
68 Chwi heddiw sy'n haeddol,
      Wawr freiniol ar fryn;
      Nid tyn ydyw eich tasg
      Roi ataf ryw ateb
72 Cyn purdeb y Pasg.

Thomas Edwards 'Twm o'r Nant' (1739–1810)

You, Beti Roberts,
36 Please me prettily
As a tender Valentine,
Truly generous and pure of gift.
Through your readiness and your radiance
40 I beg the assistance,
The greater aid, of Buarth Mawr.
A boy, if I have not
Settled down,
44 You have heard that a boy
Remains a boy for a while,
It is not a fault to fashion praise
For you who are grown-up,
48 By God, according to right.

For all that I have heard
Or spoken concerning love
Dear young woman [...]
52 In very sincere love
And true [...]
To demand your presence, in restless keenness,
Is always desirable,
56 It is pleasant to enjoy
Your consent and your blessing,
Choice [...]
Ancient nation of glory,
60 Of the nobility of [...]
In the lineage of Cynfarch ap Meirion,
Righteous [and] valiant gifts,
Excellent family, of innate ability,
64 The noble lineage of Llanrhaeadr
Is the best word [of authority] that we shall acquire;
Whatever the gentry used to be,
In splendour, before this [time],
68 Today it is you who are privileged,
Noble dawn over a hilltop;
Your task is not [too] difficult [a task]
To send me some reply
72 Before the purity of Easter.

Thomas Edwards 'Twm o'r Nant' (1739–1810)

Source
NLW 348B, 97–8

Date
Not noted; the manuscript is dated *c.*1787.

Locality

The poem was written on behalf of Peter Jones of Prion in the parish of Llanrhaeadr-yng-Nghinmeirch, Denbighshire, to be sent to Beti Roberts, Buarth Mawr, Prion.

Measure

'Ymdaith Newydd' or 'New March' was not found in the collections.

31   I ofyn Falentein

John Simon, gyda'ch cennad,
Rwy'n gyrru fel o gariad
Atoch berffaith, lanwaith *line*
4   O Falendein yn dyniad.

Yr amser hwn mae'r adar
Yn dewis cymwys gymar,
Ac yn canu o dwyn i dwyn
8   O frig y llwyn yn llafar.

Ac felly mae'r ifienctid
Mor hyfion yn eu rhyddid
Yn dewis annerch, naill y llall,
12   Yn ddiwall mewn addewid.

Os gwnewch mor fwyn â derbyn
Fy ngharedicaf docyn,
Rhaid i chwi gofio cyn y Pasg
16   Bydd arnoch dasg yn disgyn.

Robert Davies 'Bardd Nantglyn' (1769–1835)

Source
Bangor 952, 10

Date
Undated; the author's dates are 1769–1835.

Locality
Not noted; the poet lived in Nantglyn, Denbighshire.

31 In request of a Valentine

John Simon, with your permission,
I send you, out of love,
A perfect, well-wrought line
4   Of a Valentine to evoke your interest.

At this present time the birds
Are choosing a suitable partner,
And are singing from hill to knoll
8   Loudly from the topmost branch of the grove.

And so too the young people
So bold in their freedom
Choose to greet one another
12   And make vows with no restriction.

If you should be so kind as to accept
My most amiable token [of love],
You must bear in mind that before Easter
16   A demand will be made of you.

Robert Davies 'Bardd Nantglyn' (1769–1835)

Note
A poem to be sent to John Simon, on behalf of an anonymous young woman.

Measure
Triban.

32 Pennill Malandein ar 'Charity Mistress'

Derbyniwch, seren siriol,
   Gysonol sein
   O luniedd lein,
4   Bur loyw beredd leuad,
   Drwy dyniad falandein.
Ystyriwch chwi fy stori,
   Mun heini hael, dda, ffel, ddi-ffael,
8   Drwy gariad rwyf i'n gyrru
   Ac nid er meddu mael,
Ond dangos caredigrwydd,
   Cymdeithas hylwydd eitha serch,
12   Drwy loyw hedd, i deg ei gwedd,
   Rieinaidd, fwynaidd ferch;
Gwnewch gofio amdana i'n dyner,
   Feinwen syber, Fenws wen,
16   Ymhob rhyw le nes mynd i'r ne,
   Ac felly minne, Amen.

Dienw

Source
Cwrtmawr 41B, i, 177

Date
Undated; Cwrtmawr 41B, i, is dated to the second half of the eighteenth and the first half of the nineteenth century.

32 A Valentine stanza on 'Charity Mistress'

Accept, joyful star,
    A sign of constancy
    In a graceful line [of poetry],
4   Pure bright sweet moon,
    Through the drawing of a Valentine.
Consider my story,
    Vivacious, generous young woman, good, sagacious,
        without blemish,
8   I send [this] out of love
    And not for want of gain,
But to show kindness,
    A prosperous companionship of extreme affection,
12   In shining peace, to the fair of countenance,
    Chaste, gentle young woman;
Remember me kindly,
    Wise, slender young woman, bright Venus,
16   In every place until you reach heaven,
    And so will I do [you], Amen.

Anonymous

Locality

Not noted; the manuscript was written in the Llansilin/Llan-
rhaeadr-ym-Mochnant area of Powys.

Measure

For the tune 'Charity Mistress' (a corruption of the tune title 'Gerard's
Mistress') see Kinney, 'Tunes (I)', 43–4; 'Elusenni Meistres', in Kinney
and Evans, *Hen Alawon*, number 26.

33   Penillion i ddiolch am rodd Falantein: 'Leave Land'

Siân Humphrey fwyn galon, pur feddwl, pêr foddion,
Can diolch, mun dirion, awch union, i chwi;
Mi'ch cofia chwi yn ddilys, y wiwdda fun weddus,
4   Chwi fuoch haelionus eleni.

Rwyf fi yn rhwymedig a phur ostyngedig,
Chwi fuoch garedig nodedig o'r da,
I mi yn rhywiogedd, yn hylaw ac yn haeledd
8   A gweddedd, mwyn agwedd, mynega'.

Mi gefais rodd hynod, yn Falandine barod,
Yn ôl y pur amod, gwych eurglod fo i chwi,
A diolch yn dirion o w'llys fy nghalon,
12   Mun ffyddlon nod union, amdani.

Am gael y rhodd yma diolchgar a fydda
I chwi, meinir wiwdda, mi a'i gwisga yn ddi-gudd
I'ch cofio, lliw hinon, o w'llys fy nghalon,
16   Pur foddion, yn dirion, da arwydd.

Siân weddol, Siân wiwdda, Siân barod, Siân bura,
Siân hylaw, Siân haela, anwyla mewn nod,
Siân fanwl, Siân fwynedd, Siân burion, Siân buredd,
20   Siân wedded, Siân beredd, Siân barod.

Teg iechyd fo ichwi a gras a daioni,
Mun hynod, yn heini, y lili fwyn, lon,
Am i chwi fy nghofio yr ydwi yn gweddïo,
24   Mae'n hawdd i chwi goelio, o'm gwir galon.

John Jones

33   Stanzas in gratitude for a Valentine gift: 'Leave Land'

Tender-hearted Siân Humphrey, pure of mind, sweet of manners,
Thank you a hundred times over, gentle young woman [of] honest
    ardour;
I will remember you steadfastly, the good and worthy, seemly
    young woman,
4   You have been generous this year.

I am obliged [to you] and [feel] truly humble,
You have been distinctively kind, out of the goodness [of your
    heart],
You have been noble towards me, obliging and generous
8   And of seemly, courteous conduct, I do declare.

I have received an excellent gift, a prepared Valentine,
In accordance with the sincere promise, magnificent golden praise
    be to you,
And I thank you tenderly from the bottom of my heart,
12   Faithful young woman of honest renown, for it.

For having been given this gift I will be grateful
To you, good and worthy young woman, I shall wear it openly
In remembrance of you, [one with a complexion] the colour of
    sunshine, wholeheartedly,
16   [One of] pure disposition, tenderly, a good sign.

Comely Siân, good and worthy Siân, eager Siân, purest Siân,
Skilful Siân, most generous Siân, most loving in her objective,
Meticulous Siân, gentle Siân, perfect Siân, pure Siân,
20   Modest Siân, sweet Siân, willing Siân.

May you have good health and grace and goodness,
Excellent young woman, vivacious, courteous [and] happy lily,
Because you remembered me I pray,
24   It is easy for you to believe, from my true heart.

John Jones

Source
NLW 346B, 171

Date
John Jones was a schoolteacher in Llanddeiniolen, near Caernarfon in Gwynedd, and lived during the second half of the eighteenth century; the manuscript's date of composition is late eighteenth and early nineteenth century.

Locality
Llanddeiniolen, Gwynedd.

Note
A poem for Siân Humphrey.

Measure
Tri thrawiad sengl; on 'Leave Land' or 'Gadael Tir y ffordd hwyaf' see
Kinney, 'Tunes (II)', 11–13; Kinney and Evans, *Hen Alawon,* number 42.

34 [Dideitl]

Dyma lythyr gwedi ei selio
    Â sêl aur a chusan ynddo,
O na allwn gan fy ngofid
4   Roi fy nghalon ynddo hefyd.

Nid wyf yn rhoddi arnoch dasg
    Ond ichwi nghofio o hyn i'r Pasg
Â macyn sidan cyfan coch
8   Neu bâr o fenig, yr un a fynnoch.

Haws yw hela'r môr ar lwy
    A'i ddodi oll mewn plisgyn ŵy
Nag yw troi fy meddwl i
12   F'anwylyd fach oddi wrthy' chwi.

Fallai d'wedwch chwi amdanaf
    Mai hen benillion sosi yrraf,
Dweud yn wir a allaf finnau
16   Mai hen ffasiwn yw ffolantau.

Dienw

Sources
SFAWC 33.335.1 held in St Fagans National Museum of History, Cardiff
Catrin Stevens, *Arferion Caru* [Courting Customs] (Llandysul: Gwasg Gomer, 1977), p. 88
For an English translation see Trefor M. Owen, *Welsh Folk Customs* (Cardiff: National Museum of Wales/Welsh Folk Museum, 1974), pp. 153–4

Date
The beginning of the nineteenth century.

34   [Untitled]

Here is a letter that has been sealed
    With a golden seal with a kiss inside it,
Oh! that I could, on account of my grief,
4   Put my heart in it too.

I am not setting you any task
    Save that you should remember me between now and Easter
By giving me a large, red silk handkerchief
8   Or a pair of gloves, whichever you choose.

It is easier to collect the sea into a spoon
    And to place it all into an eggshell
Than it is to turn my thoughts,
12   My dear little one, away from you.

Perhaps you may say of me
    That I send you saucy old verses,
I, for my part, can truly say [in reply]
16   That valentines are an old custom.

Anonymous

Locality
Llanbryn-mair, Powys. These four stanzas, inscribed in a Valentine card sent within the historical county of Montgomeryshire, are followed by the words 'O Cofiwch fi | Da chwi | I Mary' [O remember me | I beg of you | To Mary]. It was fashioned in the family home by the sender's father, and it remains one of the few home-made Welsh Valentine cards held at the St Fagans National Museum of History.

Measure
Hen bennill.

35 Y Folantein

Fe ddarfu'r gaeaf creulon,
Tawelach yw'r awelon,
A'r adar bach gan fywiocáu
4   Sy'n dechrau gwau caneuon.

Holl anian gain sy'n gwenu
Gan neisied ymgynhesu,
Ac nid yw'n deilwng rhoddi sèn
8   I minnau, Gwen, am ganu.

Wrth weld dy hun mor laned,
Pa fab all dewi dywed?
O rho i lanc ar soddi i lawr,
12   O'i ddolur mawr ymwared.

Yn dewis y mae'r adar
Yn awr bob un ei gymar,
I fyw mewn undeb eithaf llon
16   Uwch pob argoelion galar.

Un, un ddewisaf finnau,
A hon wyt ti, lliw'r blodau;
Yn rheudol les O! rho dy law
20   I dorri'm braw a'm briwiau.

Yr eneth fwyn eiriannaf,
Tydi yw'r lana' welaf;
Na ad, a mi mor wael fy nrych,
24   Fath bwn o oernych arnaf.

Rho'th law'n addewid i mi,
Rho'th gusan i'm sirioli,
Rho'th galon rydd, yn glodydd glân,
28   Diderfyn gân cei gen i!

35 The Valentine

The harsh winter is over,
The winds are calmer,
And the little birds as they become invigorated
4   Begin to weave songs.

All nature, [so] beautiful, is smiling
On account of how nice it is to warm oneself,
And it is not worthy [of you] to rebuke
8   Me, Gwen, for singing.

Seeing you so fair,
Tell me, what young man can keep silent?
O allow a young man who is on the point of sinking [down
        in despair]
12   Deliverance from his great pain.

The birds are now choosing
Each one his mate,
To live in unity of the utmost cheerfulness
16   Beyond all signs of sorrow.

It is one, one that I too choose,
And you are she, [one with a complexion] the colour of blossoms;
For [my] essential benefit O! give [me] your hand
20   To put an end to my fear and my pains.

The gentle, most beautiful young woman,
You are the fairest I behold;
Do not permit, and I so wretched my plight,
24   Such a burden of miserable torment to rest upon me.

Give [me] your hand as a pledge to me,
Give [me] your kiss to cheer me,
Give [me] your unrestrained heart, in pure praises,
28   You will receive unending song from me!

Y mae dy wedd yn waddol,
Deg Wen, o werth digonol;
Uwch unrhyw bris yw'th lygaid pêr
32   Sydd fel y sêr yn siriol.

O tro yn awr, tra'n iraidd,
I rwymyn cariad puraidd;
Cawn fyw mewn tes yn gynnes, Gwen,
36   A'n byd yn hufen hafaidd.

Mae'r gwanwyn ar egino,
Daw blodau'r haf i'w rhifo,
Anturia, Gwen, mae natur gain
40   Yn cymell sain cydsynio.

Daniel Evans 'Daniel Ddu o Geredigion' (1792–1846)

Sources
Ceredigion, 'Valentine', *The Carmarthen Journal and South Wales Weekly Advertiser*, 13 February 1829, 4
Daniel Evans, *Gwinllan y Bardd* [The Poet's Vineyard] (Llanbedr: J. Davies, 1872), pp. 233–5
'Y Folantein (The Valentine)', *JWFSS*, 2 (1914–25), 51–2
Welsh Folk-Songs/Caneuon Gwerin Cymru, arranged by W. Hubert Davies (Wrexham: Hughes and Son, *c*.1919), pp. 16–17

Date
1829.

Your countenance is a dowry,
Beautiful Gwen, of abundant value;
Your sweet eyes are beyond any price,
32   [And] are as cheerful as the stars.

O turn now, while young and fresh,
To the knot of pure love;
We shall live affectionately in the summer heat, Gwen,
36   And our world will be like summer cream.

The spring is about to swell into bud,
The summer flowers will [soon] come to be counted,
Venture, Gwen, [since] beautiful nature
40   Compels a note of agreement.

Daniel Evans 'Daniel Ddu o Geredigion' (1792–1846)

Locality
Mynydd Bach (the Trefenter and Blaenpennal districts) in mid Ceredigion.

Note
The song was collected by Miss Jennie Williams 'Ehedydd Ystwyth' from
the singing of Mr Evan Rowlands, Aberystwyth, in April 1911; he noted
that it was very popular in the Mynydd Bach district in the 1860s.

Measure
Triban; for the tune see *JWFSS*, 2 (1914–25), 51; Davies, *Welsh Folk-
Songs*, p. 17.

36   Pennill mewn Falandein i'w ganu ar 'Belle Isle March'

Yr hawddgar gangen irwen ara,
A'r lana', fwyna fun,
Rhowch dderbyniad i hyn o ganiad,
4   Fy lleuad hardd ei llun;
Yn ôl rhyw arfer fu'n 'r hen amser
Lle bydde syber *sign*,
Rwy finne felly yn rhyfygu
8   Eich tynnu yn falandein.
Am hyn gobeithiaf fi,
Yn dyner, J a D,
O gael rhyw roddion, union eneth,
12   O'ch helaeth ddwylo chwi.
Mi fyddaf inne ym mhob rhyw fanne
Tra bwyf heb amau'n bod
Ymhlith y Gymry yn ddigelu
16   Yn deusy' glymu eich glod.
Cewch chwithe, main ei hael,
Am wrando ar gwynion gwael,
Uchel eiddo iach o lwyddiant
20   A ffyniant yn ddi-ffael,
A gwir orfoledd fyth heb ddiwedd
Mewn dinas waredd wen;
Duw a'ch dygo i dario
24   Rwyf fi'n dymuno, Amen.

Harri Humphreys (fl. *1819–24)*

Source
Cwrtmawr 41B, i, 211

Date
Not noted; *fl.* 1819–24; the manuscript was copied during the second half of the eighteenth and the beginning of the nineteenth century.

36 A verse in a Valentine to be sung on 'Belle Isle March'

The most amiable, tender, fresh young bough,
The fairest, gentlest young woman,
Accept this song,
4   My moon, so beautiful her form;
After the fashion of a custom practised in olden days
When a serious sign [that was a signifier of love] was acquired,
I too, in that same way, venture
8   To draw you as a valentine.
Because of this I hope,
With great tenderness, J and D,
To receive some gift, honest young woman,
12   From your generous hands.
I shall, in all places,
For as long as I live, without any doubt,
In the midst of the Welsh people, laying this [intention] open to view,
16   Seek to compose skilful stanzas in praise of you.
You shall receive, one with the slender eyebrows,
Because you have attended to [my] sorry plaints,
A high level of wholesome good fortune
20   And assured prosperity,
And true rejoicing for ever without end
In a gracious holy city;
May God lead you to dwell [there]
24   Is my wish, Amen.

Harri Humphreys (fl. *1819–24*)

Locality
No location is noted; however, the poet was a native of the Welshpool
area and he served as the family harpist at Powis Castle; the manuscript
derives from the Llansilin/Llanrhaeadr-ym-Mochnant area in Powys.

Measure
For 'Belle Isle March' see Kinney, 'Tunes (I)', 49–50.

37 Pennill i'w roi mewn Ffalendine i'w ganu ar fesur
a elwir 'Follow my Fancy'

Clau seren annwyl, clws eirwir eneth,
Purloyw, didwyll, perl eiriau odiaeth,
Y fun dynergalon, fwyn dirion gowled,
4   Gywreindeg, onest, gwrando ar gwynion!
Y mae'r Falendein drwy fwynlan dyniad
Yn hen arferion, mewn heini fwriad;
Llond hon, O rosyn, llawn hoyw draserch,
8   Clir, eirwir donnen, clyw air i d'annerch:
Winw'dden lawen luniedd lon
Â phiniwn annwyl ffenics,
Gwenithen dirion ffyddlon ffel,
12   Rianedd fel yr onycs,
Yr wyt yn ail i'r goleulan arglwys
Ni welai Fenws galant,
Nid eill fy nhafod tra bo chwyth
16   Gyhoeddi fyth mo'th haeddiant.
Lloer ole ei gwedd, ll[i]w'r lili gwyn,
Doeth rosyn odiaeth rasol,
Y gangen gymwys wiwlys wen,
20   Y d'wysen, gariad ysol,
Nid wy'n llysyfu dim llesâd
Am hyn o ganiad gennych,
Am hynny'n rhwyddedd dan y rhod
24   Y feinwen, dod a fynnych.

John Rees

37 A stanza to be placed in a Valentine to be sung on
the measure known as 'Follow my Fancy'

Dear honest star, pretty [and] truthful young woman,
Shining, sincere, of exquisite words [that are like] pearls,
Tender-hearted young woman, gentle, good-natured darling,
4   Artistic and beautiful, honest, attend to [my] plaints!
The Valentine custom of [names] being drawn [in a] gentle and
        pleasant [manner]
Is an old custom, having active intent;
As much as this [stanza] will hold of perfect joyful passion, O rose,
8   One of clear, truthful semblance, take notice of a verse that
        greets you:
Happy, slender, merry vine
With opinions [similar to] a cherished phoenix,
Grain of wheat, gentle, loyal, sagacious,
12   [Noble] young woman like unto the onyx,
You are comparable with the clean and bright [...],
Gallant Venus could not see
[And] my tongue can never as long as I draw breath
16   [Adequately] declare your merit.
One who has the appearance of a bright moon, [one with a
        complexion] the colour of a white lily,
Wise rose, exquisitely gracious,
The modest, beautiful and pure, blessed bough,
20   Ear of corn, passionate love,
I do not form syllables for any gain
From you [in return] for this song,
[And] because of that, readily under the sun
24   Give as you please, [fine] young woman.

John Rees

Source
NLW 1710B, 140–1

Manuscript reading
Line 17 llawr

Date
NLW 1710B is dated to 1800–49.

Locality

Not noted, but the song was copied into a Crosswood (near Welshpool) manuscript by Walter Davies 'Gwallter Mechain' (1761–1849); the poet, John Rees, lived in Llanrhaeadr-ym-Mochnant, Powys.

Measure

The tune noted is 'Follow my Fancy', see J. Lloyd Williams Papers AH1/36, f. 95ᵛ, at the National Library of Wales; Meurig, *Alawon John Thomas*, tune 371. Compare also 'Dilyn Serch', in Parry, *British Harmony*, p. 9, tune number 4, a variant form of 'Follow my Fancy'. However, it is unlikely that 'Follow my Fancy' can accommodate these stanzas.

38 Englynion: Penillion a anfonwyd mewn Valentine i Morgan Evans shop

Morgan yw cwynfan ceinferch—sy beunydd
    Tan boenau trwm traserch;
  I'w chiliau aeth saethau serch,
4   Am hynny ti yw'n hannerch.

Os arall heb ball tristgan—yw'th asen,
    Fyth isod hwy 'm dodan';
  Lledai 'nghri, llwyda 'ngra'n,
8   Mawr gwyno wnaf am Morgan!

David Evans 'Dewi Dysul'

Sources
NLW 23692A, f. 13ʳ
Ifans, 'Golwg eto ar y canu Ffolant', 25–6

Date
1850.

Locality
Llandysul parish, Ceredigion.

38 *Englynion*: Verses sent in a Valentine to Morgan Evans shop

Morgan is the plaint of a beautiful young woman – who is daily
    Suffering the pains of an intense passion;
  To the [four] corners of her being, love's arrows have gone,
4   Because of this you are the one we greet.

If it is another, ceaselessly [singing] a sad song – that is your
    [preferred] wife,
    They will put me below [in the grave] for ever more;
  My cry shall spread abroad, my looks will pale,
8   I shall lament excessively for Morgan!

David Evans 'Dewi Dysul'

Note
David Evans, writing under the pen name 'Dewi Dysul', composed two *englynion* on behalf of an anonymous woman, to be sent within a Valentine card to Morgan Evans, shopkeeper.

Measure
Englyn unodl union.

39 [Di-deitl]

Gwêl fwyn adeilad odiaeth
Gan un a gŵyn gan hiraeth
    Bob dydd oherwydd
4   Fod saethau llymion cariad
O dan fy mron yn wastad,
    Nid oes distawrwydd.
Gwir iawn, lle byddo cariad llawn,
8   Pwy all ei gelu
    Na'i lawn ddistewi,
Rhaid yw ei draethu gan faint y cyni gawn,
    A gwaelu mae fy 'mennydd
12   Foreuddydd a phrydnawn.
Yn syn am eiliad gwrando hyn:
    A yw dy galon
    Fath galed foddion
16 A rhoi'n ysgyrion fy nwyfron sydd yn dynn,
Bob amser mewn prysurdeb am weld dy wyneb gwyn?

David Evans 'Dewi Dysul'

Sources
NLW 23692A, f. 15^r
W. J. Davies, *Hanes Plwyf Llandyssul* [History of the Parish of Llandysul]
(Llandysul: J. D. Lewis, 1896), p. 254

Date
Valentine's Day 1851.

39 [Untitled]

See a fair, exquisite building,
By one who groans with longing
    Every day because
4   The sharp arrows of love
Are in my breast constantly,
    There is no silence.
True enough, where there is total love,
8   Who can disguise it
      Or fully silence it,
It must be proclaimed because the anguish is so great,
    And my brain deteriorates
12   Morning and afternoon.
Amazed for a second consider this:
    Is your heart
    Of such hard means
16 As to rend my heart, which is heavy, into pieces
[And] always anxious to see your pale face?

David Evans 'Dewi Dysul'

Locality
Llandysul parish, Ceredigion.

Measure
For 'Gwêl yr Adeilad' or 'See the Building' see Kinney, 'Tunes (I)', 34–5;
Kinney and Evans, *Hen Alawon*, number 16.

40   [Di-deitl]

Y folant hon 'wy'n anfon
Yn barchus iawn fy eirchion
        At flodau'r merched;
4   Diau na ddengys Cymru,
Nac un wlad, ferch mor wisgi
        Â'm hannwyl Farged.
Heb lai—Marged heb unrhyw fai,
8   Ei hwyneb siriol
        A'i lluniaidd ganol,
Oll mor naturiol i'w chanmol gan bob rhai:
        Rhagora'n ddiau ddigon
12   Ar flodau meillion Mai.
Deg bryd, nid allan mae i gyd
        Ei holl brydferthwch
        A'i glanwedd degwch;
16 Mwy gwerthfawr gwelwch na holl reialtwch byd
Ei greddfau da a'i natur, sydd gysur i fy mryd.

David Evans 'Dewi Dysul'

Sources
NLW 23692A, f. 33[r]
Ifans, 'Golwg eto ar y canu Ffolant', 26

Date
1856.

Locality
Llandysul parish, Ceredigion.

40 [Untitled]

> I send this Valentine
> Bearing my truly honourable requests
>   To the most superior of the young women;
> 4 It is certain that Wales will never display,
> Nor will any [other] country, such a vivacious young woman
>   As my dear Marged.
> Without doubt – faultless Marged,
> 8   Her cheerful face
>   And her shapely waist,
> It is so totally appropriate that she be praised by all:
>   Doubtless she far surpasses [in beauty]
> 12   The clover flowers [borne in] May.
> Fair of countenance, [however, her beauty] is not wholly external
>   [and superficial],
>   Her whole beauty
>   And her comely attractiveness;
> 16 Far more precious, observe, than all the world's merrymaking
> Are her good instincts and nature, which are a comfort to my mind.

David Evans 'Dewi Dysul'

Note
A Valentine poem addressed to Marged.

Measure
For the tune 'Gwêl yr Adeilad' or 'See the Building' see Kinney, 'Tunes (I)', 34–5; Kinney and Evans, *Hen Alawon,* number 16.

41 Folant

Mi gara'r enw 'Ifan'
Tra'r huan fry uwchben,
A'm gwaed yn têr ergydio
4   A gwallt yn cuddio 'mhen,
Ac yn fy oriau olaf
Bydd Ifan gen i'n gu,
Ac wrth ei ochor carwn
8   Fod yn y ddaear ddu.

Y Folant hon ddanfonir
Gan ddifyr feinir fwyn
At Ifan Tomos lwysaidd,
12   Fab c'ruaidd, lawn o swyn;
Heb ynddi unrhyw weniaith,
Trwm hiraeth garia'm bron
O eisiau bod yn wastad
16   O hyd i'w chariad llon.

David Evans 'Dewi Dysul'

Source
Davies, *Hanes Plwyf Llandyssul*, pp. 253–4

Date
Mid-nineteenth century.

Locality
Llandysul parish, Ceredigion.

41 Valentine

I will love the name 'Ifan'
While there is a sun high overhead,
And [while] my blood beats clearly
4   And [while] hair [still] hides my head,
And in my final hours
Ifan will be with me intimately,
And it is next to him I would love
8   To lie in the dark earth.

This Valentine is sent
By an agreeable, gentle young woman
To handsome Ifan Tomos,
12   Affectionate young man, full of charm;
Without any dissembling speech in her,
My heart carries a sad yearning
For want of being constantly [and]
16   Perpetually [on hand] for her cheerful lover.

David Evans 'Dewi Dysul'

Note
The poem was written on behalf of an anonymous young woman to be
sent to Ifan Tomos.

Measure
7.6.7.6.D.

42 Ateb Merch i Ffolant

Mor brydferth oedd eich Ffolant,
Mae'n ddarlun pur o serch,
Ac un fel hyn ddyfeisant
4   Gael hudo meddwl merch;
Ond cofiwch hyn, fy nghariad,
Ynfydrwydd yw i chwi
Ragrithio mor ddideimlad,
8   A thorri'm calon i.

Nis gallaf lai nag edrych
Trwy'r dydd ar Ffolant hon,
Ond amau'r wyf yn fynych
12   Y purdeb dan eich bron;
Pwy ŵyr na byddaf eto
Yn gasbeth gennych chwi,
A'ch anian i'm difrïo
16   Ar ôl fy nhwyllo i.

Gwrandewch, fy nghariad annwyl,
Peth mawr yw meddwl merch,
Yn wresog rwyf yn teimlo
20   At fab 'n ôl seilio'm serch;
Os na fydd hwn yn fodlon,
Ac yn ei gynffon dro,
Wrth un fel hyn rwy'n digio
24   Pan gyrraedd frig y to.

A chwithau sydd yn treio
Rhyw lawer gyda fi,
Trwy hyn, peth doeth ffarwelio
28   Am byth â'ch cwmni chwi;
Dymunaf i chwi lwyddiant
Gael merch fo wrth eich bodd,
Gadewch i finnau'n llonydd –
32   Mi deimla hyn yn rhodd.

John Jenkins 'Cerngoch' (1820–94)

42 A Woman's Response to a Valentine

Your Valentine was so beautiful,
It is a true illustration of love,
And it is such a one as this that they invented
4   To charm a woman's mind;
But remember this, my sweetheart,
It is foolishness for you
To dissemble in such a callous way,
8   And to break my heart.

I cannot do anything other than look
At this Valentine all day,
But I frequently suspect
12   The purity of your heart;
Who knows that I will yet be
An object of hatred to you,
And that it is in your nature to discredit me
16   After having deceived me.

Listen, my dear sweetheart,
A woman's mind is a noble thing,
I have warm feelings
20   Towards the man on whom I have lain my affections;
If he is not satisfied
And there is a twist in his tail [i.e. if he is untrustworthy],
I will take offence at such a one
24   When he reaches the heights [and deems me unworthy of his love].

And you try
Very hard with me,
Because of this, it is wise to bid farewell
28   To your company forever;
I wish you success
In acquiring a woman who pleases you,
Leave me alone –
32   I consider this to be a gift.

John Jenkins 'Cerngoch' (1820–94)

Sources

Dan Jenkins and [David Lewis] 'Ap Ceredigion' (eds), *Cerddi Cerngoch: gyda detholion o waith 'Amnon II', 'Hywel' ac 'Aeronian'* [The Poems of Cerngoch: with selected pieces from the works of 'Amnon II', 'Hywel' and 'Aeronian'] (Lampeter: Cwmni y Wasg Eglwysig Gymreig, 1904), pp. 14–15

D. Islwyn Edwards (ed.), *Cerddi Cerngoch: sef cyfrol o waith John Jenkins (1820–94)* [The Poems of Cerngoch: that is a volume of work by John Jenkins (1820–94)] (Felinfach: Pwyllgor Coffa Cerngoch, 1994), pp. 57–8

Date
Mid- or second half of the nineteenth century.

Locality
The author was born in Blaenplwyf, Llanfihangel Ystrad, a village and ecclesiastical parish in Dyffryn Aeron, Ceredigion, six miles from Lampeter; John Jenkins later farmed Penbryn-mawr, Bronnant, Ceredigion.

Measure
7.6.7.6.D.

43 Y Ferch a'r Valantine

Daeth merch fach lawn o gariad
Ar noswaith lawn o wlaw
A'i henaid yn ei llygad
4   A'i chalon yn ei llaw
I geisio – i geisio ceisio,
Am ysgrifennu *line*
O rywbeth wna ('os gwelwch chwi fod yn dda'),
8   I roi ar y Valantine.

'Pa beth,' gofynnais iddi,
'Pa beth y'ch chwi am ddweud?
Pa fath yw'r pennill ichwi
12   Am i mi geisio wneud?'
Er na ches fawr o reswm,
Darllenais yn y gwrid
Ar y rhosyn coch ydoedd ar ei boch –
16   'Ei garu e' – dyna gyd.

'A gaf fi ddweud y carech
Gael ateb yn yr ôl?
Beth i chwi'n feddwl, fyddech
20   Chwi'n 'styried hynny'n ffôl?'
Roedd dwedyd beth i ddwedyd
Yn ormod iddi o dreth!
Ond dwedodd wrth fynd am ddwedyd fel ffrind,
24   'Ei garu fe, ta beth.'

Mor wirion ydyw cariad,
Mor onest, hyn yw'r gân;
Er nas gall ddweud ei deimlad
28   Nis gall ei guddio'n lân;
Mae rhywbeth ynddo'n gadarn
A rhywbeth ynddo'n feth;
Er bod y byd yn ei gelu i gyd,
32   Dangosa beth, ta beth.

Watkin Hezekiah Williams 'Watcyn Wyn' (1844–1905)

43   The young woman and the Valentine

A young woman brimming with love came by
On an evening full of rain,
Her soul in her eyes
4   And her heart in her hand
To seek – to try to seek
To write a line
Of something that would do ('If you please')
8   To place in the Valentine.

'What,' I asked her,
'What do you want to say?
What sort of stanza do you
12   Want me to try to write?'
Although I did not get much sense,
I read in the blush
On the red rose that was on her cheek –
16   'Love him' – that is all.

'May I say that you would like
To receive an answer back?
What do you think, would
20   You consider that foolish?'
Telling me what to say was
For her too taxing!
But she said as she was leaving for [me] to tell him as a friend,
24   'Love him, no matter what.'

How innocent love is,
How honest, this is [the object of] the song;
Even though it cannot express its emotion
28   It cannot completely hide it [either];
There is something in it that is steadfast
And something in it that is irresolute;
Even though the world hides it completely,
32   Reveal a little of it, no matter what.

Watkin Hezekiah Williams 'Watcyn Wyn' (1844–1905)

Source

Watcyn Wyn, *Caneuon Watcyn Wyn* [The Songs of Watcyn Wyn] (Llandilo: D. W. and G. Jones, [1871]), p. 65

Date

Sometime during the period 1860–71.

Locality
Not noted; the author lived in Carmarthenshire.

Measure
7.6.7.6.7.6.10.6. with some fluidity in lines 7 and 8.

44 Dechre pennill i ofyn Malandein ar fesur a elwir
'Young Watkin's Delight'

Rwy'n danfon, dros eich geneth fedydd, dwys arwydd i chwi
o serch,
Dan enw Malandein, modd doniol, o ddwylo'r foddol ferch;
Y lawen seren loyw sydd yn swnio heb wâd, a sôn y bydd
4   Ac aml gofio, ni wn i a wyddoch, amdanoch nos a dydd.
Hi ŵyr fod gan'och galon ethol o styriol w'llys da,
Yr hon heb ffael a wrendy'n ffyddlon bob cwynion, ni nacâ;
Ac felly'n wir fe alle fod hyn yma'n rhwyddedd dan y rhod
8   Yn annog peth ar ferch ifienedd, awch clirwedd, ganu'ch clod;
Naturiaeth geneth gu sydd am ymwychu'n wir
Gael bod yn hoyw fenyw feinael, lwys arael, blodau'r sir.
Os gwnewch chwi jeinio, John, at helpu harddu hon
12   Hi fydd gan falched â'r aderyn, yn gryno forwyn gron,
A'i swydd hi tua'r Pasg, main ei gwasg, meinwen gu,
A fydd eich ca'mol yn ddiamgen, modd llawen ymhob llu.
Mae'r gangen ffraethwen ffri yn deud y gw'rantiff hi
16   Y ceiff hi anrheg wiwdeg odiaeth, wych, helaeth, gennych chwi.

John Rees

Source
Cwrtmawr 41B, i, 17

Date
14 February 1873.

44 The commencement of a stanza requesting a Valentine
on the measure known as 'Young Watkin's Delight'

I am sending you, on behalf of your goddaughter, a serious token
of love
In the name of Valentine, in eloquent style, from the hands of the
fine young woman;
The happy bright star speaks without denial, and she mentions
4 And frequently calls to mind, I do not know whether you are
aware of this, [matters] concerning you night and day.
She knows that you have a choice heart, [one] of thoughtful
goodwill,
Which unfailingly attends faithfully to all plaints, it does not refuse;
And so indeed it is possible that this, easily under the sun,
8 Encourages a young woman somewhat to sing your praise [with]
bright eagerness;
It is in the nature of a cherished young woman to beautify herself
indeed
In order to become a vivacious woman with slender eyebrows,
comely [and] pleasant, the most superior in the county.
If you, John, will join [us] to assist in adorning her
12 She will be as happy as the bird, a trim young woman,
And at about Easter her task will be, slim of waist, beloved young
woman,
To praise you, no less, in a joyous manner in every assembly.
The readily eloquent bough declares that she will guarantee
16 That she will receive from you a very worthy and flattering,
excellent, generous gift.

John Rees

Locality
The poem was written on behalf of Mary Williams, the daughter of
Dafydd Williams of Cwm Cilan, to be sent to John (line 11), her godfather.
Cwm Cilan is a farm in Llanrhaeadr-ym-Mochnant in Powys.

Measure
'Young Watkin's Delight' was not found in the collections.

45 [Dideitl]

Fenyw fwyn, gwrando gŵyn
Un ar farw er dy fwyn.

Evan Evans 'Ieuan Glan Geirionydd' (1795–1855)

Sources
'Ymdrech Serch a Rheswm' [The Conflict between Love and Reason], in
Evan Evans, *Geirionydd: cyfansoddiadau barddonol, cerddorol, a rhydd-
ieithol, y diweddar Barch. Evan Evans, (Ieuan Glan Geirionydd)* [Geir-
ionydd: the poetic, musical, and prose compositions of the late Rev.
Evan Evans, (Ieuan Glan Geirionydd)] (Rhuthun: I. Clarke, 1862), pp.
172–4 Isaac Foulkes 'Llyfrbryf', 'Y Ddau Efell' [The Twins], *Y Traethodydd*
[The Essayist] (1875), 199, published in 1875 as a book entitled *Y ddau
efell neu Llanllonydd: rhamant* [The twins or Llanllonydd: a romance]
(Treffynnon: P. M. Evans, 1875?)
[Isaac Foulkes 'Llyfrbryf', 'Llanllonydd: ei ddau efaill, a rhai o'i bobl
eraill' [Llanllonydd: its twins, and some of its other inhabitants], *Y Cymro*,
26 October 1899, 2

Date
1875.

Locality
Written by a Caernarfonshire (now Gwynedd) man, and featured in
Llanllonydd, a fictional village.

Note
A couplet sent in a Valentine card by the lovesick Ifan to Jemima Sophia
Rees in a 'rhamant' (romance) first published in *Y Traethodydd* [The
Essayist], a quarterly literary journal, later the same year as a novel, and
in 1899 in *Y Cymro* [The Welshman], a national weekly newspaper. It
is the opening couplet of a six-stanza song entitled 'Ymdrech Serch a
Rheswm' [Conflict between Love and Reason], written by Evan Evans

45 [Untitled]

Darling young woman, listen to the plaint of
One who is at the point of death because of you.

Evan Evans 'Ieuan Glan Geirionydd' (1795–1855)

'Ieuan Glan Geirionydd' (1795–1855), to be sung to 'Roslin Castle'.
The opening stanza is as follows:

Fenyw fwyn, gwrando gŵyn
Un sy'n curio er dy fwyn;
Mae i mi ddirfawr gri
Ddydd a nos yn d'achos di.
Wylo'r dŵr rwy' eiliw'r don,
Gwêl fy mriw o tan fy mron:
Nid oes arall feddyg imi,
Ond tydi, lili lon;
Dy bryd, flodau'r byd,
Sydd o hyd i'm pruddhau:
Cofio'th lendid hyfryd di
Wna i mi fawr drymhau:
Rwy' fel un mewn carchar caeth,
Drwy fy oes yn dioddef aeth,
Ac o blegid saethau Ciwpid,
Darfu'm gwrid, gofid gwaeth.

Measure

Rhyming couplet, 6.7; noted by Benjamin Jones in the village of Pont-
rhyd-y-bont [Four Mile Bridge] near Holyhead, Anglesey, the tune
'Fenyw Fwyn' (Gentle Damsel) appears in a letter to the editor in a
journal edited by William Thomas Rees 'Alaw Ddu', *Cerddor y Cymry*
[The Musician of the Welsh] (Medi [September], 1886), 136; see also
Rhidian Griffiths, 'Ystafell yr Hen Alawon' [The Old Tunes' Room],
CG, 7 (1984), 46.

46 [Dideitl]

Nelly annwyl, mawr fu'm ffwdan
I gael darlun o dy hunan,
Y tebycaf gefais allan
4   I dy lun yw llun dylluan.

Cymer hon, a dod hi'n gynnes,
Ddarlun cywir, yn dy fynwes
Nes y caffot un fwy tebyg
8   I foddloni dy ddychymyg.

Dienw

Source
Twr y Dderi, 'Nodion o Geredigion' [Notes from Ceredigion], *Llais y Wlad* [Country Voice], 25 February 1876, 7

Date
1876.

Locality
Possibly Betws Bledrws near Lampeter in Ceredigion. The pseudonym 'Tŵr y Dderi' relates to the Derry Ormond Tower, a Grade II listed folly erected between 1821 and 1824 by unemployed men and funded by John Jones, squire of Derry Ormond, the local mansion.

46 [Untitled]

Dear Nelly, I have gone to great trouble
To find a picture of you,
The item I found that is most
4   Like a picture of you is the picture of an owl.

Take this, and place it warmly,
True picture, in your bosom
Until you find one that is more likely
8   To satisfy your imagination.

Anonymous

Note
Verses sent to Nelly Jones allegedly by the son of the neighbouring farmer, but local rumour suggested that it was Nelly's jealous cousin who sent them in the hope of gaining the farmer's son for herself. The inevitable reply arrived at the farmhouse in two days' time (see poem 47).

Measure
Hen bennill

47   [Dideitl]

Mae dy rodd yn ddiogel ddigon
A chredaf ddyfod hon o'th galon,
Ond pam anghofiaist gadw'i thafod
4   I grio'r nos ar ôl rhianod?

Ystlum du y nos a wrendy
Gri'r ddylluan rhwng y llwyni;
Cymer rhain a gweld a ddaw
8   'R noson nesaf y cei groesaw.

Myn rhai adael eu perthnasau
Ar y plwy i dreulio'u dyddiau;
Yn lled debyg mynnaist tithau
12   Daflu'th nain i'm cwpwrdd innau.

Nelly Jones

Source
Twr y Dderi, 'Nodion o Geredigion', 7

Date
1876.

Locality
Ceredigion, see poem 46, *Locality*.

47 [Untitled]

Your gift is safe enough
And I believe that it came from your heart,
But why did you forget to keep its tongue
4   To cry after the young women at night?

The black bat of the night listens to
The cry of the owl in the woods;
Take these and see if it comes
8   The next night when you are welcomed.

Some insist upon leaving their relatives
To spend their remaining days on the parish [i.e. in receipt of
     poor relief];
In quite a similar vein, you insisted on
12   Throwing your grandmother into my cupboard.

Nelly Jones

Note
Verses sent by Nelly Jones to the son of the neighbouring farmer, in reply to two stanzas alledgedly sent to her by him (see poem 46).

Measure
Hen bennill

48 Valentine's Day

Mae bechgyn a merched *on Valentine's Day*
Yn rhyfedd mewn gwaith ac mewn siarad,
Fe'u gwelir drwy'r wlad, yn y pentref a'r dre',
4   Yn wallgo addoli 'duw Cariad';
Bydd hogyn fan yma, a hogen fan draw,
Yn sibrwd 'Hoi! dwed, gest ti folant?'
A'r ateb fydd, 'Do, cefais ddwsin neu ddau,
8   A gyrrais un iawn i fy Rolant.'

A diwrnod neilltuol yw'r *Valentine's Day*,
Mae'n cynnwys yn gyfan fis Chwefror,
A gwn trwy hanesiaeth, o lwybr *Fair play*,
12   Ei fod weithiau ddyddiau yn rhagor;
Ac oni buasai grwgnachrwydd ein Dick,
A phrinder mawr arian ffyddloniaid,
Byddai'r ŵyl aflêr yma yn glynu mewn bod
16   Hyd ddydd cyntaf Ebrill, 'Gŵyl ffyliaid'.

Mae y si ar led trwy ein tref fawr ni
Fod rhai wedi bron â llewygu,
A hynny wrth dderbyn yn sydyn i'w rhan
20   Gynhyrchion tlws talaith y Bwci;
Ca'dd merch lân rhyw *farmer* 'r anrhydedd, medd Mam,
O dderbyn trwy'r post *pretty baby*;
A 'nawr y mae honno *in practice to come*
24   *A splendid and beautiful Mammy.*

Daeth darlun hynod i'r tŷ draw
I'r luniaidd Hannah Murphy,
Sef clamp o garw, goeliaf fi,
28   A'i drwyn fel cynffon milgi;
Am hyn mae Hannah, druan un,
Yn wallgo rodio allan,
A bygwth mae *Poor Dick* y Post
32   Am gludo'r darlun aflan.

48 Valentine's Day

Young men and young women on Valentine's Day
Are strange in work and speech,
They are to be seen throughout the land, in village and town,
4   Crazily worshipping the 'god of Love';
A young man here, a young woman there,
Whispering 'Hey! Tell me, did you get a Valentine?'
And the answer comes, 'Yes, I received a dozen or two,
8   And I sent a proper one to my Rolant.'

Valentine's Day is a special day,
It includes the whole of the month of February,
And I know from history, from the path of Fair play,
12   That it is sometimes days more;
And but for our Dick's grumbling,
And a great shortage of money on the part of the faithful,
This disorderly festival would remain in existence
16   Until the first day of April, 'Festival of Fools'.

There is a rumour abroad in our large town
That some were almost on the verge of fainting,
And that was when they received unexpectedly
20   The fair fruits of the land of the Phantom;
A farmer's pretty daughter had the honour, so Mam says,
Of receiving in the post [an image of] a pretty baby;
And now she in practice is to become
24   A splendid and beautiful Mammy.

A remarkable picture arrived at the house over there
[Addressed] to the comely Hannah Murphy,
Namely a great big deer, so I believe,
28   With a nose like a greyhound's tail;
And because of this, Hannah, poor girl,
Has stormed off in a fury,
And is threatening Poor Dick the Post
32   For delivering the vile picture.

Ca'dd rhai fabanod mewn *long dress*,
Bron medru galw '*Mammy*';
Ond am eu *Daddies*, druain bach,
36 Nis gwyddent pwy oedd rheiny.

A gyrrodd Marged Uwch-y-fron
At John o Dan-yr-allt
Rhyw ddarlun gwych ohoni ei hun,
40 Pan wedi colli ei gwallt.

Cynhyrfodd John wrth weld y peth,
A gyrrodd nôl yn union,
Iawn ddarlun iddi ohono ei hun
44 Heb drwyn, a'i goesau'n geimion.

Ac O! bu rhai mor benwan ffôl
Â mofyn folant ddimai
A gyrru honno gyda'r Post
48 Dan effaith drwg dymherau;

I geisio dial, os bai modd,
Ar y derbynnydd, druan,
Am na wnâi'r cariad fod yn bur:
52 At glacwydd, neu hen wylan.

Hoi! ferched, peidiwch bod mor ffôl
Â chredu mewn folantau
Yn bethau nerthol er eich gwneud
56 Yn enwog am gariadau;
A chwithau, fechgyn, yr un modd,
Gochelwch ferch y folant,
Oblegid mentraf ddweud a fydd,–
60 *A Tower for a Tyrant.*

Hen Slym, Aberteifi

Some had babies in long dress,
Almost able to call out 'Mammy';
But as for their Daddies, poor things,
36   They did not know who they were.

And Marged Uwch-y-fron sent
John of Dan-yr-allt
Some fabulous picture of herself
40   When she was bald.

John became agitated on seeing the thing,
And he sent back immediately
A true picture of himself
44   Without a nose, and with bandy legs.

And O! some were so ridiculously foolish
As to buy a comic Valentine
And send it through the Post
48   Under the influence of a bad temper.

In an attempt, if that were possible, to take revenge
On the recipient, poor wretch,
Because the lover refused to be true:
52   To a gander, or an old gull.

Hey! young women, do not be so foolish
As to believe that Valentines
Are powerful devices for making you
56   Notorious for having lovers;
And similarly you, young men,
Beware of the Valentine girl,
For I venture to state how it will turn out, –
60   A Tower for a Tyrant.

Hen Slym [Old Slum], Cardigan

Source
'The Poet's Corner', *The Cardigan Observer*, 15 March 1879, 1

Date
1879.

Locality
Probably Cardigan in the county of Ceredigion.

Note

The poem narrates the story of the inhabitants of a particular town, probably Cardigan, on St Valentine's Day morning and recounts some of the experiences of Dick the Postman as he delivers cards and parcels on 14 February 1879. The pen name 'Hen Slym' suggests a female author: 'slym' can mean a squalid urban area, but is also a derogatory word for a woman of loose sexual morals.

Measure

Stanzas 1–3: 11.9.11.9.11.9.11.9.; stanza 4: 8.7.8.7.D; stanza 5: 8.7.8.7.; stanza 6: 8.6.8.6.; stanzas 7–9: 8.7.8.7.; stanza 10: 8.7.8.7.D.

49 Valentine 'r hen ferch

Priodi, priodi mae'r merched o hyd,
Os na chânt briodi ni thâl hi ddim byd;
Ond gwell fyddai gennyf na hynny, 'rwy'n siŵr,
4   Fyw ar gardota fy mara a dŵr.
       Mi fyddaf hen ferch, mi fyddaf hen ferch,
       Mor hyfryd yw bywyd a rhyddid hen ferch.

Mi welais rhai bechgyn lled ddifyr eu sgwrs
A chwyddent fy nghalon i weithiau wrth gwrs,
A gwelais rai eraill hardd, heinyf ar droed,
8   Ond undyn a briodwn, ni welais erioed.
       Mi fyddaf hen ferch, mi fyddaf hen ferch,
       Mor hyfryd yw bywyd a rhyddid hen ferch.

Mae dyn mor anwadal ag wyneb yr aig
A'i galon mor galed â chalon hen graig;
Mae'i feddwl hunanol yn chwyddo fel ton
12   A'i ben sydd mor feddal â phen *my chignon*.
       Mi fyddaf hen ferch, mi fyddaf hen ferch,
       Mor hyfryd yw bywyd a rhyddid hen ferch.

Daw Siôn y gŵr adref gan holi mewn brys,
'Shân, ble mae fy sanau? Shân, ble mae fy nghrys?'
A druan o Shani, rhwng cannwyll a nos,
16   Mewn penbleth yn ceisio rhoi clwt ar ei glos.
       Mi fyddaf hen ferch, mi fyddaf hen ferch,
       Mor hyfryd yw bywyd a rhyddid hen ferch.

Edrycha o'i gwmpas gan sythu mor *larch*
Â phe bai o wedi ei drochi mewn *starch*;
A gwnewch iddo giniaw, ni thâl hi ddim byd,
20   Mae gormod neu fychan o rywbeth o hyd.
       Mi fyddaf hen ferch, mi fyddaf hen ferch,
       Mor hyfryd yw bywyd a rhyddid hen ferch.

49 The old maid's Valentine

Getting married, the women are always getting married,
If they cannot get married it's no good;
But I would prefer over that, I'm sure,
4   To beg for my bread and water.
        I'll be an old maid, I'll be an old maid,
        How lovely is the life and the freedom of an old maid.

I have met a few boys whose conversation was quite interesting
And of course they sometimes made my heart swell,
And I have met a few others who are handsome, fleet of foot,
8   But a man whom I would marry, I have never seen.
        I'll be an old maid, I'll be an old maid,
        How lovely is the life and the freedom of an old maid.

Man is as fickle as the surface of the sea
And his heart as hard as the heart of an old rock;
His selfish mind surges like a wave
12   And his head is as soft as the head of my *chignon*.
        I'll be an old maid, I'll be an old maid,
        How lovely is the life and the freedom of an old maid.

Siôn, the husband, comes home inquiring in a flurry,
'Shân, where are my socks? Shân, where is my shirt?'
And poor Shani, between candle and night,
16   In a quandary trying to patch his trousers.
        I'll be an old maid, I'll be an old maid,
        How lovely is the life and the freedom of an old maid.

He looks about him and stands up straight as a larch
As if he had been immersed in starch;
And cook him a dinner, it won't do at all,
20   There is always too much or too little of something or other.
        I'll be an old maid, I'll be an old maid,
        How lovely is the life and the freedom of an old maid.

Yr hwyr fe eistedda'n un Cadi tan ddeg
I swnio ac ordro heb daw ar ei geg;
Na soniwch fod Shani yn neb, *dear me!*
24 Siôn bia'r dodrefn, a Siôn bia'r tŷ.
    Mi fyddaf hen ferch, mi fyddaf hen ferch,
    Mor hyfryd yw bywyd a rhyddid hen ferch.

Ond peidiwch â meddwl na chefais i chwaith
Gynigion rhagorol, do, do, lawer gwaith,
Ond tra byddo bywyd i mi a fy nghath
28 Gwrthodaf bob cynnig gaf eto 'run fath.
    Mi fyddaf hen ferch, mi fyddaf hen ferch,
    Mor hyfryd yw bywyd a rhyddid hen ferch.

William Thomas Rees 'Alaw Ddu' (1838–1904)

Sources
NLW, Baledi a Cherddi, vol. 25.128
NLW, Baledi a Cherddi, vol. 38.60
SFNMH 2038/114a held in St Fagans National Museum of History, Cardiff

Date
1880.

Locality
The copy held at St Fagans National Museum of History was printed by W. Jones, Gazette Office, Troed-y-rhiw, Merthyr Tydfil, in 1880. The author, William Thomas Rees 'Alaw Ddu' (1838–1904) was born in Pwll-y-glaw near Pont-rhyd-y-fen in Glamorgan.

Of an evening he sits in Cadi's [chair] until ten [o'clock]
To clamour and give orders without ever holding his tongue;
Don't mention that Shani is somebody, dear me!
24   Siôn owns the furniture, and Siôn owns the house.
        I'll be an old maid, I'll be an old maid,
        How lovely is the life and the freedom of an old maid.

But don't think that I also have not had
Excellent offers, yes, yes, many times,
But while there is life for me and my cat
28   I will refuse every offer that I will yet have, just the same.
        I'll be an old maid, I'll be an old maid,
        How lovely is the life and the freedom of an old maid.

William Thomas Rees 'Alaw Ddu' (1838–1904)

Note

The poem is subtitled 'Siân Llwyd, Bwth Unig, at yr hen lanc, Siôn Wmffre, Llwyn Dedwydd: y Bwthyn yng nghanol y Wlad' [Jane Lloyd, Lonely Cottage, to the bachelor, John Humphrey, Grove of Contentment: the Cottage in the depths of the Countryside].

Measure

The song can be sung to the popular 'Mae Robin yn swil' ['Robin's so shy']; the music was composed by John Owen 'Owain Alaw'.

50 Valentine

Cyflwynedig i W. Owen, mebyn ieuangaf Mr a Mrs Owen, New Inn,
Llanrwst, delw brydferth o'i ddiweddar daid o Drefriw

O! fy hollol afallen, – dew agwedd,
　　Digon o *ddau* fachgen;
　　Dod di, er mwyn dy daid hen,
4　　Law i mi, William Owen.

Fy nghariad bach, gwell bachgen – nis gwelais
　　Ei gael dan law'r awen;
　　Ar wybr New Inn, ni cheir wên
8　　Haul mwy na William Owen.

Hardd yw'r fad leuad lawen, – hardd yw'r wawr
　　Ar ddring drwy'r ffurfafen;
　　Mil harddach boch goch, a gwên, –
12　　Liwiau Mai, William Owen.

Ei god fo'n llawn defnydd gwên, – a'i hen boc
　　Byth yn cynnwys sofren;
　　Na ddoed dim, hyd ddyddiad hen,
16　　I lymhau William Owen.

Crea'i ysbryd, drwy'r Croesbren – O! Dduw hael,
　　Ar dy ddelw loyw-wen;
　　Pwys fyth na foed, hyd oed hen,
20　　Ym meiau William Owen.

Maddeuant, meddai awen, – ac hir oes
　　O'r cryd i'r Iorddonen;
　　A Duw, mewn cyfamod hen,
24　♥　I mi a William Owen.

Robert Williams 'Trebor Mai' (1830–77)

50 Valentine

*Presented to W. Owen, youngest infant of Mr and Mrs Owen, New Inn,
Llanrwst, a beautiful image of his late grandfather from Trefriw*

O! my absolute apple tree, – plump in appearance,
    The equal of *two* baby boys;
  Give me, for the sake of your elderly grandfather,
4   [Your] hand, William Owen.

My little darling, I have not seen a better young boy
    Under the authority of the muse;
  Under the New Inn sky, there is no smile
8   Of the sun that is brighter than William Owen.

The joyous, auspicious moon is beautiful, – the dawn is beautiful
    As it climbs through the firmament;
  A thousand times more beautiful a rosy cheek, a smile, –
12   Colours of the month of May, William Owen.

May his purse be full of cause to smile, – and his old pocket
    Always contain a gold sovereign;
  Let nothing come, until he is a person of great age,
16   To impoverish William Owen.

Create his spirit, through the merits of the Cross, – O! bountiful God,
    In the image of your bright-white self;
  Never let there be emphasis, until old age,
20   On the transgressions of William Owen.

Forgiveness, says the muse, – and longevity
    From the cradle to the river Jordan;
  And God, in ancient covenant,
24   For me and William Owen.

Robert Williams 'Trebor Mai' (1830–77)

Source
[Robert Williams], *Gwaith Barddonol Trebor Mai* [The Poetic Works of Trebor Mai] (Liverpool: I. Foulkes, 1883), p. 164

Date
Published in 1883.

Locality
The Llanrwst–Trefriw area, in the Conwy Valley, north Wales.

Measure
Englyn unodl union.

51 Valentine i Dewi Havhesp

Dod reswm, wedi'i drwsio – ag awen
    Gywir, goeth, da Deio;
    Temlyddiaeth, dibabaeth bo, – os gelli,
4   Oherwydd enwi holl urddau honno.

Hyder eich holl ddefodau, – yw'r faner
    Rufeinig, yn ddiau,
    Godwch, chwi gerddwch ffyrdd gau,
8   Sodom y dyfeisiadau.

Nid 'twng', 'teilwng', a phob tâl, – hyd diras,
    Phylacterau hafal,
    Urddenwau swyddau'r dyn sâl,
12   A etyb i'r titotal.

Er dawn hyflawn, i aflwydd – â pobol,
    Braich y Pabau newydd;
    A balchder, gwacter, o'n gwŷdd
16   Is abred, – lwydda sobrwydd.

Yn y ceubren. *John Williams, Llangernyw 'Llenor o'r Llwyni'
(1827–1909)*

Sources
[Williams], *Gwaith Barddonol Trebor Mai*, pp. 315–16
'Yr Ysmaldod Dirwestol' [The foolishness of Temperance], *Y Drafod* [The
Transactions], 27 September 1918, 6

Date
Published in 1883.

Locality
Llangernyw, Conwy, north Wales.

Notes
Poems 51 and 52 form part of a poetic debate between John Wil-
liams 'Llenor o'r Llwyni' and David Roberts 'Dewi Havhesp' regarding

51 A Valentine for Dewi Havhesp

Do articulate reason, clothed – with the
      Sincere, exquisite muse, good Deio;
    Templarism, may it be free of papacy, – if you are able,
4   On account of the naming of all its (religious) orders.

The (self-)assurance of all your ritualism, – is the banner
      Of Rome, indubitably,
    Which you raise, you walk erroneous paths,
8   The very Sodom of inventions.

It is not 'oaths', 'worthy', and all payments, – wicked extent,
      Equal to phylacteries,
    Titles of honour for the offices of a contemptible man,
12   That form appropriate answers for the teetotaller.

In spite of an abounding blessing, people go to destruction,
      The arm of the new Popes;
    And pride, vanity, from our presence
16   Under deliverance, – will make sobriety prevail.

In a hollow tree. *John Williams, Llangernyw 'Llenor o'r Llwyni'
['Littérateur of the Groves'] (1827–1909)*

teetotalism, John Williams writing in support of abstinence and Dewi Havhesp arguing against.

Line 2 Deio, diminutive of Dafydd; a reference to David Roberts 'Dewi Havhesp' (1831–84).

Line 3 Temlyddiaeth, Templarism, refers to the establishing of Temples, non-denominational societies, to counteract the effects of a perceived increase in drunkenness in Wales.

Line 9 tâl may refer to the payment of indulgences.

Line 10 Phylacterau is used figuratively for a hypocritical observance of religious practices.

Measure
Englyn unodl union.

52 Valentine Dewi Havhesp

Wele ardeb, ac ebwch,
'Deryn nos – dwndwr hen hwch.

Valentine o fawl, yntê?
4   Awen biglwyd mewn bagle;
Llun hyll, cyw dylluan wen
Wincia obry mewn ceubren.

Valentine o foliant dall,
8   A Deio'n methu'i deall;
Rhy enwog, Deio, gŵyr dyn,
I gadw sŵn gyda Sionyn.

O.Y. Os oes gŵr wedi blino ar ei breswylfod, ac yn hoffi ei newid, yr wyf newydd dderbyn 'Hysbysiad o bwys'. Dyma fe: – 'Yn eisieu yn ddioed' –

Gwanwr barddoniaeth Gwynedd, – hyf gorrach
12   Yf gwrw'n ddiddiwedd,
    Yn Pen[ll]yn, i ganlyn gwedd
    Daw'r asynnod i'r Senedd.

Ymofynner yn Llety'r Awen. *David Roberts 'Dewi Havhesp'*
(1831–84)

Sources
[Williams], *Gwaith Barddonol Trebor Mai*, pp. 316–17
'Yr Ysmaldod Dirwestol', *Y Drafod*, 4 October 1918, 5

Date
Published in 1883.

Locality
The Llanfor–Llandderfel area near Y Bala in the former civil parish of Penllyn, Gwynedd.

52 Dewi Havhesp's Valentine

See here an image, and a groan,
Nightbird – bluster of an old sow.

A Valentine of praise, is it not?
4   An ashen muse on crutches;
An ugly image, a white owl chick
Winks from the lowest point in a hollow tree.

A Valentine of blind praise,
8   And Deio failing to understand it;
Too famous, Deio, goodness knows,
To make noises with Sionyn.

P.S. If a man has become weary of his dwelling place, and
would like to change it, I have just received an 'Important noti-
fication'. Here it is: – 'Wanted immediately' –

Penetrator of Gwynedd's poetry, – impudent dwarf
12   Who endlessly drinks beer,
At Pen[ll]yn, following a team of horses yoked together
The donkeys come to the Parliament.

Inquire at Llety'r Awen [The Muse's Dwelling Place]. *David Roberts
'Dewi Havhesp' (1831–84)*

Notes
Poems 51 and 52 form part of a poetic debate between John Williams
'Llenor o'r Llwyni' and David Roberts 'Dewi Havhesp' regarding teetotal-
ism, John Williams writing in support of abstinence and Dewi Havhesp
denouncing teetotalism.
Lines 8, 9: Deio, diminutive of Dafydd; a reference to David Roberts
'Dewi Havhesp' (1831–84).
Line 10: Sionyn, a version of Siôn, Welsh for John; a reference to John
Williams, the author of poem 51.
Line 13: Pen[ll]yn, a former civil parish in Gwynedd.

Measure
Ten lines of *cywydd*, followed by one *englyn unodl union*.

53 Cyflwynedig i'm cyfaill hoff Mr John Pritchard Parry,
Melbourne, Awstralia (gynt o Bryntirion, Nanmor,
Beddgelert)

Hed fy meddwl ar gyfeiliorn
Beunydd i dy gwmni, John,
Hed ar wibdaith tua Melbourne
4   Drwy'r gagendor dros y don;
Adgof am yr hen gyfeillach
Gynt fodolai rhyngom ni
Wna im' anfon fy nghyfrinach
8   Fel rhyw *valentine* i ti!

Torraf reol fanol ffasiwn
'Cyfraith caru' mab a merch,
Ond disgwyliaf y caf bardwn
12   Am wneud hyn at 'wrthrych serch';
Wel, fy annwyl hen gydymaith,
Sut mae'n dyfod – wyt ti'n iach?
Wyt ti dywed ar 'dir gobaith'
16   Ar ôl gadael Cymru fach?

Wyt ti eto'n dal i garu
Iaith a defion dy 'hen wlad'?
Wyt ti wrthynt yn ymlynu
20   A chael drwyddynt rhyw fwynhad?
Fydd gwladgarwch weithiau'n tanio –
Wedi llwyr orlenwi'th fron
Nes gwneud iti ddifyr seinio
24   Cerddi 'Gwlad y Bryniau', John?

Wyt ti yna'n mhresenoldeb
Gwyneb euraidd duwies Ffawd,
Ddim yn teimlo peth diddordeb
28   Yn 'r hen greigiog 'Nanmor dlawd'?

53 Presented to my dear friend Mr John Pritchard Parry,
    Melbourne, Australia (formerly of Bryntirion, Nanmor,
    Beddgelert)

    My thoughts fly astray
    Daily into your company, John,
    [They] fly on a trip to Melbourne
4   Across the wide abyss of the waves;
    Memory of the old friendship
    That existed between us in times past
    Makes me send my deliberation
8   As a sort of valentine to you!

    I am breaking the detailed rule of habit
    [Regarding] 'courtship customs' between a young man
            and woman,
    But I expect to be pardoned
12 For this [since] it concerns a 'love object';
    Well, my dear old friend,
    How is it going – are you well?
    Are you, tell me, in the 'land of hope'
16 Having left dear Wales?

    Do you yet still love
    The language and customs of your 'old country'?
    Do you hold on to them
20 And obtain some pleasure from them?
    Does patriotism sometimes fire [you] –
    Having completely filled your heart to excess
    Until it compels you to sing joyously
24 [The] songs of 'The Land of the Hills', John?

    Are you there, in the presence
    Of the golden face of the goddess of Fortune,
    Not feeling a little interest
28 In the old [and] craggy 'poor Nanmor'?

Ynte ydyw'th fro gynhenid
Eto'n annwyl gennyt, John?
Rhyfyg gofyn; digyfnewid
32   Fydd dy gariad byth at hon![1]

Dyma'r llannerch bu y beirddion
Rhys a Dafydd[2] gynt yn byw,
Ac o'i chreig a'i ffrydion gwylltion
36   Yn dadlennu meddwl Duw!
Lle i'r awen gael ei hafiaith
Yw'r baradwys farddol hon;
Wrth ddweud hyn, nid codi hiraeth
40   Ynot ti yw f'amcan, John!

Hon yw'r ardal bu'th gyndeidiau
Yn trigiannu er 'cyn co' –
Rhai aeth oll yng nghwrs blynyddau
44   Draw i'r llen, yn do 'rôl to;
Heddiw maent yn tawel huno
Yn hen fynwent oer y plwy',
A tho arall yn ymgrwydro
48   Hyd y lle troediasant hwy!

Dilys gyfaill, bydd dy galon
Dros y dyfnfor yn rhoi llam
I'th gartrefle yn Bryntirion
52   Lle y triga'th dad a'th fam –
Lle y treuliaist ran o'th fywyd
Heb un loes yn blino'th fron,
Gyda'th riaint, oriau'th febyd –
56   Nefoedd iti ydoedd, John!

---

[1] Mewn byr fywgraffiad o Rhys Goch, yn 'Ngorchestion Beirdd Cymru', dywed y clodfawr hynafiaethydd Cynddelw a ganlyn mewn perthynas â'i gartrefle: 'Saif Hafodgaregog, ei dreftadaeth, mewn man ag y gallai anian yn ei mawredd a'i gogoniant gorwylltaf o'r tir a'r môr ddylanwadu arno. Nis gwn am un gongl yn Nghymru a ddeil gymhariaeth am eiliad â'r lle hwn!'

[2] Rhys Goch Eryri a Dafydd Nanmor.

Or is your native haunt
Still dear to you, John?
[It is] a presumption to inquire; forever unchanging
32   Will your love be for this [country]![1]

This is the glade where the poets
Rhys and Dafydd[2] lived of old,
And from its rocks and wild rivers
36   Disclosed the [very] mind of God!
A place where poetic inspiration acquires its vigour,
[This] is [what] this poetic paradise [is];
In saying this, it is not my intention
40   To create in you a deep longing [for Wales], John!

This is the area in which your forefathers
Have lived from 'ancient times' –
All of whom have passed during the course of the years
44   Through the veil [dividing this world from the next], generation
        after generation;
Today they sleep silently
In the cold old parish graveyard
And another generation is roaming
48   The area where they [once] walked.

True friend, your heart
Will leap across the ocean
To your home in Bryntirion
52   Where your father and mother live –
Where you spent part of your life
Without one ache to fret your heart,
With your parents, your childhood hours –
56   It was heaven for you, John!

---

[1] In a short biography of Rhys Goch, in 'Gorchestion Beirdd Cymru' (lit. exploits or achievements of the Welsh bards), the celebrated antiquarian Cynddelw states as follows in respect of his home: 'Hafodgaregog, his birthright, stands in a location in which nature in all its force and wildest grandeur, from the earth and the ocean, influence him. I know not of one corner of Wales that can compare for one second with this place!'

[2] Rhys Goch Eryri and Dafydd Nanmor.

Gwell yw gadael yr encilion,
Y difyrrus amser gynt,
A chofnodi hen gyfeillion
60   Aeth o'n bro i'w bythol hynt;
Croes i hynny yw fy nheimlad,
Ond rhag rhoi i'th galon glwy'
Ni chroniclaf gyfnewidiad
64   Na chawn weld mohono mwy!

Y mae rhywun yn wastadol,
'Nôl y drefn, yn mynd tan len
Yn dy ardal enedigol
68   Sydd wrth droed y Wyddfa wen;
Os ei *phlant* sydd yn 'cyfnewid',
'Run o hyd yw'r bryniau ban –
'Run o hyd yw Moel Dyniewyd,
72   'Run yw'r Arddu a Chraig Llan!

Bellach, gyfaill, mae Namoriaid
Ddigon yn y wlad 'rwyt ti
(Bron mor amled â'r Madogiaid[3]
76   Sy'n Amerig yn ddi-ri);
I sefydlu Nanmor Newydd
Ac i gadw cynnyrch hon
Arni'n Bennaeth rhowch Namorydd,
80   Tithau'n Rhaglaw iddo, John!

Ond y 'pechod mawr' fydd wedyn
Y gwnewch, ar ôl cael eich rhan,
Godi rhyfel yn ein herbyn,
84   Fel y Mahdi yn Swdan!
Ni phroffwydaf ddim yn rhagor
(Waeth heb ddechreu 'cynneu tân'),
Neu cyhyd â'r daith o Nanmor
88   I Awstralia fydd fy nghân!

---

[3] Hiliogaeth Madog ab Owen Gwynedd, sef yr Indiaid Cymreig. – C.

It is better to leave the bygones,
The pleasant times of yore,
And record [the fortunes of] old friends
60   Who have left our neighbourhood [and gone] on their eternal way;
My inclination is contrary to that,
But to avoid wounding your heart
I will not chronicle change
64   That we shall never again see!

Someone or other is constantly,
According to divine providence, passing through the veil
In your home neighbourhood
68   At the foot of white[-tipped] Snowdon;
[Even] though her *children* 'change',
The lofty hills are ever the same –
Moel y Dyniewyd is still the same,
72   Yr Arddu and Craig y Llan [remain] the same!

Now, friend, there are Nanmorites
Aplenty in the land where you [live]
(Almost as numerous as the Madogwys [or Padoucas][3]
76   Who are in America, too many to be counted);
To establish New Nanmor
And to defend its prosperity
Appoint a Nanmorite as its Ruler,
80   [And] you yourself as his Regent, John!

But the 'great sin' that would then follow
Is that you, having obtained your position,
Would declare war against us,
84   As did the Mahdi in Sudan!
I will prophesy no more
(It is no use 'kindling a fire [of contention]'),
Or as far as the journey from Nanmor
88   To Australia will be the length of my song!

———

[3] The descendants of Madog ab Owen Gwynedd, namely the Welsh Indians. – C.

Cofion atoch, cofia dithau
Fyw o hyd yn fachgen da;
Boed i'th gwrddyd hirfaith ddyddiau,
92 A'r rhai hynny oll yn ha';
'Rwy'n dymuno yn ddiragrith
Y cei olud, parch a bri,
Ac wrth ddweud 'Amen' i'r fendith,
96 'Brysia adre', John, da chdi!'

Richard Griffith 'Carneddog' (1861–1947)

Sources
Barddoniaeth [Poetry column], *Y Genedl Gymreig* [The Welsh Nation],
24 June 1885, 6
Richard Griffith 'Carneddog', *Ceinion y Cwm* [The Beauties of the Valley]
(Tremadog: R. I. Jones, [1891]), pp. 49–51

Variant reading
Title: Valentine, cyflwynedig i'm cyfaill hoff Mr John Pritchard Parry,
Melbourne, Awstralia (gynt o Bryntirion, Nanmor), Chwefror 14eg, 1885
[Valentine, presented to my dear friend Mr John Pritchard Parry, Mel-
bourne, Australia (formerly of Bryntirion, Nanmor), February 14th, 1885]
(Griffith, *Ceinion y Cwm*, p. 49)

Date
14 February 1885.

Locality
Nantmor, between Beddgelert and Llanfrothen, Gwynedd.

> Greetings to you! Remember
> To live [life] always as a good young man;
> May you meet with a vast [number of] days [i.e. be blessed with
>   longevity]
> 92 And may they all be heydays;
> I sincerely wish
> That you should attain wealth, esteem and renown,
> And as I say 'Amen' to the benediction,
> 96 'Hurry home, John, I beg of you!'

Richard Griffith 'Carneddog' (1861–1947)

Notes

Lines 33–40 were omitted from Griffith, *Ceinion y Cwm*, pp. 49–51.

Line 34: Rhys Goch Eryri (*fl.* 1385–1448) and Dafydd Nanmor (born before 1440, died *c.*1490) were two local poets. Rhys Goch Eryri was possibly Dafydd Nanmor's bardic teacher. Dafydd Nanmor believed in tradition and aristocracy, and supported the political aspirations of the Tudors; Rhys Goch Eryri's poems reflect on the origin and purpose of Welsh poetry. See Dylan Foster Evans (ed.), *Gwaith Rhys Goch Eryri* [The Works of Rhys Goch Eryri] (Aberystwyth: Canolfan Uwchefrydiau Cymreig a Cheltaidd Prifysgol Cymru, 2007); Thomas Roberts and Ifor Williams (eds), *The Poetical Works of Dafydd Nanmor* (Cardiff: University of Wales Press, 1923).

Line 84 Mahdi: In 1881 Muhammad Ahmad bin Abd Allah proclaimed himself the Mahdi, redeemer of the Islamic faith.

Measure

8.7.8.7.D.

54 Fy Valentine

Byth, byth nid anghofiaf y boreu
Derbyniais y *valentine* fach
Wnaeth i mi anghofio'm blinderau,
4   Wnaeth glefyd fy nghalon yn iach;
Mi glywn sŵn troed yr hen gludydd
Tra troediai'r ystryd ar ei hynt,
A churo ein drws wnâi'r negesydd,
8   Ond curodd fy nghalon yn gynt.

I'm stafell, gan deimlo yn ddedwydd,
Yr euthum, a chloais y drws
Er mwyn im gael hamdden a llonydd
12   I farnu a oedd yn un dlws;
Rôl agor y blwch bach a'i gweled,
Llawenydd a lanwodd fy mron,
A theimlwn fy nghalon yn myned
16   I ofal 'r hwn roes imi hon.

Ni fedraf yn gywir ddisgrifio
Yr oll a gynhwysai i chwi;
Ond rhoddaf, er ceisio eich boddio,
20   'R hyn ganodd fy mhrydydd i mi:
Efallai mai gwawdio wna rhywun
Wrth ddarllen, ond gwawdied a fyn,
Nid oes is y nefoedd yr undyn
24   Ond bardd allai ganu fel hyn,

'Pa raid imi wrido wrth anfon
(Brydferthaf o ferched y byd)
I ddweud mai mwy annwyl i'm calon
28   Yw'th gariad na phopeth ynghyd;
Pe bawn yn cael cynnig ar Brydain,
A'i choron, er cymaint ei bri,
A chyfoeth holl wledydd y dwyrain,
32   Di-werth fyddai'r oll hebot ti.

54 My Valentine

Never, ever will I forget the morning
I received the little valentine
Which caused me to forget my troubles,
4   Which healed my lovesick heart;
I could hear the footsteps of the old bearer [of letters]
As he walked the street on his travels,
And the courier knocked on our door,
8   But my heart beat more rapidly.

I went to my room, feeling fortunate,
And I locked the door
So that I could have some respite and peace
12   To judge whether it was a pretty [valentine];
After opening the little box and seeing it
My heart was filled with joy,
And I could feel my heart enter
16   Into the care of the one who had given it to me.

I cannot exactly describe
To you all that it contained;
But, hoping to satisfy you, I will share
20   What my poet composed for me:
Someone may perhaps mock
On reading [it], but mock as they may,
There is no one under the heavens
24   Except a poet who could sing in this manner.

'Why should I blush as I send
(Most beautiful of all the women in the world)
To say that your love is more dear to my heart
28   Than everything [else] together;
If I were offered Britain
And her crown, as great as her reputation might be,
And the wealth of all the lands of the Orient,
32   It would all be worthless without you.

Y ddaear sychedig dderbynia
Yn llawen i'w mynwes y glaw,
Y ddafad a lama pan glywa
36 Ei hoen bach yn brefu fan draw;
Ond er mor anwyled a siriol
I'r ddafad ei hoenig fach hi,
Mae clywed dy lais di'n anhraethol
40 Mwy annwyl, fy oenig, i mi.

Mwy annwyl i mi ydyw'th gariad
Na rhyddid i'r caethwas bach du;
Mewn blinder mae'th fwyn gydymdeimlad
44 Fel olew ar glwyfau i mi;
Mae gweled dy lygaid serennol
A'th berson angylaidd, di-ail,
I mi yn gan mil mwy derbyniol
48 Nag ydyw i'r llygad yr haul.'

Os nad yw yn medru barddoni
Fe fedrodd ddweud rhywbeth a wnaeth
Im deimlo fy mod yn ei garu,
52 Ac ato fy nghalon a aeth;
Ei garu yr wyf yn angerddol,
A'i garu a wnaf tra bwyf byw,
A theimlo yr wyf mai hanfodol
56 I fwyniant fy mywyd i yw.

D. P. D. Aberdâr

Source
Barddoniaeth [Poetry column], *Tarian y Gweithiwr* [The Worker's Shield],
20 April 1877, 6

Date
1887.

Locality
Aberdare in the Cynon Valley area of Rhondda Cynon Taf.

Notes
A Valentine poem sung by D. P. D. of Aberdare on behalf of an

The parched earth receives
The rain happily into her bosom,
The ewe leaps when she hears
36   Her little lamb bleating yonder;
But despite how dear and delightful
Her own little lamb is to the ewe,
Hearing your voice is inexpressibly
40   Dearer, my little lamb, to me.

Your love is dearer to me
Than the freedom of the little black slave;
In adversity your gentle sympathy
44   Is as oil to my wounds;
Seeing your starry eyes
And your angelic character, without peer,
Is to me a hundred times more acceptable
48   Than the sun is to the eye.'

Even if he is unable to write poetry
He has succeeded in saying something that made
Me feel that I love him,
52   And my heart flew to him;
I love him passionately,
And I will love him all the days of my life,
And I feel that he is essential
56   To my enjoyment of life.

D. P. D. Aberdare

anonymous woman to her lover on receiving a Valentine offering in the post. David Price Davies (1843–1922), Ynys-lwyd, Aberdare, was a well-known public figure in the Aberdare area and gave his support to the Eisteddfod and other events: he is probably the author of this poem.
Line 12 A reference to the sending of 'pretty' and 'ugly' valentines.
Line 42 A rare reference to current affairs: The Slavery Abolition Act was passed in the UK in 1833; slavery was formally abolished in the US in 1865.

Measure
9.8.9.8.D.

55 [Dideitl]

Nid oes i mi ond dau elyn –
B'le bynnag af gwna rhain fy nilyn;
Nid y'nt ond dy lygaid tirion
4   A'm trywanant trwy fy nghalon.

Clywais unwaith enwi rhywun
Oedd â blodau yn ei dilyn;
Hawdd yw credu hynny'n ddilys
8   Gan bob un a welodd Gladys.

Melys ydyw addfed 'falau
Pan yn byngad mewn perllannau;
I fy meddwl mil mwy melys
12   Ydyw cusan pur fy Ngladys.

Pleth o fellt yw gwallt fy meinwen,
Eira purwyn yw ei thalcen;
Ceirios cochion ei dwy wefus, –
16   Dyna lun fy nghariad Gladys.

W. Llewelyn Williams (1867–1922)

Source
W. Llewelyn Williams, *Gwr y Dolau: neu Ffordd y Troseddwr* [The
Gentleman of Dolau: or The Way of the Criminal] (Caernarfon: Cwmni'r
Wasg Genedlaethol Gymreig, 1899), pp. 65–6

Date
1899.

Locality
A fictional village in the novel. W. Llewelyn Williams was born in Brown-
hill, Llansadwrn in the Tywi Valley in Carmarthenshire.

55 [Untitled]

I have only two enemies –
Wherever I go these follow me;
They are but your gentle eyes
4   That pierce me through my heart.

I once heard a person named
Who was followed by flowers;
It is easy to believe that to be true
8   By each one who has seen Gladys.

Ripe apples are sweet
When they grow in clusters in orchards;
A thousand times sweeter to my mind
12   Is Gladys's pure kiss.

My slender and beautiful woman's hair is a flash of lightening,
Her forehead is pure-white snow;
Her two lips are red cherries, –
16   That is how my sweetheart Gladys looks.

W. Llewelyn Williams (1867–1922)

Notes
Robert Williams, Robin y Teiliwr [Robin the Tailor] writes four Valentine
stanzas on behalf of William Rowlands, the local curate, to send to Gladys
Bowen.
Lines 5–6: a reference to the beautiful Olwen in the medieval Welsh tale
'Culhwch and Olwen'; wherever she walked, four white trefoils sprang
up in each of her footsteps.

Measure
Hen benillion to be sung to the tune 'Nos Galan', 'a typical *penillion*
tune used extensively in New Year's Eve gatherings. Traditional verses
and harp interpolations or nonsense syllables could be interwoven in
the air', see Kinney, *Welsh Traditional Music*, p. 54; for the tune see
Parry, *British Harmony*, p. 12, tune number 7.

56 [Dideitl]

Os fy llygaid yw'r gelynion
A'th drywanant drwy dy galon,
Gochel rhagddynt, enaid gwirion, –
4   Gwell yw cadw rhag gelynion.

Blodau gwynion oedd yn dilyn
Olion camrau ysgafn Rhywun;
Ni ches i'r fath dynged felys–
8   'Deryn du sy'n canlyn Gladys.

Os fy ngwefus sy fel ceiros
Yn dy ddenu ati'n agos,
Cofia'r 'deryn du, mor galed
12   Yw calonnau ceiros addfed!

Gwyn yw'r eira ar Eryri–
Gwynder sydd yn cuddio oerni;
Oerach nag oer eira'r mynydd
16   Calon Gladys at y prydydd.

Gwir fod 'falau pêr Glan Tywi
Dan y dant fel mêl yn toddi;
Her it ddweud ai pêr ai melys
20   Ydyw'r cusan sydd gan Gladys!

W. Llewelyn Williams (1867–1922)

56 [Untitled]

If it is my eyes that are the enemies
That are piercing you through your heart,
Avoid them, simple soul,–
4   It is better to keep away from enemies.

White flowers followed
The light footsteps of Someone;
I did not come by such a sweet fate –
8   It is a black bird that follows Gladys.

If my lip is like a cherry
That attracts you to draw close to it,
Keep in mind, black bird, how hard
12   The hearts of ripe cherries are!

The snow on Snowdonia is white –
A whiteness that conceals a coldness;
Colder than the cold mountain snow
16   Is Gladys's heart towards the poet.

It is true that the sweet apples of Glan Tywi
Are on the tooth similar to melting honey;
I challenge you to say whether it is delicious or sweet,
20   Gladys's kiss!

W. Llewelyn Williams (1867–1922)

Source
Williams, *Gwr y Dolau*, p. 70

Date
1899.

Locality
A fictional village in the novel; Glan Tywi is noted in line 17 and may be a reference to Glan Tywi, Abergwili in Carmarthenshire; Glan Tywi, Llanarthne in Carmarthenshire; Glan Tywi near Llandeilo Fawr in Carmarthenshire; Glan Tywi near Llanegwad in Carmarthenshire; Glan Tywi near Llanwrda in Carmarthenshire; Glan Tywi near Llanymddyfri in Carmarthenshire; or Glan Tywi near Myddfai in Carmarthenshire. W. Llewelyn Williams was a radical Liberal Party politician and became Member of Parliament for Carmarthen in 1906.

Notes

Five Valentine stanzas written by the fictional Gladys Bowen in reply to the four Valentine stanzas sent to her by the fictional William Rowlands, the local curate. Gladys Bowen, in the novel, returns the card that had cost him half a crown with the above stanzas written on it.

Lines 5–6: a reference to the beautiful Olwen in the medieval Welsh tale 'Culhwch and Olwen'; wherever she walked, four white trefoils sprang up in each of her footsteps.

Measure

Hen benillion to be sung to the tune 'Nos Galan', see poem 55 *Measure*.

57 Y Falenten Hyll

Rwy'n diolch am eich darlun,
  Y mae e'n ddarlun da;
Rwyf wedi torri'm hesgyrn
4   Efo Ha! Ha! Ha!
Pwy wnaeth eich darlun, Catrin,
  Darlun mor dda?
Mae'n werth y byd o chwerthin,
8   O Ha! Ha! Ha!

Yr wyf yn fachgen gwirion,
  Heblaw yn fachgen da,
Oherwydd torri'm calon
12   Efo Ha! Ha! Ha!
Ni thorraf byth fy nghalon
  O eisiau 'ch llaw fach wen,
Ond gallaf dorri'm calon
16   Wrth chwerthin am eich pen.

J. Ceiriog Hughes (1832–87)

Sources

J. Ceiriog Hughes, *Oriau'r Hwyr* [The Evening Hours] (Wrexham: Hughes and Son, 1872), p. 100

Stevens, *Arferion Caru*, p. 87

Date

The second half of the nineteenth century.

57   The Ugly Valentine

> I thank you for your picture,
> > It is a good picture;
> I have broken my bones
4 > > With Ha! Ha! Ha!
> Who drew your picture, Catrin,
> > Such a good picture?
> It is worth the [whole] world in laughter,
8 > > Oh Ha! Ha! Ha!
>
> I am a simple boy,
> > As well as being a good boy,
> Because my heart has been broken
12 > > With Ha! Ha! Ha!
> I shall never break my heart
> > For the want of your small white hand,
> But I can break my heart
16 > > By laughing at you.

J. Ceiriog Hughes (1832–87)

Locality

Not noted; the author lived in Caersws in Powys in 1872, the year *Oriau'r Hwyr* was published.

Notes

Catrin received this poem in response to the photograph (of herself) she had previously sent Ceiriog.

Measure

7.6.7.4.D with some fluidity in lines 4, 6, 12 and 16.

58   [Dideitl]

Ni fuasai'n rhaid it yrru
Dy lun ar bapur wedi'i dynnu,
Gan fy mod i'n gwybod gystled
4   Nad oedd yr un i'w chael gyn hylled.

Gwell gen i yw cael fy ngalw
'N gi cynddeiriog, daliwch sylw,
Neu'n beth hylla' dan yr wybren
8   Nag yn gariad Meri o Gorwen.

Isaac Jones, Pedair a Dime, Uwchaled

Sources
Robin Gwyndaf Jones, 'Y Cwlwm sy'n Creu' [The Tie that Creates],
Transactions of the Denbighshire Historical Society, 15 (1966), 208–9
Stevens, *Arferion Caru*, p. 86

Date
The second half of the nineteenth century.

58 [Untitled]

You did not have to send
Your picture taken on paper,
Since I know all too well
4   That there is no one in existence that is so ugly.

I would prefer to be called
A mad dog, take notice,
Or the ugliest thing under the sky
8   Than to be called Mary of Corwen's sweetheart.

Isaac Jones, Pedair a Dime, Uwchaled

Locality
Historically Uwchaled rural district, now part of the district of Colwyn, Clwyd.

Measure
Hen bennill

59   [Dideitl]

       Folant fach, O! cerdd yn fuan,
       Paid ag aros dim yn unman;
       Disgyn lawr ar bost y gwely
4   Lle mae nghariad fach i'n cysgu.

       Dyma'r Folant wyf yn anfon
       Atat ti o fodd fy nghalon
       Gan obeithio caiff roesawiad
8   Gyda ti, fy annwyl gariad.

       Dienw

Source
Davies, *Hanes Plwyf Llandyssul*, p. 255

Date
The nineteenth century.

59 [Untitled]

Dear Valentine, O! travel swiftly,
Do not tarry at all in any place;
Alight on the bedpost
4 Where my dear love sleeps.

This is the Valentine that I send
To you out of the goodwill of my heart
Hoping that it receives a welcome
8 From you, my dear love.

Anonymous

Locality
Llandysul parish, Ceredigion.

Measure
Pennill telyn.

60 [Dideitl]

Hed y Ffolant, rhed yn fuan,
Paid ag aros dim yn unman;
Disgyn lawr ar bost y gwely
4   Lle ma nghariad fach i'n cysgu.

Mae llawer cnwc a llawer pant
A llawer cant o bethau
A llawer twmpath bach o frwyn
8   Rhyngdda i a 'nghariad.

Dienw

Source
A Valentine card in the ownership of Miss Mair Jenkins, Aberystwyth

Date
The nineteenth century.

Locality
Tal-y-bont, Ceredigion.

60 [Untitled]

Fly Valentine, travel swiftly,
Do not tarry at all in any place;
Alight on the bedpost
4   Where my dear love sleeps.

There are many hillocks and many valleys
And many hundreds of things
And many little clumps of rushes
8   Between me and my sweetheart.

Anonymous

Note
The lover offers two floating stanzas to convey his message: line 8 does
not rhyme with line 7 and examples a poet breaking off from the original
line to convey his own sentiment.

Measure
Pennill telyn.

61 Y Folant salw

Mae'r Folant yma'n dangos
Shwt fachan wyti, Tomos;
Pwy all roi cusan fyth ar swch
4   Sy'n fwrfwch fel yr andros?

Mi rown lapswchad iti
Pe gwisget shilcen deidi,
A britsh ben-lin, a gwasgod flot
8   A cot fel Ianto Cati.

Dienw

Source
D. R. Rees and Z. S. Cledlyn Davies, *Hanes Plwyf Llanwenog: y Plwyf a'i
Bobl* [The History of the Parish of Llanwenog: the Parish and its People]
(Aberystwyth: Welsh Gazette, 1939), p. 117

Date
The nineteenth century.

61 The ugly Valentine

This Valentine shows
The sort of lad you are, Tomos;
Who can ever plant a kiss on a snout
4   That is devilishly hairy?

I would give you a long wet kiss
If you would wear a tidy silk hat,
And knee breeches, and a plaid waistcoat
8   And a coat like Ianto Cati.

Anonymous

Locality
Llanwenog parish, Ceredigion.

Measure
Triban.

62 Y folant lân

Nid oes gennyf bunt i'w wario
Arnat, Cati;
Dim ond CALON alla i sbario –
4   Cymer ati.

Aeth saeth trwyddi i'r man pella,
Fel y gweli;
Dim ond ti a all ei gwella –
8   Ti sy â'r eli.

Dienw

Source
Rees and Davies, *Hanes Plwyf Llanwenog*, p. 117

Date
The nineteenth century.

62 The pretty Valentine

I do not have a pound to spend
On you, Cati;
It is but a HEART that I can spare –
4   Take a liking to it.

An arrow has pierced it to its furthest point,
As you see;
It is only you who can heal it –
8   It is you who has the healing ointment.

Anonymous

Locality
Llanwenog parish, Ceredigion.

Measure
8.4.8.4.

63 [Dideitl]

> Os wyt ti'n fy ngharu i
> Fel rydw i'n dy garu di,
> Bydd yn falantein i mi.

Dienw

Source

Betsan Jones, 'Betsan Jones ar Bobol a Phethau (Gyni Hi ei Hunan)' [Betsan Jones on People and Places (By She Herself)], *Y Clorianydd* [The Arbiter], 17 February 1910, 3

Date

The nineteenth century.

63 [Untitled]

If you love me
As I love you,
Be my Valentine.

Anonymous

Locality
Anglesey, or the historical county of Caernarvonshire, now Gwynedd.

Note
Y Clorianydd was a weekly Welsh-language conservative newspaper that circulated in Anglesey, Liverpool and Manchester.

Measure
7.7.7.

64   [Dideitl]

Mae'r rhosyn yn goch
Ac felly mae'th foch;
Ond y lle mwya'i swyn
4   Yw reit dan dy drwyn.

Dienw

Source
Jones, 'Betsan Jones ar Bobol a Phethau', 3

Date
The nineteenth century.

Locality
Anglesey, or the historical county of Caernarvonshire, now Gwynedd.

64 [Untitled]

The rose is red
And so is your cheek;
But the place of greatest charm
4   Is right under your nose.

Anonymous

Note
Y Clorianydd was a weekly Welsh-language conservative newspaper
that circulated in Anglesey, Liverpool and Manchester.

Measure
Hen bennill.

65 [Dideitl]

Y mae pwdin reis yn dda,
Gwell yw tatws, cig, a ffa;
Ond mae cariad sy'n parhau
4   Yn ganmil gwell na'r un o'r ddau.

Dienw

Source
Jones, 'Betsan Jones ar Bobol a Phethau', 3

Date
The nineteenth century.

Locality
Anglesey, or the historical county of Caernarvonshire, now Gwynedd.

65   [Untitled]

Rice pudding is tasty,
Potatoes, meat and beans are better;
But true love
4   Is a hundred times better than either.

Anonymous

Note
Y Clorianydd was a weekly Welsh-language conservative newspaper that circulated in Anglesey, Liverpool and Manchester.

Measure
Hen bennill.

66 Cerdd Ffolant i'r Beirniad

Yr wyt ti, JANE, yn ferch fach glên,
Yr wyf reit FONDA 'honat
A wir, rhen Siân, i ti mae nghân,
4   Ie wir, ti yw fy Ffolant.
Fe geisiais gofio'n santes *ni*
Yn Ionawr, ond anghofies
A nawr ar ŵyl yr estron Val
8   Fe geisiaf anfon neges.

Rwyf fi'n hen Gardi, weli di,
Meddyliais anfon cerdyn,
Fe wnes i 'styried bocs o *chocs*
12   A blode o siop Kevin,
Ond gan fod papur Gaynor fach
Mor lân a gwyn a handi
Fe steddes lawr a llunio cerdd
16   A dyma fi'n barddoni!

Wel cofia nawr, pan weli fi
Yn prynu stampiau'n ddyddiol,
Tu ôl i'r gwydr dyro wên,
20   'Rhen Jên, i ddyn bach fforddiol;
Ac os mai fi enillith Ted
Yn atgof bydd i aros,
Cans rhatach cadw tedi bêr
24   Na gwraig a'i gêr, a phlantos.

Dafydd Ifans (1949–)

Source
Ifans, 'Golwg eto ar y canu Ffolant', 33

Date
1996.

Locality
Penrhyn-coch, Aberystwyth, Ceredigion.

66 A Valentine Poem to the Adjudicator

You, JANE, are a fine young woman
I am quite FONDA you
And indeed, dear Siân, my song is for you,
4   Yes indeed, you are my Valentine.
I tried to remember *our* saint
In January, but I forgot
And now on the foreign Val's feast
8   I will try to send [you] a message.

You see, I am an old Cardi,
I had considered sending a card,
I thought of a box of chocs
12   And flowers from Kevin's shop,
But as dear Gaynor's paper
Is so clean and white and handy
I sat down and wrote a poem
16   And here I am writing poetry!

Now remember, when you see me
Buying stamps every day,
Behind the glass partition, give a smile,
20   Dear Jane, to a miserly little man;
And should it be I who wins Ted
He will be a permanent reminder [of our love],
For it is cheaper to keep a teddy bear
24   Than a wife and her gear, and little children.

Dafydd Ifans (1949–)

Notes
A Valentine poem written for Jane Ebenezer by Dafydd Ifans.
Line 5 santes *ni*, the Welsh patron saint of lovers is Saint Dwynwen
whose feast day is celebrated on 25 January.

Measure
8.6.8.6.D.

67   Ar Ŵyl Sant Ffolant

O na bai fy mhen yn feipen
Fel y gallet dan fy nhalcen
Lunio llyged, trwyn a gwefus
4   Sydd wrth fodd dy gusan melys.

O na bait yn llyn o gyrri
Llawn o sbeis a ffrwythau lyfli,
Llosgi nghorff a llosgi nhafod
8   A byth yn blino byta gormod.

Vernon Jones (1936–)

Source
Ifans, 'Golwg eto ar y canu Ffolant', 34

Date
1997.

Locality
Bow Street, Ceredigion.

O na bai fy mhen yn feipen
Fel y gallet dan fy nhalcen
Lunio llyged, trwyn a gwefus
4   Sydd wrth fodd dy gusan melys.

O na bait yn llyn o gyrri
Llawn o sbeis a ffrwythau lyfli,
Llosgi nghorff a llosgi nhafod
8   A byth yn blino byta gormod.

Ti yw'r corryn cyfrwys creulon
Sy'n nyddu gwe o gylch fy nghalon,
Tithe wrth dy fodd yn wherthin
12   O ngweld i'n strancio fel gwybedyn.

67   On Saint Valentine's Day

O that my head were a turnip
So that you could, under my forehead,
Craft eyes, nose and lip
4   That are pleasing to your sweet kiss.

O that you were a lake of curry
Full of spice and lovely fruit,
Burning my body and burning my tongue
8   And never tiring of eating too much.

Vernon Jones (1936–)

Note
The above two stanzas were added to and entered into a competition
at the National Eisteddfod of Wales in 2017 to write six stanzas enti-
tled 'Cariadon' [Lovers]. Some years previously the same two open-
ing stanzas had also served as the commencement of a longer series
of *hen benillion* entered into a competition at the National Eisteddfod
of Wales.

[O that my head were a turnip
So that you could, under my forehead,
Craft eyes, nose and lip
4   That are pleasing to your sweet kiss.

O that you were a lake of curry
Full of spice and lovely fruit,
Burning my body and burning my tongue
8   And never tiring of eating too much.

You are the cunning, cruel spider
That spins a web around my heart,
You delight in laughing
12   On seeing me struggle like a fly.

Rhoist ti sialens galed imi
Wedi iti 'fynd amdani'
Ar fy mhedwar yn y pwdel
16 Byth ers 'ny rwy'n fyr fy ngafel.

Ti, fy mara ffres, fy nghariad
Ti yw 'nhoes ym mhob cynhyrfiad,
Dwmplen ydwyt mewn daioni
20 A wynwnsen pob drygioni.

O na bawn yn feic Suzuki
Rhwng dy goesau'n canu grwndi;
Byddai'n nefoedd ar ben Trichrug
24 Wedi moelyd yn y mangrug!

Sbïwch yma, Mr Ynad!
Torres ffenest lloft fy nghariad
Cofiwch chi ma gwydr tene
28 Byth ers 'ny yw nghalon inne.

Dim ond pen yn drwm fel meipen,
Dim ond gwres fel tân eithinen,
Dim ond nicer dan y pilo,
32 Sycha ddeigryn wrth noswylio.

Measure
Hen bennill.

You presented me with a difficult challenge
After you 'went for it'
On all fours in a puddle
16   Ever since then my reach is short.

You, my fresh bread, my sweetheart,
You are my [lump of] dough in every excitement,
You are a dumpling in goodness
20   And the onion of every evil.

O that I were a Suzuki bike
Purring between your legs;
It would be heaven on Trichrug summit
24   After rolling about in the fine heather!

Look here, Mr Magistrate!
I broke my sweetheart's bedroom window;
Remember that my heart,
28   Ever since then, is thin glass.

Nothing but a head as heavy as a turnip,
Nothing but heat like gorse fire,
Nothing but a knicker under the pillow,
32   Wipe away a tear as you go to bed.]

68 Ar Gerdyn Gŵyl Sain Folant

> Rhowch heddiw yn dorch iddi – y gwyrda
> Ar gardiau eich cerddi;
> Addef wyf y rhoddaf i
> Harddach ganmoliaeth erddi.

4

John Emyr (1950–)

Source
Personal e-mail from John Emyr

Date
2005.

68 On a Saint Valentine's Day Card

> Present her today with a bouquet, – good men,
>> Of your songs on cards;
>> I avow that I shall give
4   More beautiful praise for the love of her.

John Emyr (1950–)

Locality
Cardiff.

Measure
Englyn unodl union.

69 Aberystwyth *I Gwen*
   (ar Ddydd Gŵyl Sain Folant)

Nid y môr 'rwy'n 'drysori, – nid hanes
    Y tonnau a'u torri
    Ar gerrig sy'n rhagori,
4   Ond golud oes dy gael di.

John Emyr (1950–)

Source
Robat Powell (ed.), *Awen Tawe* [Tawe Muse] (Castell-nedd: Gwasg Mor-gannwg, 2013), p. 14

Date
2013.

69   Aberystwyth *To Gwen*
     (on Saint Valentine's Day)

    It is not the sea that I treasure – it is not the story
          Of the waves breaking
       On rocks that excels,
4   But a lifetime's richness of having you [for my wife].

John Emyr (1950–)

Locality
Written in Cardiff, with Aberystwyth, Ceredigion, in mind.

Measure
Englyn unodl union.

Bibliography

Primary sources

Aberystwyth, National Library of Wales

Bangor Diocesan Wills, Bangor 1710/37.

Cwrtmawr 41B, i 'Barddoniaeth' [Poetry].

Cwrtmawr 128A, 'Llyfr Ofer Gerddi Margaret Davies 1738' [A Book of Frivolous Poems by Margaret Davies 1738].

Cwrtmawr 171D 'Casgliad o Hen Gerddi' [A Collection of Old Poems].

Cwrtmawr 225B 'Llyfr Dafydd Marpole' [The Book of Dafydd Marpole].

Cwrtmawr 231A 'Barddoniaeth Huw Morys a Robert Jones ...' [The Poetry of Huw Morys and Robert Jones ...].

J. Lloyd Williams Papers.

NLW 9B 'Welsh Songs and Ballads'.

NLW 19B 'The Poetical Works of John Jenkins ("Ioan Siengcyn"), of Cardigan'.

NLW 312D 'Brut, Poetry'.

NLW 346B 'Welsh Poetry by John Jones, Thomas Edwards, and Others'.

NLW 348B 'The Poems of Thomas Edwards (Twm o'r Nant)'.

NLW 431B 'Welsh and English Poetry'.

NLW 1062B 'Anterliwt a Barddoniaeth' [Interlude and Poetry].

NLW 1710B 'Poems'.

NLW 1940Ai 'Melus-seiniau Cymru' (1817–25) available online, digitized
     by the National Library of Wales.
NLW 1940Aii 'Per-seiniau Cymru' (1824–25) available online, digitized
     by the National Library of Wales.
NLW 4697A 'Llyfr Robert Evans, Syrior' [The Book of Robert Evans of
     Syrior].
NLW 9047A 'Ail Biser Sioned' [Sioned's Second Pitcher].
NLW 11987E, Gwilym H. Jones, 'Gweithiau Siôn Brwynog' [The Works
     of Siôn Brwynog], a typescript submitted to the National Eisteddfod
     of Wales held at Holyhead in 1927.
NLW 11990A 'Barddoniaeth ...' [Poetry].
NLW 21738B 'Daniel Jones: Cerddi [Poems]'.
NLW 23692A 'Dewi Dyssul: Barddoniaeth ...' [Dewi Dyssul: Poems].
NLW Baledi a Cherddi [Ballads and Poems].
Peniarth 244B 'The Book of Richard Wiliam, clochydd Llan Llyvni'.
The Penrice and Margam Estate Records, Literary Papers.
Sir John Williams's Ballad Collection.

Bangor, Bangor University

Bangor 952 'Copïo gwaith hen feirdd' [Copying the works of old poets]
     in the Lewis Davies Jones 'Llew Tegid' collection of manuscripts.
Cerddi Bangor.

Cardiff, Central Library

Cardiff 2.14 'Barddoniaeth ...' [Poetry ...].
Cardiff 3.68 'Cywyddau ...'.
Cardiff 4.10 'Gwaith Beirdd Cymru' [Works by the Poets of Wales].
Cardiff 4.156 'Barddoniaeth' [Poetry].

Cardiff, St Fagans National Museum of History

SFAWC 14.159.271.
SFAWC 33.335.1.
SFNMH 2038/114a.

London, British Library

'Valentine's day love letter, February 1477', British Library [Online].
     Available at: *http://www.bl.uk/learning/timeline/item126579.html*
     (accessed 20 March 2018).

Secondary sources

'Anghofio Hen Arfer', 'Y Golofn Gymraeg', *The Cambrian News and Merionethshire Standard*, 21 February 1919, 6.

Andronicus, 'Nodion Cartrefol', *Y Genedl Gymreig*, 17 February 1892, 5.

Barddoniaeth, *Tarian y Gweithiwr*, 20 April 1877, 6.

Barddoniaeth, *Y Genedl Gymreig*, 24 June 1885, 6.

Baring-Gould, S., and J. Fisher, *The Lives of the British Saints*, 4 vols (London: The Honourable Society of Cymmrodorion, 1907–13).

Barlow, Jeremy (ed.), *The Complete Country Dance Tunes from* Playford's Dancing Master (1651–ca.1728) (London: Faber Music Limited, 1985).

Bennett, Nicholas, *Alawon fy Ngwlad. The Lays of my Land. Collected by Nicholas Bennett of Glanyrafon. Arranged for the harp or pianoforte by D. Emlyn Evans*, 2 vols (Newtown: Phillips and Son, 1896), available online, digitized by the National Library of Wales.

Benson, Larry D. (ed.), *The Riverside Chaucer* (Oxford: Oxford University Press, 2008).

The Bible: The Book of Genesis; The Book of Joshua; The Song of Solomon; The Gospel according to Saint Luke.

Blackburn, B., and L. Holford-Strevens, *The Oxford Companion to the Year* (Oxford: Oxford University Press, 2003, repr. with corrections).

Bowen, Geraint, 'Ystyriaethau Drexelivs ar Dragywyddoldeb, Elis Lewis, Rhydychen, 1661', *Journal of the Welsh Bibliographical Society*, 8/2 (July 1955), 81–3.

Brookner, Anita, *A Misalliance* (London: Cape, 1986).

Butler, Alban, *Lives of the Fathers, Martyrs and Other Principal Saints* (London, 1756–9).

Canu Gwerin (Folk Song) (Cymdeithas Alawon Gwerin Cymru/The Welsh Folk-Song Society, 1978–).

Ceredigion, 'Valentine', *The Carmarthen Journal and South Wales Weekly Advertiser*, 13 February 1829, 4.

Charles, Thomas, *Geiriadur Ysgrythyrol* (Wrexham: Hughes and Son, 1892).

Cooper, Diana, and Norman Battershill, *Victorian Sentimental Jewellery* (Newton Abbot: David and Charles, 1972).

Crampin, Martin, 'Gwydr Lliw yng Nghymru/Stained Glass in Wales' [Online]. Available at: *http://stainedglass.llgc.org.uk/object/1796* (accessed 22 March 2018).

Cross, F. L., and E. A. Livingstone (eds), *The Oxford Dictionary of the Christian Church* (Oxford: Oxford University Press, 2005; third edition revised).

Crossley, Alice, 'Paper Love: Valentines in Victorian Culture', in Helen Kingston and Kate Lister (eds), *Paraphernalia! Victorian Objects* (London: Routledge, 2018).

Cyfraith Hywel [Online]. Available at: *http://cyfraith-hywel.cymru.ac.uk/ en/index.php* (accessed 22 March 2018).

Dafydd, Rhys, 'Rhys Dafydd Sy'n Deyd', *Y Clorianydd*, 25 February 1904, 3.

Davies, J. H., *A Bibliography of Welsh Ballads Printed in the Eighteenth Century* (London: The Honourable Society of Cymmrodorion, 1910).

Davies, W. Hubert, *Welsh Folk-Songs/Caneuon Gwerin Cymru* (Wrexham: Hughes and Son, *c.*1919).

Davies, W. J., *Hanes Plwyf Llandyssul* (Llandysul: J. D. Lewis, 1896).

D[avies], W[alter], *Eos Ceiriog, sef Casgliad o Bêr Ganiadau Huw Morys*, 2 vols (Wrexham: I. Painter, 1823).

Dictionary of the Welsh Language [Online]. Available at: *http://geiriadur. ac.uk/gpc/gpc.html* (accessed 23 March 2018).

Dictionary of Welsh Biography down to 1940 (London: The Honourable Society of Cymmrodorion, 1959) [Online]. Available at: *http://yba. llgc.org.uk/en* (accessed 22 March 2018).

'Digwyddiadau yr Wythnos: Cartrefol', *Baner ac Amserau Cymru*, 26 December 1906, 8.

'Dygwyl Falentein', *Y Cymro*, 18 February 1897, 5.

Edwards, D. Islwyn (ed.), *Cerddi Cerngoch: sef cyfrol o waith John Jenkins (1820–94)* (Felinfach: Pwyllgor Coffa Cerngoch, 1994).

Edwards, O. M. (ed.), *Beirdd y Berwyn 1700–1750*, Cyfres y Fil (Llanuwchllyn: Ab Owen, 1902).

Emyr, John (ed.), *Lewis Valentine, Dyddiadur Milwr a Gweithiau Eraill* (Llandysul: Gomer, 1988).

Encyclopaedia Britannica [Online]. Available at: *https://www.britannica. com/topic/Lupercalia* (accessed 22 March 2018).

Evans, Daniel, *Gwinllan y Bardd* (Llanbedr: J. Davies, 1872).

Evans, Dylan Foster (ed.), *Gwaith Rhys Goch Eryri* (Aberystwyth: Canolfan Uwchefrydiau Cymreig a Cheltaidd Prifysgol Cymru, 2007).

Evans, Evan, *Geirionydd: cyfansoddiadau barddonol, cerddorol, a rhyddieithol, y diweddar Barch. Evan Evans (Ieuan Glan Geirionydd)* (Rhuthun: I. Clarke, 1862).

Evans, Meredydd, *Hela'r Hen Ganeuon* (Talybont: Y Lolfa, 2009).

Evans, Meredydd, and Phyllis Kinney, 'Dauganmlwyddiant John Parry Ddall', *Y Casglwr*, 17 (1982), 8–9.

Evans, William (ed.), *Diary of a Welsh Swagman, 1869–1894* (South Melbourne: Macmillan Company of Australia, 1975).

Evening Express, 19 February 1895, 2; 15 February 1900, 4.

Fabian's Bay, 'Good Templarism', *The Cambrian*, 12 July 1872, 8 [Online]. Available at: *http://newspapers.library.wales/view/3331460/3331468/69/templarism* (accessed 6 December 2017).

Feeney, D., *Caesar's Calendar: Ancient Time and the Beginnings of History* (Berkeley and London: University of California Press, c.2007).

'The Festival of St. Valentine', *The North Wales Chronicle*, 17 February 1877, 3.

'Y Folantein (The Valentine)', *Journal of the Welsh Folk Song Society*, 2 (1914–25), 51–2.

Foulkes, Isaac 'Llyfrbryf', 'Y ddau efell; rhamant', *Y Traethodydd* (1875), 176–204, 261–87.

_____ *Y ddau efell: rhamant* (Treffynnon: P. M. Evans, 1875?).

[_____] 'Llanllonydd: ei ddau efaill, a rhai o'i bobl eraill', *Y Cymro*, 26 October 1899, 2.

Glasgow University Library Special Collections Department [Online]. Available at: *http://special.lib.gla.ac.uk/exhibns/month/feb2002* (accessed 5 April 2017).

Glenn, Thomas Allen (ed.), *The Family of Griffith of Garn and Plasnewydd in the County of Denbigh, as Registered in the College of Arms from the Beginning of the XIth Century* (London: Harrison and Sons, 1934).

Griffith, Richard 'Carneddog', *Ceinion y Cwm* (Tremadog: R. I. Jones, [1891]).

Griffiths, Rhidian, 'Alaw Ddu: o'r pwll at y gân', *Y Casglwr*, 35 (1988), 3.

_____ 'Ystafell yr Hen Alawon', *Canu Gwerin (Folk Song)*, 7 (1984), 39–57.

Griffiths, William Hughes (ed.), *Diliau'r Awen; sef, Crynodeb o waith Awenyddol y Diweddar Ardderchog Brydydd Evan Thomas Rhys, o Lanarth, Ceredigion (…) ac eraill* (Aberystwyth: D. Jenkins, 1842).

Haycock, Marged, *'Where Cider Ends, there Ale begins to Reign': Drink in Medieval Welsh Poetry* (Cambridge: Cambridge University Press, 1999).

'House of Commons Select Committee On Administration of Justice in Wales', *Parliamentary Papers*, 2 (London: House of Commons, 1820).

Howell, John (ed.), *Blodau Dyfed* (Caerfyrddin: J. Evans, 1824).

Hughes, Hugh (ed.), *Barddoniaeth Edward Morris Perthi Llwydion* (Liverpool: Isaac Foulkes, 1902).

Hughes, J. Ceiriog, *Oriau'r Hwyr* (Wrexham: Hughes and Son, 1872), p. 100.

Huws, Bleddyn Owen, and A. Cynfael Lake (eds), Genres *y Cywydd* (Aberystwyth: Bleddyn Owen Huws and A. Cynfael Lake, 2016).

Huws, Daniel, 'Gwisgo Merched â Mesurau'/'Dressing Women in Tunes', in Sally Harper and Wyn Thomas (eds), *Cynheiliaid y Gân: Ysgrifau i anrhydeddu Phyllis Kinney a Meredydd Evans/Bearers of Song: Essays in honour of Phyllis Kinney and Meredydd Evans* (Cardiff: University of Wales Press, 2007), pp. 180–8.

______ 'Melus-Seiniau Cymru', *Canu Gwerin (Folk Song)*, 8 (1985), 32–50.

______ 'Melus-Seiniau Cymru: Atodiadau', *Canu Gwerin (Folk Song)*, 9 (1986), 47–57.

Iago ab Dewi, 'Selection of Welsh Poetry', *Y Cymmrodor, the Magazine of the Honourable Society of Cymmrodorion*, 9 (1888), 1–38.

Ifans, Rhiannon, *Awstralia, Gwlad yr Aur: Teithiau i Awstralia drwy lygad y baledwyr Cymraeg* (Aberystwyth, Cymdeithas Lyfrau Ceredigion, 2008).

______ *Canu Ffolant* (Aberystwyth: Cymdeithas Alawon Gwerin Cymru, 1996).

______ '"O na bai fy mhen yn feipen ...": golwg eto ar y canu Ffolant', *Canu Gwerin (Folk Song)*, 21 (1998), 25–34.

J., J. Bronygadfa, 'Ancient Valentines', *Bye-gones*, 26 December 1894, 508–9.

Jenkins, Dan, and [David Lewis] 'Ap Ceredigion', *Cerddi Cerngoch: gyda detholion o waith 'Amnon II', 'Hywel' ac 'Aeronian'* (Lampeter: Cwmni y Wasg Eglwysig Gymreig, 1904).

Jobbins, Siôn T., *The Phenomenon of Welshness or 'How many aircraft carriers would an independent Wales need?* (Llanrwst: Gwasg Carreg Gwalch, 2011).

Jones, Benjamin, 'Fenyw Fwyn', *Cerddor y Cymry*, 4 (Medi 1886), 136.

Jones, Betsan, 'Betsan Jones ar Bobol a Phethau (Gyni Hi ei Hunan)', *Y Clorianydd*, 17 February 1910, 3.

Jones, Dafydd, *Blodeu-gerdd Cymry* (Amwythig: Stafford Prys, 1779; first edition 1759).

Jones, Dafydd Glyn, 'Hawl ac Ateb', *Efrydiau Athronyddol*, 57 (1994), 27–49.

Jones, Edward, *The Bardic Museum, of primitive British literature; and other admirable rarities; forming the second volume of the musical, poetical, and historical relicks of the Welsh bards and druids* (London: A. Strahan for the author, 1802); available online, digitized by the National Library of Wales.

_____ *Hên Ganiadau Cymru. Cambro-British melodies, or the national songs, and airs of Wales (…) never before published (…) to which are added variations for the harp, or the piano-forte, violin, or flute (…) this third volume is a continuation of the former two volumes of the Musical and Poetical Relicks of the Welsh Bards* (London: printed for the author, 1825); available online, digitized by the National Library of Wales.

_____ *Musical and Poetical Relicks of the Welsh Bards preserved by tradition, and authentic manuscripts, from remote antiquity, never before published* (London: printed for the author, 1784); available online, digitized by the National Library of Wales.

_____ *Musical and Poetical Relicks of the Welsh Bards preserved by tradition, and authentic manuscripts, from remote antiquity, never before published*, 2 (London: printed by A. Strahan for the author, 1794); available online, digitized by the National Library of Wales.

Jones, Gwenllian, 'Bywyd a Gwaith Edward Morris Perthi Llwydion' (unpublished MA thesis, University of Wales [Aberystwyth], 1941).

Jones, John, *Llên Gwerin Sir Gaernarfon* (Caernarfon: Cwmni y Cyhoeddwyr Cymreig, Swyddfa Cymru, [1908]).

Jones, R. M., 'Mesurau Cerdd Dafod', *Bulletin of the Board of Celtic Studies*, 27/4 (1978), 533–51.

Jones, Robin Gwyndaf, 'Y Cwlwm sy'n Creu', *Transactions of the Denbighshire Historical Society*, 15 (1966), 186–215.

Jones, T. Gwynn, 'Welsh Song Writing', *Journal of the Welsh Folk Song Society*, 2 (1914–25), 139–51.

Jones, Tegwyn, *Tribannau Morgannwg* (Llandysul: Gwasg Gomer, 1976).

Jôns, Jini, 'Sisial Godre'r Berwyn', *Llangollen Advertiser, Denbighshire, Merionethshire, and North Wales Journal*, 20 February 1914, 6.

Journal of the Welsh Folk Song Society (Bangor: Welsh Folk Song Society, 1909–77), vols 1–5.

Kerr, Rosemarie, 'Cywyddau Siôn Brwynog' (unpublished MA thesis, University of Wales [Bangor], 1960).

Kinney, Phyllis, 'The Tunes of the Welsh Christmas Carols (I)', *Canu Gwerin (Folk Song)*, 11 (1988), 28–57.

_____ 'The Tunes of the Welsh Christmas Carols (II)', *Canu Gwerin (Folk Song)*, 12 (1989), 5–29.

_____ *Welsh Traditional Music* (Cardiff: University of Wales Press in association with Cymdeithas Alawon Gwerin Cymru, 2011).

—, and Meredydd Evans, *Hen Alawon (Carolau a Cherddi)* (n.p.: Welsh Folk Song Society in association with the National Museum of Wales (Welsh Folk Museum), 1993).

Lamb, Charles, 'Valentine's Day', *The Essays of Elia*, Project Gutenberg, *www.gutenberg.org/files/10343/10343.txt* (accessed 20 March 2018).

Latham, Robert, and William Mathews (eds), *The Diary of Samuel Pepys*, 9 vols (London: HarperCollins, 1995).

Lee, Ruth Webb, *A History of Valentines* (London: Studio Publications, 1952).

Lewis, Elis, *Ystyriaethau Drexelivs ar Dragywyddoldeb* ([Oxford], 1661).

Lloyd, J. Y. W., *The History of the Princes, the Lords Marcher and the Ancient Nobility of Powys Fadog and the Ancient Lords of Arwystli, Cedewen and Meirionydd*, 6 vols (London: T. Richards, 1881–7).

Lloyd-Jones, J., *Geirfa Barddoniaeth Gynnar* (Caerdydd: Gwasg Prifysgol Cymru, 1931–63).

Love, Harold, 'That Satyrical Tune of "Amarillis"', *Early Music*, 35/1 (1 February 2007), 39–48.

Meurig, Cass, *Alawon John Thomas: a fiddler's tune book from eighteenth-century Wales* (Aberystwyth: National Library of Wales, 2004).

Millward, E. G. (ed.), *Blodeugerdd Barddas o Gerddi Rhydd y Ddeunawfed Ganrif* ([Abertawe]: Cyhoeddiadau Barddas, 1991).

Mitford, Mary Russell, Our Village: Sketches of Rural Character and Scenery [Online]. Available at: *https://books.google.co.uk/books?id=Fow7AAAAYAAJ&pg=PA505&dq=wooings+begun+on+the+Fourteenth+of+February&hl=en&sa=X&ved=0ahUKEwiSx4XcyI7aAhXEL1AKHfFeBPYQ6AEIKTAA#v=onepage&q=wooings%20begun%20on%20the%20Fourteenth%20of%20February&f=false* (accessed 26 May 2017).

Morgan, D. Densil, *Cedyrn Canrif: Crefydd a Chymdeithas yng Nghymru'r Ugeinfed Ganrif* (Caerdydd: Gwasg Prifysgol Cymru, 2001).

Morris-Jones, John, *Cerdd Dafod* (Rhydychen: Gwasg Prifysgol Rhydychen, 1930).

Morse, Fflur, 'Be my Valentine: Victorian Comic Valentines', 9 August 2018, Amgueddfa Blog: Amgueddfa Cymru – National Museum Wales, *https://museum.wales/blog/2016-02-09/Be-My-Valentine-Victorian-Comic-Valentines/* (accessed 3 April 2017).

New Catholic Encyclopaedia (New York: McGraw-Hill, 1967–96).

'North West Wales Dendrochronology Project: Dating Old Welsh Houses', *http://datingoldwelshhouses.co.uk/library/Hhistory/HHHafod-Ysbyty.pdf* (accessed 20 March 2018).

'Nuremberg Chronicle' [Online]. Available at: Cambridge Digital Library, University of Cambridge *http://cudl.lib.cam.ac.uk/view/PR-INC-00000-A-00007-00002-00888/1* (accessed 20 March 2018).

Obituary [for John Williams 'Llenor o'r Llwyni'], *The North Wales Weekly News*, 19 March 1909, 12.

Oruch, Jack B., 'St Valentine, Chaucer, and Spring in February', *Speculum*, 56 (1981), 534–65.

Owen, Trefor M., 'Three Merioneth Valentines', *Journal of the Merioneth Historical and Record Society*, 4 (1961–4), 72–4.

_____ *Welsh Folk Customs* (Cardiff: National Museum of Wales/Welsh Folk Museum, 1974).

Parry, John, *British Harmony, being a collection of antient Welsh airs, the traditional remains of those originally sung by the bards of Wales* (Ruabon and London: John Parry and P. Hodgson, 1781); available online, digitized by the National Library of Wales.

_____ 'To the Editor of the Cambro-Briton', *The Cambro-Briton*, 2 (London: John Limbird, 1821).

_____ *The Welsh Harper, being an extensive collection of Welsh music, comprising most of the contents of the three volumes published by the late Edward Jones*, 2 vols (London: D'Almaine and Co., 1839 and 1848); available online, digitized by the National Library of Wales.

_____ and Evan Williams, *Antient British Music; or, a collection of tunes, never before published, which are retained by the Cambro-Britons* (London: Mickleborough, 1742); available online, digitized by the National Library of Wales.

Parry, Rhian, 'An Ardudwy Crown Rental of 1623', *Journal of the Merioneth Historical and Record Society*, 15 (2009), 365–89.

Parry, Thomas (ed.), *Gwaith Dafydd ap Gwilym* (Caerdydd: Gwasg Prifysgol Cymru, 1979; third edition).

_____ (ed.), *The Oxford Book of Welsh Verse* (Oxford: Oxford University Press, 1962).

Parry-Williams, T. H., *Hen Benillion* (Llandysul: Gomer, 1988).

Pearsall, Derek, *John Lydgate* (London: Routledge and Kegan Paul, 1970).

Peate, Iorwerth C., *Diwylliant Gwerin Cymru* (Dinbych: Gwasg Gee, 1998; third edition).

Phillips, Bethan, *Pity the Swagman: The Australian Odyssey of a Victorian Diarist* (Aberystwyth: Cymdeithas Lyfrau Ceredigion, 2001).

______ *Rhwng dau fyd: y swagman o Geredigion* (Aberystwyth: Cymdeithas Lyfrau Ceredigion, 1998).

'The Poet's Corner', *The Cardigan Observer*, 15 March 1879, 1.

Pollen, Annebella, '"The Valentine has fallen upon evil days": Mocking Victorian valentines and the ambivalent laughter of the carnivalesque', *Early Popular Visual Culture*, 12 (2014), 127–73, available online at: *http://www.tandfonline.com/doi/ abs/10.1080/17460654.2014.924212?journalCode=repv20 DOI: 10.1080/17460654.2014.924212* (accessed 23 March 2018).

Powell, Robat (ed.), *Awen Tawe* (Castell-nedd: Gwasg Morgannwg, 2013).

Rasmussen, Ann Marie, 'Fathers to Think Back Through: The Medieval German Mother-Daughter and Father-Son Conduct poems known as *Die Winsbeckin* and *Der Winsbecke*', in Kathleen Ashley and Robert L. A. Clark (eds), *Medieval Conduct* (Minneapolis: University of Minnesota Press, 2001), pp. 106–34.

Rees, Brinley, *Dulliau'r Canu Rhydd 1500–1650* (Caerdydd: Gwasg Prifysgol Cymru, 1952).

Rees, D. R., and Z. S. Cledlyn Davies, *Hanes Plwyf Llanwenog: y Plwyf a'i Bobl* (Aberystwyth: Welsh Gazette, 1939).

Rees, William Thomas, 'Alaw Ddu', *Cerddor y Cymry* (Medi, 1886).

Reske, Christoph, *Die Produktion der Schedelschen Weltchronik in Nürnberg/The Production of Schedel's Nuremberg Chronicle*, Mainzer Studien zur Buchwissenschaft, 10 (Wiesbaden: Harrassowitz, 2000).

Roberts, Elizabeth Gloria, 'Bywyd a Gwaith Ioan Siencyn (1716–1796)' (unpublished MA thesis, University of Wales [Aberystwyth], 1984).

Roberts, Thomas, and Ifor Williams (eds), *The Poetical Works of Dafydd Nanmor* (Cardiff: University of Wales Press, 1923).

Roberts, W., *Crefydd yr Oesoedd Tywyll* (Caerfyrddin: A. Williams, 1852).

The Royal Commission on the Ancient and Historical Monuments in

Wales and Monmouthshire: County of Merioneth, 6 (London: HMSO, 1921).

'Sant Falantein', *Tarian y Gweithiwr*, 13 February 1896, 5.

Shipley, Joseph T. (ed.), *Dictionary of World Literature – Criticism, Forms, Technique* (New York: The Philosophical Library, 1943).

Simpson, Claude M., *The British Broadside Ballad and its Music* (New Brunswick: Rutgers University Press, 1966).

Smith, J. Beverley, and Llinos Beverley Smith, *History of Merioneth, volume II: The Middle Ages* (Cardiff: University of Wales Press on behalf of the Merioneth Historical and Record Society, 2001).

Stephens, Meic (ed.), *The New Companion to the Literature of Wales* (Cardiff: University of Wales Press, 1998).

Stern, S., *Calendars in Antiquity: Empires, States and Societies* (Oxford: Oxford University Press, 2012).

Stevens, Catrin, *Arferion Caru* (Llandysul: Gwasg Gomer, 1977).

Thomas, John, *Telyn Arian* (Llanrwst: J. Jones, 1857).

Trevelyan, Marie, *Folk-lore and Folk-Stories of Wales* (London: Elliot Stock, 1909).

Twr y Dderi, 'Nodion o Geredigion', *Llais y Wlad*, 25 February 1876, 7.

Vincent, David, *Literacy and Popular Culture: England 1750–1914* (Cambridge: Cambridge University Press, 1989).

Vittle, Arwel, *Valentine: Cofiant i Lewis Valentine* (Talybont: Y Lolfa, 2006).

Walters, Huw, 'Cerddi ymddiddan ynghylch ymfudo i Awstralia', *The National Library of Wales Journal*, 31 (Winter 2000), 381–400.

Wiliam, Aled Rhys (ed.), *Llyfr Iorwerth* (Caerdydd: Gwasg Prifysgol Cymru, 1960).

Williams, Arthur Howard, 'Adar yng Ngwaith y Cywyddwyr' (unpublished PhD thesis, Aberystwyth University, 2014).

Williams, D. G., 'Casgliad o Lên Gwerin Sir Gaerfyrddin', in E. Vincent Evans (ed.), *Transactions of the National Eisteddfod of Wales Llanelly, 1895* (London: National Eisteddfod Association, 1898).

Williams, G. J., *Hanes Plwyf Ffestiniog* (Wrexham: Hughes and Son, 1882).

Williams, Gruffydd Aled, 'Edmwnd Prys ac Ardudwy', *The National Library of Wales Journal*, 22 (1981–2), 282–303.

Williams, J. Lloyd, 'The Earlier Collections of Traditional Welsh Melodies', *Journal of the Welsh Folk Song Society*, 3 (1930–41), 14.

[Williams, Robert], *Gwaith Barddonol Trebor Mai* (Liverpool: I. Foulkes, 1883); reviewed in *Y Traethodydd* (January 1884), 132.

Williams, W. Llewelyn, *Gwr y Dolau: neu Ffordd y Troseddwr* (Caernarfon: Cwmni'r Wasg Genedlaethol Gymreig, 1899).

Williams, Watkin Hezekiah [Watcyn Wyn], *Caneuon Watcyn Wyn* (Llandilo: D. W. and G. Jones, [1871]).

Wilson, Adrian, assisted by Joyce Lancaster Wilson, *The Making of the Nuremberg Chronicle* (Amsterdam: A. Asher, 1976).

Wlock, Violet A., *Valentines* (York: Castle Museum, York for York Corporation, 1979).

Woodward, Marcus (ed.), *Gerard's Herbal: The History of Plants* (London: Studio Editions, 1994).

'Yr Ysmaldod Dirwestol', *Y Drafod*, 27 September 1918, 6; 4 October 1918, 5.

Verse forms

1. Strict-metre Welsh poetry

Cywydd (pl. *cywyddau*): a poem consisting of lines of seven syllables composed in rhyming couplets, one accented the other unaccented, and each line in full *cynghanedd* (consonance).

> Y pedwerydd dydd, diau,
> Wir adde' clod, ar ddeg clau
> O Chwefror oedd a chyfri,
> Ddwyn mawr ddaioni i mi. (Poem 1.45–8)

[The fourth day, doubtless, | Sincerely acknowledging praise, on ten swiftly | Of February it was by count, | That brought me great goodness.]

Englyn unodl union (direct monorhyme *englyn*) (pl. *englynion* unodl union): it has four lines of ten, six, seven and seven syllables, each line in full *cynghanedd* (consonance). The last syllable of lines 2–4 rhyme with the sixth, seventh, eighth or ninth syllable of line 1. The syllables in line 1 that follow the rhyme alliterate with the first part of line 2.

> Morgan yw cwynfan ceinferch—sy beunydd
>> Tan boenau trwm traserch;
>> I'w chiliau aeth saethau serch,
>> Am hynny ti yw'n hannerch. (Poem 38.1–4)

[Morgan is the plaint of a beautiful young woman – who is daily | Suffering the pains of an intense passion; | To the [four] corners of her being, love's arrows have gone, | Because of this you are the one we greet.]

On strict-metre verse forms see further:

John Morris-Jones, *Cerdd Dafod* [Welsh Poetic Art] (Rhydychen: Gwasg Prifysgol Rhydychen, 1930).
R. M. Jones, 'Mesurau Cerdd Dafod' [Metres of Welsh Poetic Art], *Bulletin of the Board of Celtic Studies*, 27/4 (1978), 533–51.

2. Free-metre Welsh poetry

Hen bennill (old stanza) (pl. *hen benillion*): a traditional quatrain popularly used to convey folk wit and wisdom: 'cynnyrch celfyddyd ddihyfforddiant, ddiddiwylliant, "anymwybodol", i raddau helaeth ... at eu canu, a hynny gan amlaf gyda'r delyn, y cedwid hwy gan rai pobl ar y cof ' (largely the product of an untrained, uncultivated, 'unconscious' art ... some people knew them by heart so that they could sing them, most often to harp accompaniment) and that to such an extent that they were referred to as *penillion telyn* (harp stanzas), see T. H. Parry-Williams, *Hen Benillion* [Old Stanzas] (Llandysul: Gomer, 1988), p. 9.

> Dyma lythyr gwedi ei selio
> Â sêl aur a chusan ynddo,
> O na allwn gan fy ngofid
> Roi fy nghalon ynddo hefyd. (Poem 34.1–4)

[Here is a letter that has been sealed | With a golden seal with a kiss inside it, | Oh! that I could, on account of my grief, | Put my heart in it too.]

Pennill telyn (verse for harp) (pl. *penillion telyn*): see *Hen bennill* (old stanza).

Triban (triplet) (pl. *tribannau*): an epigramatic stanza in Welsh folk poetry,

> one of the metres used by the non-professional poets, the min-
> strels or the *Clêr*. It consists of two seven-syllable lines, fol-
> lowed by a third line of seven or eight syllables which rhymes
> with the caesura of the fourth line; the fourth line ends with an
> unaccented syllable rhyming with the first two lines

See Meic Stephens (ed.), *The New Companion to the Literature of Wales* (Cardiff: University of Wales Press, 1998), p. 735.

> Yr eos dewrfost diddig,
> Cenhadwr ffraeth arbennig,
> Tegwawdydd mwyn, pruddlais ben,
> Dydi yw Capten coedwig. (Poem 29.1–4)

> [The genial nightingale, [with his] long boast [to potential
> mates], | A matchlessly fluent messenger, | A beautiful poet,
> wise-voiced ruler, | You are the Captain of the forest.]

See further Tegwyn Jones, *Tribannau Morgannwg* [Glamorgan *Trib-annau*] (Llandysul: Gwasg Gomer, 1976), and the tunes and notes on the tunes by Daniel Huws, pp. 209–15.

Tri thrawiad sengl:

> so called because there are only 3 accents in the last line. It
> consists of dactyllic half lines of 6, 6, 6, 5; 6, 6, 6, 3 syllables
> rhyming *aaab*; *cccb* (or *aaab*), the 4th ending in a masculine
> and the others in unaccented rhymes. The *a* rhyme is repeated
> in the middle of the 4th half line

See Joseph T. Shipley (ed.), *Dictionary of World Literature – Crit-icism, Forms, Technique* (New York: The Philosophical Library, 1943), s.v.

Y liwgar olygus, gain seren gysurus,
Lon, heini, lân, hoenus a dawnus ar dw',
Mi fydda, mae'n fuddiol, ['n] eich cofio yn wastadol,
Bun weddol, dda, foesol, ddifasw. (Poem 2.1–4)

[The fair in appearance, beautiful [one], handsome joyous star,
| Happy, vivacious, pretty, spirited, and blessed in form, |
I will remember you constantly, it is fitting, | Beautiful of
countenance, good, high-principled young woman, devoid of
wantonness.]

Index to first lines

Index to poets

Index to tunes

General index